2022年度教育部人文社科青年项目（项目编号：22YJC740002）
2021年度上海理工大学国家社科基金培育基金项目（项目编号：21SKPY11）
2021年度上海理工大学博士启动基金项目

# 语料库辅助的中国英语学习者汉英交替传译中的语篇意义显化研究

阿力亚·艾尼◎著

天津大学出版社
TIANJIN UNIVERSITY PRESS

**图书在版编目（C I P）数据**

语料库辅助的中国英语学习者汉英交替传译中的语篇意义显化研究 / 阿力亚•艾尼著. -- 天津 : 天津大学出版社, 2023.9
ISBN 978-7-5618-7418-9

Ⅰ. ①语… Ⅱ. ①阿… Ⅲ. ①语料库－应用－英语－口译－教学研究 Ⅳ. ①H315.9

中国国家版本馆CIP数据核字(2023)第038712号

YULIAOKU FUZHU DE ZHONGGUO YINGYU XUEXIZHE HANYING JIAOTI CHUANYI ZHONG DE YUPIAN YIYI XIANHUA YANJIU

| | |
|---|---|
| 出版发行 | 天津大学出版社 |
| 地　　址 | 天津市卫津路92号天津大学内（邮编:300072） |
| 电　　话 | 发行部:022-27403647 |
| 网　　址 | www.tjupress.com.cn |
| 印　　刷 | 北京虎彩文化传播有限公司 |
| 经　　销 | 全国各地新华书店 |
| 开　　本 | 787mm×1092mm　1/16 |
| 印　　张 | 11 |
| 字　　数 | 332千 |
| 版　　次 | 2023年9月第1版 |
| 印　　次 | 2023年9月第1次 |
| 定　　价 | 49.00元 |

# 前　言

显化研究在翻译领域备受关注，尤其是自 Mona Baker（1996：175-186）将显化置于“翻译共性”的高度后，大量的翻译研究也将目光锁定在显化现象。总体而言，显化研究主要集中在笔译层面，口译中的显化现象鲜有涉及。此外，显化研究多围绕显化策略的使用，很少有学者深入探究显化背后的原因。在基于语料库的口译显化研究中，研究对象多为职业译员，很少谈及中国英语学习者。鉴于口译和笔译之间的差异，职业译员与学生译员在显化策略应用方面的不同，本书以大量的中国英语学习者汉英交传语料为研究对象，探究中国英语学习者在汉英交传中的语篇意义显化特征。

本书以系统功能语言学的语篇语义为分析框架，采用定性分析与定量方法、描写和解释相结合的语料库方法，探讨中国英语学习者在汉英交传中的语篇意义显化特征。具体而言，本书不仅探讨了语际语篇显化（inter-language textual explicitation），即源语文本（source text）与目标语文本（target text）对比基础上的显化，还研究了英语翻译文本（English translated text）与英语原创文本（English original text）对比的语内语篇显化（intra-language textual explicitation）。关于语际显化，作者借助平行语料库，对比分析了中国英语学习者和职业译员在汉英交替传译中衔接手段的使用频率和显化。为分析语内显化，本书使用类比语料库，统计分析了中国英语学习者的英语翻译文本和英语原创

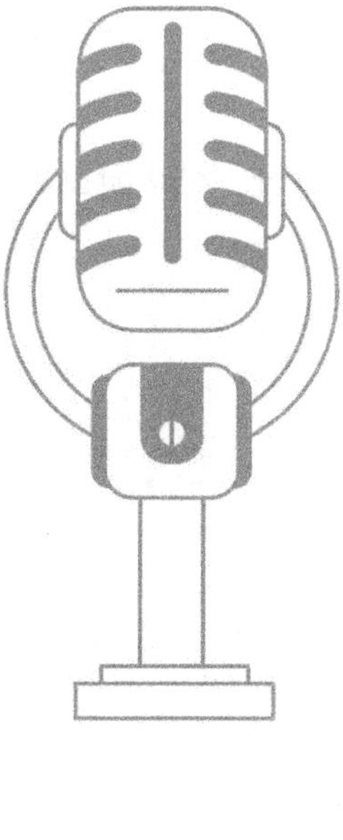

文本中衔接手段以及引导从句的连接词“that”的出现频率。

本书首次使用语料库方法对中国英语学习者在汉英交传中的显化特征进行综合分析，探索了职业译员与中国英语学习者在汉英交传中的显化特征，比较了它们显化特征的差异。研究结果显示，关于语际显化，与职业译员相比，中国英语学习者使用显化手段更为少见；中国英语学习者更倾向于将每个句子作为一个孤立的个体来处理，未能在句子的各个部分之间建立前后逻辑关系；中国英语学习者较少显化原文隐含的逻辑关系，从而增加了听众的理解难度。至于语内显化，统计结果显示，与原创英语相比，在中国英语学习者的英语翻译文本中较少出现衔接手段和引导从句的连接词“that”。中国英语学习者的口译译文中不存在语内显化，这与前人谈及的翻译语言特征相反（Baker 1995，1996；Olohan and Baker 2000：142）。

研究结果还显示，中国英语学习者在汉英交传中所出现的语际显化可归因于语言差异、口译规范以及认知差异。本文还从源语的影响、职业译员的认知等方面解释了学生的英译文中较少出现衔接手段和引导从句的连接词“that”的原因，并探讨了导致中国英语学习者与职业译员在语篇显化方面存在差异的根本原因。

本书的创新之处在于：

首先，将中国英语学习者视为研究对象，而不仅仅关注职业译员。

其次，在方法论上既利用平行语料库，又依赖类比语料库进行分析，以研究学习者的汉英交传口译语料的语际显化和语内显化。

再次，还在语篇意义显化方面对中国英语学习者和职业译员进行了比较，以便为职业译员培训设计提供新的教育启示。

最后，本书还探寻了语际显化和语内显化背后的动机，以及研究了中国英语学习者和职业译员产生语际显化异同的原因。

# Contents



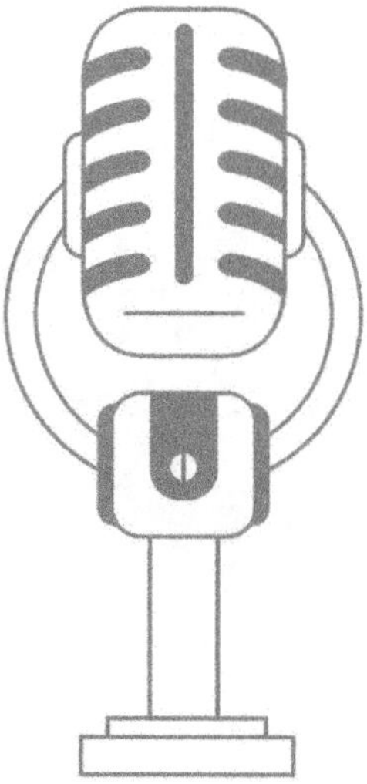

# List of Tables

# List of Figures



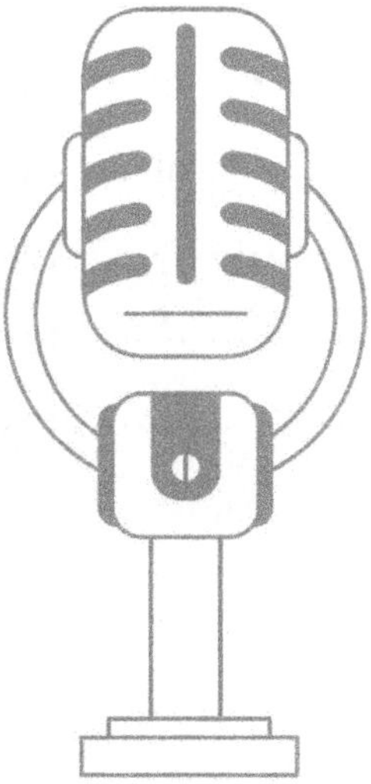

# List of Abbreviations

| | |
|---|---|
| BNC | British National Corpus |
| C-E | Chinese-English |
| CEL | Chinese EFL Learner Corpus |
| CECIC | Chinese-English Conference Interpreting Corpus |
| CI | Consecutive Interpreting |
| CIS | Corpus-based Interpreting Studies |
| CTF | Corpus of Translated Finnish |
| CTS | Corpus-based Translation Studies |
| CTIS | Corpus-based Translation and Interpreting Studies |
| DTS | Descriptive Translation Studies |
| EFL | English as a Foreign Language |
| NC | Non-finite Constructions |
| NT | Non-translated Text |
| OEC | Original English Corpus |
| PIC | Professional Interpreters Corpus |
| SFL | Systematic Functional Linguistics |
| SI | Simultaneous Interpreting |
| SL | Source Language |
| ST | Source Text |
| TL | Target Language |
| TT | Target Text |
| TEC | Translational English Corpus |
| TEM | Test for English Major |

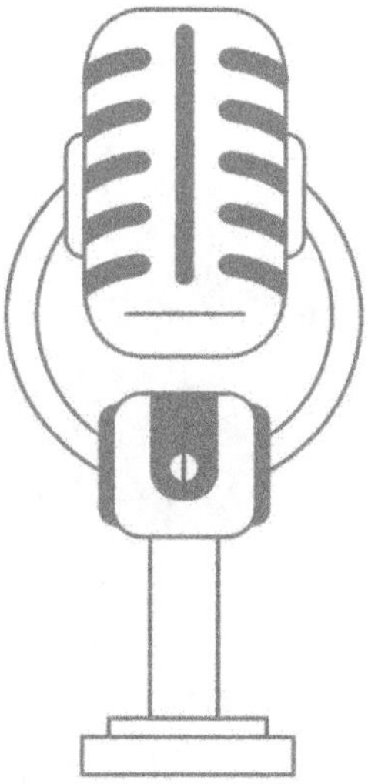

# Chapter One Introduction

## 1.1 Research Background

Explicitation is regarded one of the universal features in the process of translation. Vinay and Darbelnet (1995) first introduced the term when they made a comparison between French and English from the stylistic perspectives. It is defined as the technique of making explicit in the target language (TL) information which is implicit in the source language (SL), but clear from its context or situation (ibid: 9, translated from French by Englund-Dimitrova (2005: 34)).

Explicitation strategies are generally relevant to the strategy of addition. Nida (1964) has further developed the concept of explicitation, although he does not actually employ the term "explicitation". Nida observes major techniques of adjustment in the process of translation, such as additions, subtractions, and alterations. Russian scholar Barkhudarov (1975: 223) identified addition as one of the transformations used in translation from English into Russian. In Bulgarian scholar Vaseva's (1980) view, "linguistic asymmetry" makes explicit expressions necessary in Bulgarian-Russian bidirectional translation from the perspectives of pragmatic additions.

Like Nida, neither Vaseva nor Barkhudarov actually used the term "explicitation" itself. It is Russian professor Komissarov (1969) who employed the Russian equivalent, *Eksplitsiroaniye.* Thereafter, the term is widely applied in Russian linguistic approach to translation (Kukharenko 1988; Chernov 1988; Gak 1988).

Blum-Kulka (1986: 19) formulates "the explicitation hypothesis" which postulates "an observed cohesive explicitness from ST (source text) to TT (target text) regardless of the increase traceable to differences between the two linguistic and textual systems involved" (ibid: 300). She takes a discoursal and communicative approach to the study of translation and argues that the process of translation necessarily entails shifts both in textual and discoursal relationships, rather than by differences between particular languages:

> The process of interpretation performed by the translator in the source text might lead to a TL text which is more redundant than the SL text. This redundancy can be expressed by a rise in the level of cohesive explicitness in the TL text. This argument may be stated as "the explicitation hypothesis", which postulates an observed cohesive explicitness from SL to TL texts regardless of the increase traceable to differences

between the two linguistic and textual systems involved. It follows that explicitation is viewed here as inherent in the process of translation. (ibid)

Numerous studies have been further conducted to examine the explicitation hypothesis on translation among different language pairs (Séguinot 1988; Weissbrod 1992; Klaudy 1993; Englund-Dimitrova 1993; Øverås 1998; Olohan & Baker 2000; Whittaker 2004). These studies deal with explicitation of one kind or another.

Klaudy (1993; 2008) was the first one to put forward an explicitation typology based on factors that cause the occurrence of explicitation. These factors fall into four specific categories: obligatory, optional, pragmatic, and translation-inherent explicitation. There is seldom a clear-cut distinction among them, particularly, between the last three categories due to the arbitrariness of choices made by the translator/interpreter during processes of translation.

In short, from an inter-lingual perspective, explicitation is considered a translation technique that refers to the ways in which structures or content implicit in the source text are made more explicit in the target text. It concentrates on the ST-TT comparison, which involves clearing up ambiguity, increasing the cohesiveness of the ST and adding linguistic and extra-linguistic information. In general, translators will make intentionally or unintentionally certain content in the ST explicit in order to meet target readers' expectations. From an intra-lingual perspective, explicitation designates a text feature contributing to a higher level of explicitness established between target texts and non-translated texts in the same language. Explicitation manifests itself either in linguistic features used at a higher frequency in translated texts than in non-translated texts (NT)① or in added linguistic and extra-linguistic information in translated texts in relation to non-translated texts (Mauranen 2004).

It is a common belief that the large scale of electronic texts in corpora is an appropriate testing ground for hypotheses about translation universals. The following processes or operations have the potential as preferred candidates for translation universals, which include simplification, explicitation, normalization, repetition avoidance, leveling out, disambiguation and standardization, among which, explicitation in translation has been attracting much attention (Mauranen 2005). Electronic corpora are an optimal methodology that provides the researcher with more "objective" data than subjective one that lays the groundwork for manual comparisons of translations between language pairs. Thus, it is necessary to have sufficient quantities of translation texts in electronic corpora to analyze quantitatively translational features.

Consequently, Corpus-based Translation Studies (CTS), first advocated by Baker in her seminal 1993 paper, has motivated many researchers to investigate universal features in translated

① The abbreviation NT complies with Chesterman (2004)

texts (TrT). Experts acknowledge that translated texts are systematically distinguishable both from their source texts (ST) and from non-translations (NT) in similar domains in the target language (TL). An increasing number of scholars, by means of new techniques and methodologies in corpus linguistics, are compiling their own corpora to investigate translations in terms of an empirical and descriptive view. Most of the results achieved so far have further verified the target-oriented approach to translations in descriptive translation studies (Toury 1985).

Apart from the explicitation studies in Indo-European languages mentioned above, some researchers have conducted studies of explicitations by means of corpus methodologies in Chinese (Wallace 2004; Ke 2005; Zhou 2007; Hu & 2008; Huang 2008). However, the vast majority of studies on explicitation in translation basically concentrate upon written translation, with few focusing on explicitation features in interpreting (Zhang 2009; Hu & Tao 2009; Tang & Li 2013), let alone explicitation features demonstrated in students' interpreted texts. This is mainly due to the comparatively small scope of interpreting studies that seem to lag behind the research on written-translation. Therefore, the number of articles about the research on explicitation in interpreting is relatively limited, not to mention the corpus-based study of interpreting learners. To fill the research gap, this paper attempts to probe the explicitation features of textual meaning by Chinese EFL (English as a Foreign language) students in C-E (Chinese-English) CI (Consecutive Interpreting) compared with professional interpreters, and to seek possible motivations for such explicitation and to shed some new light for interpreters' training. The following sections will provide further explanation.

## 1.2 Rationale for the Present Study

Corpus-based Translation Studies (CTS) has been recognized a well-grounded paradigm that has transformed empirical approaches to translation studies since Mona Baker introduced corpus methodologies into translation studies over two decades ago. A number of significant studies focus on translation-related investigations, among which explicitation studies alone cover 20 more investigations since 1993 (Englund-Dimitrova 2005: 35). Other empirical CTS probe translation universals (Laviosa 1998; Olohan & Baker 2000; Xiao & Dai 2010), explicitation features of translated Chinese texts (Huang 2008; Hu 2009), translation shifts (Munday 1998), translator style in particular (Baker 2000; Winters 2009), and translation teaching (Zhu & Mu 2013) as well as the research on diachronic change of the translated literacy language (Xia 2013). These findings of these studies suggest that CTS has been and will remain the most effective and productive research methodology for identifying common linguistic features and behaviors in translation across a wide range of language pairs.

Moreover, Interpreting Studies has been subsumed as a subdiscipline under Translation

Studies, so there is no reason to exclude the corpus-based approach to interpreting studies. In a pioneering article on corpus-based interpreting studies (IS) by Shlesinger —— *Corpus-based interpreting studies as an offshoot of corpus-based translation studies*, he proposed that "corpus-based interpreting studies offer a tool which is both viable and revelatory not only for the study of interpreting, but for translation studies as a whole" (Shlesinger 1998: 1). However, the scant corpus-based interpreting studies place the primary focus on simultaneous interpreting (SI) in the European setting, including typical papers related to interpreting studies that adopted a corpus methodology in *Breaking Ground in Corpus-based Interpreting Studies* edited by Sergio & Falbo (2012).

In interpreting studies, explicitation is also regarded the technique of making explicit the target language information that is implicit in the source language. It seems that whether explicitation can be established as present or absent in the target text depends on the translator/interpreter and his/her process of interpretation. The representation of explicitation in the target text is diverse. Klaudy (1998) distinguishes such categories as obligatory, optional, pragmatic and translation-inherent explicitations. The obligatory explicitation occurs because of syntactic and semantic differences of languages; optional explicitation is due to differences in text-building strategies and stylistic preferences between languages; and pragmatic explicitation is present due to assumed differences in culture and world knowledge, while translation-inherent explicitation attributes to the nature of translation process itself. However, there is seldom a clear-cut distinction among four types of explicitation mentioned above, particularly between the latter three categories, because pragmatic or translation-inherent explicitations could be either obligatory or optional.

In view of this, this study adopts a combination of a parallel corpus approach and a comparable corpus approach to investigate inter-language and intra-language explicitation in C-E CI by interpreting learners majoring in English. In light of the typology of language functions proposed by M. A. K. Halliday, this study focuses exclusively on explicitation features of textual meaning from multi-layered dimensions in C-E texts interpreted by Chinese EFL students.

It is of great significance that this study can yield critical insights into translation mechanism in dealing with explicitations from a new perspective, through an attempt to provide motivations for both inter-language explicitation and intra-language explicitation and to seek explanations for different textual explicitations between Chinese EFL students and professional interpreters in C-E CI. Hopes are high that this study can enrich the literature on students' explicitations in C-E interpreting studies. Moreover, practically speaking, this study attempts to shed new light on C-E CI performed by Chinese EFL students compared with professional interpreters and to offer useful and practical educational implications for interpreter training.

## 1.3 Significance of the Present Study

Despite a considerable number of corpus-based interpreting studies centering around Indo-European languages, enlightening studies have been conducted by Chinese scholars to explore norms and strategies of CI (Wang 2012; Hu & Tao 2012), paralinguistic features of interpreting learners (Zhang 2015), and compilation of interpreting teaching materials as well (Tao 2010). Although the studies mentioned above are scattered and limited in number, to some degree, they could supplement the complete collection of Eurocentric Corpus-based Interpreting Studies literature that centralizes European languages.

Many studies have taken explicitation as their object in terms of different standpoints, but most of them are from the macroscopic angle. Based on previous studies, explicitation manifests itself from the perspective of addition, specification and amplification. Differences in language-specific pairs and cultural diversities are the main reasons for the explicitation. Different from previous explicitation studies, this research has been initiated for the following significance.

To begin with, most explicitation studies conducted previously depend on scattered examples in written translation, and the investigation focuses on a few words and sentences. However, this book attempts to provide a new systematic classification of explicitations in terms of Halliday's Systematic Functional Linguistics (SFL), textual explicitation in particular. This study also focuses on inter-language and intra-language textual explicitation based on a large number of C-E interpreted texts in interpreting learners' corpus, which would hopefully fill the gap in explicitation studies for interpreting learners.

In addition, explicitation strategies of great significance to the logical information flow smoothly, increase the acceptability of target texts. Therefore, the study also discusses reasons for inter-language textual explicitations and intra-language textual explicitations in C-E CI as a new topic in this book.

In the end, a comparative study of textual explicitation features, between Chinese EFL learners and professional interpreters, might serve as a general guidance to interpreting practice in language teaching. Therefore, this book intends to raise some educational implications based on a comprehensive contrastive analysis between professional interpreters and interpreting learners with regard to textual explicitations in particular.

## 1.4 Research Questions and Objectives

To be specific, the project attempts to investigate the inter-language and intra-language explicitation features of textual meaning in C-E interpreted texts by Chinese EFL students, which involves contrastive studies of the explicitness based on the comparison between Chinese source texts and their English translations, and their interpreted English in relation to the original English from different categories of explicitations. It also intends to explain the reasons for such explicitation features. Furthermore and most importantly, the current research shed light on how to design a training course for interpreters and provide lecturers in interpreting studies with some useful information in terms of the strategic dimension of interpreting learners.

This book is committed to address the following questions.

(1) What is specific to Chinese EFL students in C-E consecutive interpreting in terms of categories of inter-language textual explicitation compared with professionals?

(2) What are the characteristics of intra-language textual explicitation in Chinese EFL students' interpreted English texts in comparison with the original English?

(3) How do linguistic, cognitive and social factors motivate such explicitation features in C-E consecutive interpreting?

(4) What implications might be possibly put forward for the education of interpreters' training?

## 1.5 Organization of the Book

The book consists of eight chapters. The first chapter introduces the research background of explicitation in translation studies and rationale for the present study. After reviewing the previous studies, this research claims its significance. By doing so, it sets forth the major issues that confront contemporary explicitation research in the corpus-based interpreting studies, and raises research questions to which the present study attempts to offer answers.

Chapter Two is a comprehensive review of existing studies on explicitation. The section of literaturere view falls into three parts, which focus respectively on papers about explicitations in translation studies of written texts, publications on explicitation in interpreting studies as well as research about explicitation in Corpus-based Translation and Interpreting Studies (CTIS). However, the review points out that further research should focus on corpus-based explicitation studies, particularly on features of explicitation in interpreting, as few studies place primary focus on this area. Almost no corpus-based study deals with explicitation research on learner's interpretation.

Chapter Three introduces the theories that lay the groundwork for and give credit to the study. First, the present research is grounded on the explicitation hypothesis formulated by Blum-Kulka, and the descriptive approach to translation developed by Toury (1995; 2012). The study draws on Halliday's (2014) Systematic Functional Linguistics as the overarching analytical framework. Three Meta-meanings of Language and their respective lexico-grammatical realizations are introduced an effective approach to analyzing linguistic features in a text within a given context, with much emphasis on textual meaning. Based on this, it finally puts forward a tentative typology of explicitation applied to the present interpreting study along with working definition of explicitation.

Chapter Four, with regard to the methodology for carrying out the study, first introduces the corpus as the main methodology, consisting of both quantitative and qualitative analyses. Then it elaborates upon the different subcorpora adopted in the current study. Finally, it outlines the research procedures employed in the investigation of the data concerning explicitation features in Chinese EFL students' C-E CI, with the assistance of the analyzing software including ParaConc (269), AntConc (3.2.3), and SPSS (18.0).

The purpose of Chapter Five and Chapter Six is to present the results of inter-language textual explicitation and intra-language textual explicitation in accordance with tentative categorizations of explicitation. This study makes a systematic comparison between Chinese EFL students and professionals concerning explicitation of textual meaning. Chapter Five investigates the inter-language textual explicitations found in students' corpus compared with the professional corpus based upon multilayered classifications of explicitation. Chapter Six is devoted to analyzing intra-language explicitation in students' interpreted texts in relation to the original English texts from multi-dimensional subcategories of explicitation.

Chapter Seven, along with Chapter Five and Chapter Six constitutes the core of the book. It discusses the contributing factors behind such explicitation features in C-E CI. The first section focuses on possible reasons for inter-language explicitation of textual meaning in C-E CI from linguistic differences, interpreting and cognitive perspectives. In the second section, there is an analysis of potential shaping factors for which different intra-language explicitation features in students' English interpreted texts. The last section offers possible explanations for the differences between Chinese EFL students and professional interpreters with respect to inter-language explicitation.

As a conclusion, the final chapter summarizes major findings of the study; points out its contributions and educational implications that may assist the interpreting teaching; and offers limitations and suggestions concerning further research on explicitation in translation and interpreting for future studies.

# Chapter Two　Literature Review

This chapter reviews research on explicitation in translation, interpreting studies in general, and corpus-based approaches to explicitation studies, which includes explicitation research on Western languages and Chinese language as well. It starts with the definition of explicitation as a translation technique in the first section. Then it elaborates the first formulation of explicitation hypothesis by Blum-Kulka (1986), whose idea also contributes to the rising of descriptive translation studies (Holmes 1972) in the 1970s. In the second section, there is a review about previous studies with respect to Blum-Kulka's explicitation hypothesis. It is argued that corpora offer a more applicable resource for carrying out a corpus-based explicitation, as large quantities of translated texts can be examined and investigated in relation to source texts and non-translated texts. Since the study reported corpus-based investigation of textual explicitation in Chinese EFL students' C-E CI, there has been a detailed review of corpus-based explicitation studies, explicitation in interpreting studies as well as learner-based explicitation studies.

## 2.1　Explicitation in Translation

### 2.1.1　Defining Explicitation

The commonly acknowledged definition of explicitation is the one originally proposed by the "inventors" of the concept, Vinay and Darbelnet. They define the explicitation as "[a] stylistic translation technique which consists of making explicit in the target language what remains implicit in the source language because it is apparent from either the context or the situation." (Vinay & Darbelnet 1995: 342)

Nida (1964) seems to regard addition as a hyperonym to explicitation (as noted by Klaudy 1998; Perego 2003), although he does not discuss directly the concept of explicitation. In a detailed study on the account of the techniques of adjustment in translation, Nida equates explicitations with additions, which is a more practical description of his approach to explicitation. Øverås (1988), on the other hand, views addition as just one of manifestations of explicitation. Other scholars relate explicitation with a variety of manifestations, such as pragmatic additions (Vaseva 1980), editing strategies (Seguinot 1988), syntactic-stylistic modifications (Leuven-Zwart 1989; 1990), addition of background information (Baker 1992), expansion of meaning in a broad sense (Ke 2005), explicitation as one of syntactic operational norms (Hu & Tao 2012), and explicitation of cohesive devices in the SI (McDermid 2014).

### 2.1.2 Explicitation Hypothesis

Explicitation can be regarded a phenomenon that should be verified as a hypothesis or law. Based on discourse analysis, Blum-Kulka (2001: 300) is the first to systematically formulate a well-known "explicitation hypothesis". The hypothesis postulates from her observation about cohesive shifts in translated texts, thus expanding the source text in the translation. As Blum-Kulka (2001: 300) claims as following:

> The process of interpretation performed by the translator on the source text might lead to a TL text which is more redundant than the SL text. This redundancy can be expressed by a rise in the level of cohesive explicitness in the TL text. This argument may be stated as "*the explicitation hypothesis*", which postulates an observed cohesive explicitness from SL to TL texts regardless of the increase traceable to differences between the two linguistic and textual systems involved. It follows that explicitation is viewed here as inherent in the process of translation.

Followed by Blum-Kulka, a number of scholars carry out studies to confirm the explicitation hypothesis on translation between diverse language pairs (Séguinot 1988; Weissbrod 1992; Klaudy 1993; Englund-Dimitrova 1993; Øverås 1998; Olohan & Baker 2000; Whittaker 2004). In addition, a number of studies aim to examine explicitation in the usage of connectives in writings in the discipline of English as Second Language (ESL) or English as Foreign Language (EFL) students (Bolton et al 2002; Crewe 1990; Granger & Tyson 1996).

Seguinot (1988) not only seeks evidence for explicitations, but also looks at possible motivations behind them by investigating the addition of linking devices and converting subordinate clauses into coordinate ones based on translations between English and French. She (ibid: 108) argues that text-editing strategies might trigger the explicitation, but suggests that the longer text in the translation calls for explanation "by well-documented differences in the stylistics of English and French" (ibid: 107). In addition, she holds that the term "explicitation" should retain in cases of additions in the translated texts that could not account for "structural, stylistic, or rhetorical differences between the two languages".

In Olohan & Baker's view (2000), evidence of explicitation can emerge in the translated English through the analysis of optional *that* which is included or omitted after the reporting verbs *tell* or *say.* The instances of *that/zero* constructions are present in both Translational English Corpus (TEC) and original English texts in British National Corpus (BNC). However, the findings reveal that the TEC favors *that*-connective while the BNC prefers *zero*-connective for all the forms of both verbs. The research confirms the evidence for explicitation at syntactic level in the translated English.

Given the fact that additional connectives and cohesive devices in the target text could improve the level of readability for target readers, Toury (1995: 227) observes about correlations between explicitness and readability. He suggests that experimentation research in translation studies may help modify a hypothesis "by exploring the circumstances under which it tends to have the upper hand and other possible factors". Puurtinen (1989) also adopts an approach to testing the acceptability of translated children's books, one of which is influenced by explicitation features, such as the finite constructions in one translated text are more readable and acceptable than in the other one. Chesterman also endorses scientific methods of hypothesis generation and testing which leads "to push Translation Studies in a more empirical direction" (Chesterman 2004: 46).

As for interpreting studies, Shlesinger's (1989; 1995) study suggests that explicitation hypothesis may apply to oral as well as written translations. She finds shifts of cohesion in simultaneous interpreting, both from English into Hebrew and from Hebrew into English, which indicates that the interpreter tends to render implicit forms more explicitly, regardless of the languages concerned.

Gumul (2006) conducts an empirical research on explicitation in English-Polish simultaneous interpreting done by advanced interpreting students with Polish as their mother language. The study analyzes the wide variety of explicitating shifts ranging from lexical specification and syntaxto pragmatics. On account of both product and process data (students' retrospective comments), it is found that the vast majority of explicitating shifts are not conscious interpreting strategy but appearing to be subconscious.

Campbell McDermid (2014) detects explicitation of cohesive devices in the simultaneous interpreting from English into American Sign Language (ASL) by 12 interpreters, among which seven are recent graduate interpreters and five are nationally certified experts. There is a significant difference in the use of conjunctive devices where the experts tend to produce more additional conjunctives, which implies they go beyond the surface structure in the creation of ASL target text and indicates the relationship between sentences or paragraphs.

Within the sphere of non-European languages, Zhao (2002) touches upon the mapping of cohesion-coherence between the source text and the target text, and argues that a translator should strive for maximum mapping of cohesion-coherence. The translation scholar He (2003) identifies logical relations between some sentences in the Chinese translation of *O. Henry' s the Last Leaf*, and finds that the translation as a whole is less difficult to read, but more explicit. In a broader sense, Wang (2003) discovers that there is an overall tendency to explicitate in the translated texts regardless of translation directions between Chinese and English based on corpus-based study. Ke (2005) is also in favor of explicitation in the broad sense, and argues that explicitness manifests itself not only in the form but also in the meaning. In other words, it would increase the clarity and logic of the translated text by adding explicated expressions or making hidden information explicit in the translated text.

To sum up, this subsection elaborates the explicitation hypothesis and relevant literature, and the case studies presented above attempt to verify the assumption that there is a general tendency-towards explicitation in written translation or interpreting as a product and a process. According to previous studies, there is an inclination towards explicitness in the translated texts irrespective of the language pairs, mode of interpreting or text genres involved. The following section aims to review the research on explicitation in corpus-based approaches to translation and interpreting.

## 2.2 Studies on Explicitation in Corpus-based Translation Studies

In the early 1990s, the study of translation garnered much attention to the corpus-based approach proposed in Baker (1993; 1995; 1996), with the increasing emergence of electronic translation corpora that hold a great deal of authentic data. Since the postulation of Blum-Kulka's (1986) Explicitation Hypothesis, explicitation has found a fruitful testing ground in the framework of CTS (Laviosa 2002: 18). A growing number of corpus-based studies have been received a significant boost, so as to systematically identify explicitation features in translated texts that might confirm or falsify the explicitation hypothesis to date. In the meantime, translational features are examined based upon various types of translation corpora, ranging from the traditional data comparison between ST and TT in the parallel corpus and between TT and non-translations (NT) in the same language of comparable corpus, to the methodology that unites parallel corpora and comparable corpora. The section reviews the relevant research based on three methods mentioned above, which show how the explicitation hypothesis has been approached by using different kinds of corpora.

### 2.2.1 Studies of Explicitation Using Parallel Corpora

Explicitation, considered one of the translation universals, has received a significant boost with the emergence of CTS. Explicitation studies based on parallel corpora initiate in the form of traditional comparison between ST and TT, where the process of translation is the focus. As an initial attempt to verify Blum-Kulka's explicitation hypothesis, Øverås (1998) explores explicitationbased on the bidirectional English-Norwegian Parallel Corpus (ENPC). The results show that there is a strong tendency to explicate at lexico-grammatical level in either translated English or translated Norwegian in comparison with their source texts. Instances of explicitation occur in explicating ellipses of source text in translation and the insertion of connectives so that the translated text seems more coherent. Øverås suggests that explicitation is "a natural consequence of the joint demands of source and target" (ibid: 19). Therefore, in the transfer process, the translators very often prefer to employ explicitation to improve cohesion and coherence of the translated texts.

Becher (2011) reports on a study whose aim is to elucidate translators' motivations for performing cohesive shifts as source of explicitation, mainly focusing on the addition of connectives. The study focuses on a bidirectional parallel corpus containing translations of business texts between English and German. This research departs from the observation that "explicitations in one translation direction are often not counterbalanced by implicitations in the other direction" (ibid: 4). The results reveal that the vast majority of identified shifts are attributable to previously established English-German contrasts in terms of syntax, lexis, and communicative norms. It involves profound investigations from neighboring disciplines such as linguistic typology, contrastive linguistics and cross-cultural pragmatics.

Károly (2014) examines various types of referential cohesion in translation from Hungarian into English in a parallel corpus of news translation, and wants to uncover the relationship between shifts of reference and news content. Overall, the study is not likely to lend support to the explicitation hypothesis with no significant increasing of referential cohesion.

In the same year, Kolehmainen (2014: 46) investigates null subjects through the translation of passive predicates from Finnish into German, a language that is intolerable to subjectless clauses. The parallel corpus is composed of six Finnish fiction books, two non-fiction books, and their German translations. The research items consist of random 902 Finnish passive clauses and their German translations. In most cases, passive predicates in Finnish are translated into active predicates in German (58.6%), other cases translated into either indefinite person or a specific person. It is concluded that the expression of missing category does not always necessarily involve explicitation, and only some of them can be regarded as explicitation in those cases where covert human agents in Finnish are expressed by overt subject in German.

Another research, within the scope of non-European languages, is a corpus-based study of explicitation in two Chinese versions of Shakespeare's *Hamlet*, which also concentrates on motivations behind explicitation (Hu & Zhu 2008). The study observes explicitation from the angle of three metafunctions in two well-known Chinese versions of William Shakespeare's *Hamlet* translated by Liang Shiqiu and Zhu Shenghao respectively. The research reports the important fact that explicitation in Zhu's version is more striking than in Liang's because they are targeted at different readerships and thus different translation strategies accordingly.

Explicitation studies based on parallel corpora reveal interesting findings about the process of translation. Explicitation manifests itself by means of adding connectives, and a variety of other surface realizations as well as specification in meaning. It can be assumed that translators tend to provide more information in target texts to improve coherence of the translated text (Øverås 1998), and to remove the potential ambiguity for the target reader (Olohan 2004) as well. Some cases are unlikely to support the explicitation hypothesis (Károly 2014) and the missing category does not always involve obligatory explicitation in translation (Kolehmainen 2014). It is also rather significant to conduct explicitation studies based upon comparison between translated texts and non-translated texts in which it might yield some interesting results.

### 2.2.2 Studies of Explicitation Using Comparable Corpora

With the introduction of monolingual comparable corpora, an entirely new approach to the investigation of translated text has emerged. The second approach can be called "monolingual turn". Baker (1995: 234) formulates the merits of comparable corpora as follows:

> The most important contribution that comparable corpora can make to the discipline is to identify patterning which is specific to translated texts, irrespective of the source or target languages involved.

Within comparable corpora (Baker 1996), translations tend to be more explicit on a number of levels than original texts in a variety of ways. For instance, compared with non-translations in similar domain, translations might exhibit longer text length, more frequent use of the optional syntactic features, and causal conjunctions, as one of the important cohesive devices, such as *due to*, *reason*, *because*, *therefore* (Baker 1996: 180-181). Here is a summary of some studies based upon comparable corpora.

Olohan and Baker (2000) carry out a pioneer study of explicitation using comparable corpora, in which an extensive analysis of the use of optional *that/zero*-connective with reporting verbs SAY and TELL, with reference to TEC and BNC. In their study, the authors come to a conclusion that the *that*-connective features far more prominently in the TEC whereas the *zero*-connective is more frequent in the BNC (i.e. in original texts). The results indicate that it is likely to be a subconscious process of explicitation. Furthermore, in the case of verb PROMISE, *that*-connective occurs more frequently than the *zero*-connective in the TEC in Olohan's (2001) study. These studies mentioned above indicate that there is a distinctive pattern of preference for *that* construction in translated English texts compared with original English texts. These studies firmly anchored comparable corpora as an empirically important approach to identifying explicitation in a systematic manner within the field of CTS.

Olohan (2002; 2004) also makes a quantitative analysis of a number of other optional syntactic structures in TEC and BNC, and the results point towards a general tendency for syntactic explicitation in TEC. Instances of these syntactic features include relative pronouns, contractions, the complementizer, omission of "in order" before "to", etc. Olohan (2003) also looks at English contractions in detail and investigates the relationship between *that*-deletion and contractions.

The extensive research done by Olohan (2000-2004) indicates that optional syntactic forms show higher prevalence in TEC, thus it could be assumed that the BNC writing is more involved, more generalized, less explicit than the literary texts of TEC. In contrast, translated English in TEC is more likely to include *that* and prefer long forms over contracted ones, thus exhibiting further evidence of explicitation.

On the contrary, Puurtinen's studies from 1998 to 2004 indicate that a highly frequent featurein translation can serve as a label of explicitation rather than implicitness based on the Corpus of Translated Finnish (CTF). Non-finite constructions (NCs) occur much more frequent in translated Finnish than in non-translated Finnish in the subcorpus of children's literature in CTF. In virtue of cognitive load on the part of a translator, NCs higher occurrence in translated Finnish tends "to decrease, not increase, explicitness owing to lack of connectives" (Puurtinen 2003b: 397).

As for NCs, it is hard to signal clearly the relations between sentence elements for lack of connectives, thus decreasing explicitness and imposing a negative impact on the readability of translated literature for children. Based on these findings, Puurtinen (2003c; 2004) draws a conclusion that the higher occurrence of translational features found in the subcorpus of CTF about children's literature do not verify the explicitation hypothesis.

Zufferey and Cartoni (2014) focus on the concept of explicitation through a multifaceted study of causal connectives based on comparable corpora of French translated texts from Europarl① corpus. The corpus is made of French translations from German, Italian, Spanish and English including original French texts from the Europarl. The results indicate that the most frequently used connectives for explicitation share a similar semantic profile in both English and French. Finally, the study also demonstrates that explicitation also varies across different discourse relations, even when a single connective conveys discourse relations. As for motivations, it is likely that adding causal connectives reinforce the argumentative stance of the source text by marking causal links as obvious and thus indisputable. By doing so, translators also strengthen the coherence of a target text aiming at a different culture, in which readers may not perceive the obviousness of the causal link if this semantic feature is unmarked by the choice of a connective.

Within the area of Chinese translations, a number of scholars conduct a research on

① It is a large collection of minutes from the European parliament, and a multilingual corpus that contains 506 parallel subcorpora in 23 languages.

explicitation based on comparable corpus of translated Chinese and original Chinese in similar domain (Hu & Zeng 2009; Wang & Qin 2012; Li & Tang 2015). Hu and Zeng (2009) find that there is a higher incidence of grammatical markers in translated Chinese fictions compared with non-translated Chinese fictions, the attributive and modal marker *de* (的) in particular. Wang and Qin (2012) argue that the compilation of diachronic comparable corpora, which consist of translated Chinese and non-translated Chinese texts, could provide a powerful tool for the research of explicitation across different times. Li and Tang's (2015) study also supports explicitation hypothesis, which reveals lower density of pronouns in the comparable corpus of translated English tourism texts and non-translated English tourism ones.

It has been two decades since Baker (1995) put forward the use of comparable corpora to investigate translational features, and to find out the distinctive patterns in relation to non-translations in the same language. This methodology has undoubtedly initiated a new focus of consideration, which shifts from the traditional comparison between ST and TT to TrT and NT as the centre of enquiry (Olohan 2004: 36). Studying translation without looking at the source text can be controversial but it can be viewed a methodological exploration (ibid: 39). The comparable method in translation studies helps verify existing hypotheses and generate new ones in a scientific manner (Mauranen 2000; Tirkkonen-Condit 2002; Puurtinen 2003b; Wang & Qin 2012). However, apart from the development of the comparable approach to translation studies, it is also rather important to consider the source text. Therefore, some scholars (Bernardini & Zanettin 2004; Kenny 2003; Huang 2008; Wang 2011) began to advocate an integrated approach that incorporates the use of parallel and comparable corpora.

### 2.2.3 Studies of Explicitation Based on an Integrated Approach

An integrated approach that incorporates parallel and comparable corpora allows us to carry out a cross examination in relation not only to source texts but also to non-translated texts in the target language. In other words, comparable corpus allows researchers to pinpoint a potential translational feature by providing various statistical means, and then a parallel corpus allows researchers to distinguish the level of influence from the source text. As Bernardini & Zanettin (2004: 59) point out that:

> By examining the relevant source texts, this possibility might be checked and refuted, making the ample evidence in favour of explicitation as a "universal" feature of translation provided by Olohan all the more convincing.

A number of scholars (Kenny 2003; Krüger 2014; Huang 2008; Liu & Chen 2010) have studied explicitation by using integrated corpus methodology. Their works are elaborate in the following literature.

Adopting an integrated approach that combines parallel and comparable corpora, Kenny (2003) conducts a systematic study that examines whether patterns of inclusion or exclusion of optional *that* in translated texts emerge from their respective source texts, based on German-EnglishParallel Corpus of Literary Texts. Kenny discovers that around half of the instances of SAY + *that* have a corresponding *daß* in the German source texts, while with only 21% *daß* to *zero*-that shift in the German original. The results point to a tentative conclusion that there is a tendency towards explicitation in using reporting *that* in German-English Parallel Corpus of Literary Texts, not only in comparison with comparable corpus but also with parallel corpus for explanation.

Krüger (2014) calls for an inquiry into major strands of explicitation research, ranging from S-explicitation to T-explicitation with reference to Chesterman's (2004: 39) S-universals and T-universals. The study follows the tracks of an explicitation concept from its proposition, which leads to S-explicitation, to widespread application of explicitation in CTS that results in T-explicitation. Krüger (2014) also argues that T-explicitation "seems to fall outside the cognitive reality and the translational action of the translator", and "comparative explicitness lacks the necessary criterion of translational intertextuality" (ibid: 171).

Within the area of non-European languages, Huang (2008) investigates explicitation of personal pronoun subjects with the help of parallel and comparable corpora, which contain literary and non-literary E-C translations and their corresponding non-translated Chinese texts respectively. The findings reveal that there are more correspondences between English and Chinese personal pronoun subjects, that is to say, inter-lingual explicitation is not prominent. Compared with non-translated Chinese texts, translated Chinese texts tend to contain more personal pronoun subjects, and thus a high degree of explicitness in the comparable corpora.

Liu and Chen (2010) conduct a similar research about the phenomenon of explicitation using a parallel corpus. The corpus includes the British novel *Lady Chatterley's Lover* as the source text and three Chinese translations of the novel, and a comparable corpus consisting of three Chinese translations of *Lady Chatterley's Lover* and an original Chinese novel respectively. Features of explicitation in the three translations differ from each other in terms of lexis density, type-token ratio, the use of adversative conjunctives and mood markers (*Ni, Ma,* and *Ba*). This can be attributable to factors such as the different objectives and target readers for which the respective translations aim to design.

The integrated approach described above allows us to "construct a more complete picture of translation" (Olohan 2004: 44). An integrated approach can start either by analyzing the comparable corpus and then the parallel corpus, or vice versa. The former approach could help verify translational features between translated texts and non-translated texts in the first step, then to examine the extent to which a given instance of TT explicitness affected by ST. The latter could help identify whether operating the explicitation strategy in the translation/interpreting process would lead to TT explicitness. Thus, the comparable-parallel approach adopts a primary target text-oriented perspective, while the parallel-comparable approach adopts a source text-oriented viewpoint. Both bring the study of translation process and product under an integrated investigation on explicitation, although there is a minor difference in the initiative step of either parallel or comparable approach.

## 2.3 Studies on Explicitation in Interpreting

To date, the vast majority of explicitation studies focus on written texts. However, it is also possible to investigate explicitation extensively in interpreting. Explicitation in interpreting studies becomes apparent in Pöchhacker's view that "quite apart from its postulated status as a universal feature of translation, explicitation may be needed as a strategy to circumvent linguistic and sociocultural differences" (Pöchhacker 2004: 135). Thus, this section provides a brief introduction of relevant and significant explicitation studies conducted in CI and simultaneous interpreting both at home and abroad. In addition, Explicitation in learner's translation is also touched upon, as it is relevant to the study that investigates explicitation features in C-E CI performed by Chinese EFL learners.

### 2.3.1 Research on Explicitation in Consecutive Interpreting

Explicitation has been studied extensively in translation studies to the extent that it has been regarded one of the translation universals. Nevertheless, there are just a few studies on this phenomenon in the mode of CI, which are as follows.

Hu and Tao (2009) are the ones who make the initial attempt to expand the horizons of explicitness towards interpreting studies. They investigate the phenomenon of explicitation based on a corpus of interpreter-mediated texts in a conference setting. The investigation shows that explicitation of textual meaning is rather apparent in C-E conference interpreting. It can be said that the interpreter tends to use "that", "to" and logical connectives in C-E conference interpreting, which can facilitate audiences' comprehension of textual meaning and earn extra time for the interpreter. The motivations of the interpreter to do so have much to do with the concern about the difference between English and Chinese in terms of hypotaxis and parataxis and interpreting strategies as well.

Zhang (2009) discusses explicitation phenomenon in CI during the question and answer period. The data that informs his study consists of the speech given by Chinese former Premier Wen

Jiabao at the World Economic Forum in early 2009. The results show that the interpreted texts show a tendency towards explicitation related to affairs of China and other countries in order to make interpreting clear and sound. This phenomenon seems to bear on the interpreter's personal habit or professional cognition established with pre-employment training. He argues that the nature of conference interpreting and the different power status enjoyed by the interpreter and the speaker are important factors contributing to the interpreter's tendency to resort to explicitation when dealing with topics of bilateral affairs between China and other countries.

Adopting a descriptive perspective and informed by the concept of "norms", Wang (2012) investigates the explicitation phenomenon in the C-E interpreting of Chinese Premier Press Conferences. Focusing on the linguistic shifts manifested between/in the source and target texts, Wang conducts an inter-textual comparative analysis of 12 Chinese Premier's Press Conferences (2003-2014) using a parallel corpus that consists of the transcripts of the interpreters' words. The study identifies three primary shifts, including addition, reduction, and correction. By conducting a qualitative analysis in every type of shifts and a quantitative analysis of the statistics for the frequencies of shifts in the corpus, Wang's study also identifies four typical norms of ST-TT relations. Three of them are relevant to explicitation in this research, which includes the norm of explicitation in logic relations, the norm of specificity in information content, and the norm of explicitness in meaning as well. Wang's study can serve as a tentative exploration of explicitation based on a relatively large corpus of on-site interpretation in descriptive interpreting studies. This study may also shed new light on explicitation concerning translation norms in CI.

Tang and Li's (2015) research aims at providing both quantitative and descriptive data on the explicitation phenomenon in CI. The study has conducted a systematic investigation of explicitation in English-Chinese CI based on a comparison between ST and TT. They identify ten different forms of explicitation and four motivations for explicitation. As to the features of explicitation, half of the explicitations are relevant to experiential information; most explicitations are for clarification on the part of professional interpreters, whereas there are some instances of explicitation accounting for interpreting trainees' insufficient competence. The differences between professional interpreters and interpreting trainees with regard to explicitation indicate that interpreting trainees should try to use explicitations as a means of facilitating audiences' comprehension rather than compensating for their incompetency.

### 2.3.2 Research on Explicitation in Simultaneous Interpreting

Compared with the overwhelming majority of research on explicitness in translated texts, the amount of research on explicitation in simultaneous interpreting (SI) seems to be much smaller. It is likely that particular constraints inherent in the mode of simultaneous interpreting may pose limitations on the systematic and extensive occurrence of explicitation. Nevertheless, the studies conducted sofar (Shlesinger 1995; Niska 1999; Gumul 2006; Nicole Baumgarten et al 2008) have demonstrated that this phenomenon also exists in simultaneous interpreting. The relevant influential studies on explicitation in SI are as follows.

Shlesinger (1995) is the first to make a preliminary attempt to investigate explicitation from the perspective of cohesive shifts. With the data drawn from an eleven-minute piece of spontaneous discourse as rendered by thirteen student interpreters, this study primarily examines shifts of cohesion which occur in simultaneous interpreting. Preliminary findings suggest that shifts do occur in all types of cohesive devices, particularly in those perceived as not essential to the informational content of the text and in devices whose recognition requires knowledge that is not available to the interpreter. The research confirms that interpreters tend to explicitate implicit links by inserting additional cohesive devices.

As a product-and-process study of explicitation in interpreting, Gumul (2006) not only detects explicitation on the English-Polish language pair, but also aims at investigating the causes triggering shifts leading to greater explicitness of the target texts. The scope of the analyzed explicitating shifts encompasses all linguistic strata, ranging from lexis and syntax to pragmatics. Through the analysis of both product (target text) and process data (retrospective comments), it is found that interpreters' conscious strategic behaviors do not attribute to the vast majority of explicitating shifts in simultaneous interpreting. Instead, in most cases, explicitation in simultaneous interpreting appears to be subconscious (ibid: 187). It would be assumed that the remaining cases of explicitation can be attributed to the translation process itself and are coined in a new term of by-product of language mediation. The results demonstrate that subconscious explicitation appears to be mainly cohesion-related, while as far as conscious strategic behavior is concerned, the prevailing type of explicitating shift is meaning specification.

Another previous research on explicitation in SI by Gumul (2006b) indicates that explicitation in the mode of interpreting is mainly cohesion related. The most common changes related to explicitation are identified as follows: adding connectives, shifting from referential cohesion to lexical cohesion, replacing nominalizations with verb phrases, reiterating lexical items, filling out elliptical constructions, and shifting from reiteration in the form of paraphrase to reiteration in the form of identical or partial repetition.

Baumgarten et al (2008) investigate data from a corpus of interpreter-mediated discourse in a simultaneous setting between Brazilian and German language pair. As a point of departure, the use of proper names (e.g. Amazônia) provides an opportunity for studying explicitation by two interpreters. The focus is on different ways in which interpreters render the same word. The result of their study indicates that explicitation is a gradual phenomenon, which depends on three different types of variables: (a) the interpreting mode; (b) individual differences between interpreters such as time-lag, chunking, or experience; and (c) constellation features such as social distance, professional status, and linguistic and cultural differences between speaker and audience (ibid: 198).

Lee's (2014) research aims to examine patterns of explicitation and implicitation in simultaneous interpreting from Korean to English by eight student interpreters. In addition, Lee's study also examines explicitation patterns related to connectives in SI. Additions are the most common type of shifts regarding connectives. The preliminary findings indicate that there is a tendency towards implicitation rather than explicitation in the target language renditions. This is because of a stronger effect of the mode (i.e., simultaneous interpreting) on the phenomenon of explicitation than language-specific factors such as directionality and language pairs. For the pedagogical implications, students can learn to utilize various strategies as paraphrasing and summarizing instead of inserting connectives frequently, so as to avoid omitting important meaningful elements and interpreting key messages.

### 2.3.3 Studies of Explicitation in Learner's Translation

Since this study attempts to explore explicitation features manifested in interpreting learners carried out by English learners, it is quite necessary to review some significant and leading investigations on learner's translation or interpretation. In addition, unique items in one language very often seem to have only partially overlapping equivalents in other languages, i.e. equivalents that tend to explicate their implicit SL meaning, which is part of the world knowledge of the SL user (Tirkkonen-Condit 2000). The following section provides an overview on relevant explicitation studies that involve learners' translation and interpreting.

Klaudy (1996) adopts an experimental approach to detect instances of explicitation by using back-translation as a tool in learners' translation. In the study, the students' work is analyzed in terms of the four types of explicitation proposed by Klaudy (1993): obligatory, optional, pragmatic and translation-inherent. Klaudy (1993) finds that regarding obligatory explicitation, "the tendency for explicitation (additions) in written translations may be stronger than the tendency for implicitation (omissions)" (ibid: 110).

From the perspective of ideological content, Puurtinen (2003) focuses on explicitating and implicitating translation strategies by translation students found in English magazine articles into Finnish translations. Implicitation occurs much more frequent than explicitation. Explicitation is present in converting a source-text nominalization into a Finnish verb phrase and making clausal relations more explicit by adding connectives to the texts. While implicitation involves turning verb phrases into nominalizations and complete relative clauses into complex premodified noun phrases. These strategies play a significant role in changing the viewpoints and even modifying the opinions expressed by the ST writers. The students' non-systematic application of these strategies suggests that the source text manipulation is mainly because of insufficient skills and knowledge rather than ideological motivations.

Within the framework of CTS, Castagnoli (2009) presents a quantitative and qualitative analysis of the use of connectives in a corpus of Italian student translations, with a view to verifying the existence of explicitation in these translated texts. Moreover, the approach adopted in this thesis is novel due to the focus on learners rather than professional and seasoned translators. The proposed methodology is also new, in that it relies on the analysis of a multiple translation corpus, i.e. a special kind of parallel corpus in which several translations into the same target language are available for each source text. The study shows that explicitation is a significant characteristic of Italian student translations from both English and French. Finally, the comparison of multiple translations of the same source text proves to be an effective method for distinguishing shifts linked to target language norms/preferences from non-linguistically-motivated shifts, and a valuable support to the researcher's intuition about the appropriateness of alternative renditions.

Faber et al (2010) explores the use of explicitation in the context of legal translation for trainee translator TTs. From a cognitive point of view, we may therefore assume that explicitations are frequent in legal TTs because of the tendency to leave traces of hard-won understanding in the TT. From a legal point of view, we may conversely assume that explicitations would be relatively rare in legal TTs owing to the potential legal effect of adding or removing information. It is surprisingly to find that they did not restrict themselves to obligatory linguistic explicitations and implicitations as the safest choice; rather, in more cases they were willing to run the risk of linguistic explicitation in spite of the legal consequences and risks involved.

Within the scope of non-European languages, Lai (1995) conducts a research among translation students from Japanese into Chinese and discovers an overall higher tendency to use more conjunctions in translated Chinese, which illustrates obvious tendency towards to explicititation among university students. This is the case in adversative, additive and causal relations. Lai attributes the addition of conjunctions to an attempt by student translators to achieve greater readability.

Chen (2014) touches upon the difference between professional interpreters and student interpreters in terms of explicitation of logical links in simultaneous interpreting, and finds that this kind of explicitation is commonly used by both professional and student interpreters. Although there is not too much difference between professional interpreters and student interpreters, the average of explicitated logical links employed by professional interpreters outnumbers that of student interpreters. Because the professional interpreters are more inclined to explicitate logical links for the purpose of interpreting or of explaining the implicit logical relationship retained in the source text. He also finds that explicitated logical links as SI strategies employed by professional interpreters outnumbers that of student interpreters.

## 2.4 Summary

This chapter summarizes explicitation in both translation and interpreting studies, ranging from the introduction of explicitation as translation technique, explicitation hypothesis with its relevant literature, to explicitation research both in consecutive and simultaneous interpreting studies. Explicitation in learner's translation is also touched upon since this study attempts to investigate explicitation features in C-E interpreted texts by interpreting learners. Special interest lies in explicitation studies within the framework of new methodology — corpus-based translation studies, including those relevant studies based on parallel corpora, comparable corpora and integrated corpora respectively.

Investigating explicitation by using different kinds of corpora help identify its associated features in as many languages pairs as possible, and then an attempt is made to find out the possible factors that might lead to different kinds of explicitation at different linguistic levels. Explicitation is associated with different kinds of adjustment, such as textual redundancy (Blum-Kulka 1986), addition (Nida 1964), addition of background information (Baker 1992), pronominal shifts and explicating logical connectives (Huang 2008; Hu & Tao 2009), specification and expansion of meaning (Mesa-Lao 2011), explicitation as one of syntactic operational norms (Hu & Tao 2012), and explicitation of cohesive devices in SI (McDermid 2014).

So far, there is yet no agreement as to the nature of explicitation, in other words, whether it is universal or norm-governed. To some scholars (Toury 1978; Blum-Kulka 1986; Baker 1993; Mauranen 2000; Huang 2008), explicitation serves as a universal strategy, while others (Øverås 1998; Bernardini et al 2004; Hu & Tao 2009) consider it as a norm constrained behavior by socio-cultural factors. In general, for both cases mentioned above, extensive research supports explicitation as a translational feature, and considers it as a probabilistic feature (Toury 2004) or an approximation (Chesterman 2004), instead of a certain and stable feature.

At this stage, explicitation research and its influence on translation and interpreting are still in its infancy (Chesterman 2004: 45; Olohan 2004: 92). Therefore, it is certainly crucial to not only describe and identify explicitation features but also to explain and interpret factors behind them in translation and interpreting studies. Only by resorting to corpus-based methodology, which contains large authentic data in a wide variety of translations and interpreted texts by professionals and learners, can we have a complete picture of explicitation features and explanatory factors for explicitations.

Despite the studies related to explicitations mentioned above, very few focus on explicitation features of interpreting learners in C-E CI by employing large interpreting learners' corpus. Most studies merely investigate explicitations either in several passages or in written translated texts, or in a mini-corpus of interpreting learners. Therefore, this study attempts to concentrate on distinctive explicitation features of interpreting learners in C-E CI from the perspective of three meta-functions, namely ideational, interpersonal and textual functions with special interest in textual function compared with professional interpreters.

# Chapter Three Theoretical Framework

The current study attempts to identify explicitation features of textual meaning by Chinese EFL learners in C-E CI based on the use of the learner corpus, and then seeks explanations for such explicitation features from linguistic, interpreting and cognitive perspectives, and finally puts forward some educational implications in comparison with professional interpreters. The current chapter presents the theoretical framework upon which the descriptive-explanatory analysis of explicitation is grounded: the concept of explicitation initiated by Vinay and Darbelnet (1995) for indentifying explicitation and the three meta-functions in Systematic Functional Linguistics (SFL) proposed by Halliday and Matthiessen (2004), with much focus on realization of textual meaning. Final section introduces the Effort Models devoted in interpreting used for explaining reasons for explicitation features in C-E CI.

## 3.1 Explicitation

### 3.1.1 The Concept of Explicitation

It is quite necessary to clarify the concept of explicitation in both translation and interpreting. As pointed out by Baleghizadeh and Sharifi (2010: 59), "The examination of explicitation in a specific language pair not only raises our awareness and understanding of the very nature of translation process and product, but also contributes to the translation theory by enabling us to explain and predict a phenomenon in translation".

First introduced by Vinay and Darbelnet (1995), the concept of explicitation traditionally can be defined as a shift in translation from what is implicit in the ST to what is explicit in the TT, which are inferred from its context. Vinay and Darbelnet associate explicitation with implicitation, i.e. "making what is explicit in the source language implicit in the target language, relying on the context or the situation for conveying the meaning" (ibid: 344). Explicitation and implicitation are relevant to addition and omission in the translation process.

Nida (1964) further elaborates the concept. He argues that the process of translation involves three major techniques of adjustment, including addition, alteration and subtraction without actually mentioning explicitation. In his research, the phenomenon of explicitation is closely bound up with "addition" techniques, for instance, "additions required because of grammatical restructuring", "addition of classifiers and connectives", "filling out elliptical expressions". He also explains the motivation that triggers additions by saying that "categories of the receptor language do not exist in the source language" (ibid: 227). Explicitation, in his view, also plays the part of semantic expansion as well and meets the needs of the target culture in mind. For instance, in the example of "queen of the south", which might be obscure to the target culture, thus it should be rendered as "woman who was ruling in the south country" (ibid: 229).

The concept of explicitation is also relevant to "additions in a translated text which cannot be explained by structural, stylistic, or rhetorical differences between two languages" (Séguinot 1988: 108). The statement above illustrates the optional aspect of explicitation in the process of translation. Similar cases occur in English-Russian translation, where explicitation relates to substitution through specific words in the target text. For example, *gun license* in English is translated *license for right to carry weapon* in Russian (Barkhudarov 1975, cited in Klaudy 1998: 81).

Another type of explicitations is the addition of background information as cultural reference. Baker (1992) looks at this strategy from the perspective of translator's decision, which involves an additional reference for the needs of the target reader. In her opinion, explicitation is an alternative choice in translation, because the implied information in the source text could be left implicit in the translation at times; in other cases, it is made explicit by the addition of detailed background information in the body of the text (ibid: 244-248).

As for interpreting studies, the concept of explicitation can be found in Pöchhacker's view that "quite apart from its postulated status as a universal feature of translation, explicitation may be needed as a strategy to circumvent linguistic and sociocultural differences" (Pöchhacker 2004: 135). In other words, explicitation can be regarded a means to bridge the gap between local communicative contexts and institutional ones (Mason 2006). Wadensjö (1998) also finds different types of renditions associated with explicitation in interpreting such as "explicit coordination", "expanding translating" and "substituting translating".

For the research on explicitation in China, several translation scholars put forward their own viewpoints. Ke (2005) argues that explicitation should not only refer to the change in the form of cohesion in a narrow sense, but also should include the expansion of meaning in a broad sense. Huang (2007) holds that the level of explicitation differs in various language pairs based on their linguistic formalization at syntax level along with direction of translation and genre as variables.

As for explicitation in interpreting studies, Hu and Tao (2009) are the first scholars who systematically investigate explicitation of textual meaning from the use of "that", the infinitive "to" and logical connectives in Chinese-English conference interpreting by means of corpus approach. Hu and Tao (2012) also examine explicitation as one of syntactic operational norms and concludes that the influence of explicitation on press conference interpreting is less noticeable than on the English version of the work report of Chinese government.

In summary, from the studies mentioned above, it can be seen that explicitation in translation and interpreting functions as umbrella term (Bartolomé 2011), which covers a variety of transfer procedures, ranging from addition of modifiers, conjunctions and insertion of extra information to specification and expansion of meaning. These studies systematically compare translated texts and their source texts in order to identify instances of explicitated information. The following section introduces a systematic typology of explicitation, which covers different forms of explicitation and various categorizations of explicitation so as to better account for the phenomenon of explicitation.

### 3.1.2 Typology of Explicitation

This section offers an overview of different typologies of explicitation to cover various aspects of explicitation. The first one, Klaudy's model, initiated in her 1993 paper, has been widely used for differentiating diverse aspects of explicitation in academic and literary texts. Based on claims about language universals in linguistics and sociolinguistics, Chesterman (2004) states that there are two kinds of universal features in translation: S-universals and T-universals, which is in correspondence with Huang's (2007) typology of explicitation. The last ones, after the introduction of CTS, are Perego's (2003) model and Becher's model (2011), based upon a corpus of two movies subtitled in Hungarian and Italian, and bidirectional corpus of English-German business texts respectively. The detailed information about these classifications will be elaborate in the following sections.

#### 3.1.2.1 Klaudy's Model

The Hungarian scholar Kinga Klaudy proposed the first systematic typology of explicitation, which is widely applied for differentiating explicitation in the wide range of translations. She developed a model of explicitation based on the reasons triggering the phenomenon, with its structural manifestation. Klaudy classifies the explicitation into four types: obligatory, optional, pragmatic, and translation-inherent (Klaudy 1996: 102-103; 1998: 82-84), as clearly represented in Table 2.1.

**Table 2.1 Types and forms of explicitation in Klaudy's model**

| Explicitation | | | | |
|---|---|---|---|---|
| Types | Obligatory | Optional | Pragmatic | Translation-inherent |
| Basis | Linguistic differences | Stylistic and textual preference | Cultural gap ST and TT | Language independent |

Obligatory explicitation arises from linguistic differences at the morphological, syntactic and/or semantic level between languages. This results from structural differences between SL and

TL, especially from so-called "missing categories". For example, *three pencils* in English, translated as "三支铅笔" (San Zhi Qian Bi) in Chinese with the insertion of a classifier *Zhi* where an obligatory explicitation occurs, because without it the target language would be ungrammatical.

On the other hand, optional explicitation depends on language use. It results from differences in text-building strategies and stylistic preferences between language pairs. This type typically involves the insertion of connective elements to strengthen cohesive links, addition of emphasizers for the clarification of the sentence, and changing subordinate information into coordinate information. For instance (cited from Hu & Tao 2009):

ST: 是的，中国电信正在降价，降得还不够，还要成倍地降!

TT: Indeed, China Telecom is reducing the prices, *but* I do not think that reduction is far enough; I think the prices should be reduced continuously, and by several times.

There is no logical conjunction in the Chinese sentence, the logical relationship could be assessed from the context; while in the target text, the implicit logical relationship is explicated through the usage of the conjunction *but*.

The label "pragmatic" refers to the explicitation that serves to narrow down the cultural gap between ST and TT, where translators intervene to provide cultural explanations in the translation. Instances of pragmatic explicitation include adding background information for culture-specific terms and proper nouns either within the text or in footnotes. E.g., culture-specific name, "桃花运" (Tao Hua Yun) in Chinese is translated into *having a love affair* in English, thus avoiding ambiguity of the culture-specific information.

The last one, according to Klaudy, translation-inherent explicitation is language-independent and it depends on the nature of the translation process itself. It is namely "the necessity to formulate ideas in the target language that were originally conceived in the source language" (Klaudy 1998: 83). This type of explicitation includes expansion in the target text while the shorter information-package in the source text requires additional interpretation.

Although the typology of explicitation proposed by Klaudy is concise and practical, it is not so easy to make a clear-cut distinction between optional, pragmatic and translation-inherent explicitations that imply open choices upon the translator. It might be advisable, therefore, to subsume the pragmatic and translation-inherent explicitations under optional explicitation, as the obligatory and optional categories are quite distinguishable from each other in this model.

#### 3.1.2.2 Chesterman's/Huang's Model

The corpus-based approach to translation studies initiates a new dimension for researchers to have a descriptive analysis of translation universals. Chesterman (2004) develops a detailed schema to sort out claims about universal features of translation. The claims represent two different perspectives based on two different contrastive relations on translation. Some claims are made according to equivalence relations between translated texts and their source texts, which is called S-universals (S stands for source). Other claims are formed in correspondence with universal differences between translated texts and their comparable non-translated texts, which is called T-universals (T stands for target) (Chesterman 2004: 39).

In view of this, Huang (2007: 1) also classifies explicitation into two categories, namely inter-language explicitation and intra-language explicitation. Inter-language explicitation depends on the comparison between source texts and target texts. It is possible to identify the intra-language explicitation based on the contrast between translated texts (TrT) and their corresponding original texts, non-translated texts (NT), in the same language. Table 2.2 demonstrates the brief classification of Chesterman's/Huang's model.

**Table 2.2 Types of explicitation in Chesterman's/Huang's model**

<table>
<tr><td colspan="5">Explicitation</td></tr>
<tr><td>Basis</td><td colspan="2">Comparison between ST-TT</td><td colspan="2">Comparison between TrT-NT</td></tr>
<tr><td>types</td><td colspan="2">Inter-lingual/ Inter-language</td><td colspan="2">Intra-lingual/ Intra-language</td></tr>
<tr><td>Subtypes</td><td>Referential content</td><td colspan="2">Interpersonal relations</td><td>Textual cohesion</td></tr>
</table>

As for inter-language explicitation, the example of explicating cohesive devices is in the following sentence. The example is cited from Huang (2007: 79) with explicitated items in italic type. The implicit logical relationship in the source text is explicated with the usage of conditional connective *if* in the following example:

ST: 请的客一个都不来,就无异主人在社交生活上被判死刑。

TT: *If* none of the invited guests show up, it means the death sentence for the host as far as his social life is concerned.

(钱钟书著《围城》, Jeanne Kelly & Nathan K. Mao 译)

Another example of explicitation of personal pronouns as one of the referential content is given in the sentence below. The example is cited from Huang (2007: 39) with explicitated items in italic type.

ST: 林小姐这天从学校回来就撅(噘)起着小嘴唇。她掼下了书包,并不照例到镜台前梳头发搽粉,却倒在床上看着帐顶出神。

TT: *Miss Lin's small mouth* pouting when *she* returned home from school that day. She flung down her books, and instead of combing her hair and powdering her nose before the mirror as usual, she stretched out on the bed. Her eyes staring at the top of the bed canopy, Miss Lin lay lost in thought.

(茅盾《林家铺子》, Shapiro 译)

In the above example, *Miss Lin' s small mouth* and the first *she* are the instances of explicitation with explicating logical subject in the first sentence. The second "She" is correspondent to "她" in the source text while the third "she", "Her eyes" and "Miss Lin" are the instances of addition techniques in translation.

In terms of intra-language explicitation, the typical example is likely to occur in the usage of overt conjunctions and connectives in the translated text. The following case is an excerpt from Huang (2007: 62) with explicitated items in parentheses.

Original Chinese: 冯二成子喝足了酒,退了出来,连饭也没有吃,他打算到磨坊去睡一觉。常年不喝酒,喝了酒有些昏头。

(萧红《后花园》; 转引自朱永生等, 2001: 99)

TrT:冯二成子喝足了酒,(于是/就)退了出来,连饭也没有吃,他(就)打算到磨坊去睡一觉。(由于)常年不喝酒,(所以)喝了酒(就)有些昏头。

In a word, the explicitation typology, proposed by Chesterman/Huang, namely inter-lingual/inter-language and intra-lingual/inner-language explicitation can be largely applicable to all language pairs and languages though it is not much detailed and specific regarding its subcategories.

### 3.1.2.3 Perego's Model

According to Perego (2003: 74), three main classes of explicitation have been found on the basis of why and when explicitation occurs, in line with Klaudy's typology. These are labeled as cultural, channel-based or intersemiotic and reduction-based explicitations, and in the manifestation of addition and specification on the surface respectively, as shown in Table 2.3.

**Table 2.3 Types and forms of explicitation in Perego's Model**

| Explicitation | | | | |
|---|---|---|---|---|
| Types | Cultural | — | Channel-based | Reduction-based |
| Forms | — | Addition | — | Specification |

Cultural explicitation is similar to pragmatic explicitation in Klaudy's model, and it has already been widely studied in a wide range of translations. It results from a cultural gap between source culture and target culture, and it is extra-linguistic in nature. Cultural explicitation is very common in the material where objects or events are unknown in the target culture, thus requiring overt, unequivocal clarification (Perego 2003: 74). It is the case in the realms of history and politics due to a different political backgrounds and cultural heritage.

The term channel-based or intersemiotic explicitation is applicable to those instances of explicitation determined by the impact of shifts from one semiotic channel to another (ibid: 74). In other words, intersemiotic explicitation is very dynamic in nature, and its manifestation in the verbalization of those data is conveyed only by the visual or auditive support. Translators who employ this type of explicitation consider not only lexical and syntactical choice, but also gesture and supra-segmental features for audio-visual translation in particular.

The third class of explicitation results from the need to reduce the ST in order to meet the special requirement of placing concise information in a shorter span of time. Reduction-based explicitation, therefore, is a natural and obvious operation employed in translation of subtitling of movies. It seems that reductions trigger the informational gain, and not loss, in the TT message.

#### 3.1.2.4 Becher's Model

Becher puts forward a new classification of explicitation based on a corpus of English-German business texts, which is more objective and reliable to keep the different types separate in his PhD book. His typology is actually adapted from Halliday's three metafunctions of language and his framework is as follows (Becher 2011: 86):

> ① **Interactional shifts** concern the appearance of the source text author and the target text addressee in the target text (cf. Halliday's interpersonal metafunction).
>
> ② **Cohesive shifts** concern the cohesion of the target text compared to the source text (cf. Halliday's textual metafunction).
>
> ③ **Denotational shifts** concern the description of the states of affairs expressed by the target text (cf. Halliday's ideational metafunction).

Although his three types of explicitations do not cover the whole range of linguistic phenomena, his framework is more manageable because it is "more clearly delimited from each other and their range of application is smaller" (ibid: 87). Becher creates a framework particularly suitable to his data, which is the bidirectional corpus of English-German business texts and their translations. His typology might not be applicable to the analysis of other data, but it is still possible to set up an operative framework for the analysis of explicitation based on Halliday's three metafunctions of language.

In summary, three typologies of explicitation presented above depend on the comparison between ST and TT. In addition, there is considerable overlapping between subcategories in the same typology, and it is hard to distinguish one from another. Finally, each instance of explicitation has to put into one category or another according to the distribution of the variables that motivate the explicitation, thus it is hard to cover as many as explicitation features manifested in the translation and interpreting. Therefore, this study investigates the explicitation from the new perspectives of three meta-functions of language, textual explicitation in particular including inter-language explicitation and intra-language explicitation, to cover explicitation features as many as possible. These refer to here as explicitations of ideational meaning, explicitations of interpersonal meaning and explicitations of textual meaning, with special interest in the explicitation of textual meaning. It is also hoped that this study can enrich the literature on explicitations based on learner corpus in C-E interpreting studies.

### 3.1.3 The Working Definition of Explicitation

The acknowledged definition of explicitation is put forward by Vinay and Darbelnet (1995), who define explicitation as "the translation technique of making explicit in the target language information which is implicit in the source text (ST), but inferable from its context or situation" (1995: 342). It is apparent that this definition of explicitation relies on the comparison between source texts and target texts, which refers to inter-language explicitation in this study. However, the definition seems highly vague about what the phrase of "making explicit" refers to. Moreover, there is no specification on the term "context" or "situation".

It is understandable that when a concept is formulated for the first time, the vagueness is probably unavoidable. In addition, due to the complexity of decisions on identification of explicitation in C-E CI, it is comparatively significant to clarify the working definition as clearly as possible for the present study. Hence, the tentative definition of inter-language explicitation for this study is as follows:

> **Inter-language explicitation** refers to additions or clarifications made in target texts that are implicit in source texts, which can be derivable from the co-text and situation through contextualization.
>
> ("Contextualization" refers to the one proposed by Gumperz (1992: 230), who-claimed that "situated interpretations are intrinsically context-bound and cannot be analyzed apart from verbal sequence in which they are embedded".)

In this new definition, it elaborates the criteria by which whether the information is judged evident or not, and the general statement of "making implied information explicit" in Vinay and Darbelnet's definition is supplemented by more specific term "additional textual information".

Furthermore, a clear label "co-text" (Catford 1965: 31) is also stamped on "context", which means the wording that comes just before and after a word, phrase or statement and helps you understand its meaning.

This study investigates not only inter-language explicitation that involves the comparison of target texts with source texts, but also intra-language explicitation which is based upon the constrative analysis between translated or interpreted texts with non-translated texts. The working definition proposed above is applicable for identifying inter-language explicitation, whereas the tentative definition of intra-language explicitation for the present study is as follows:

> **Intra-language explicitation** refers to the feature that translated or interpreted texts manifest a higher frequency of the use of cohesive devices and optional syntactic elements (i.e. optional complementizer *that*) than original texts written in the same language.

The actual division of the explicitation into inter-language explicitation and intra-language explicitation occurs in the seminal article by Baker (1993) in which she highlights "the theoretical possibilities of large corpora in translation research" (ibid: 234). Her study lays the groundwork for the study of the previously mentioned "universal features of translation [...] which typically occur in translated text rather than original utterances and which are not the result of interference from specific linguistic systems" (ibid. 243).

To sum up, taking the target text as the anchor point, explicitation can be not only established relative to the source text (inter-language explicitation), but also in relation to non-translated texts originally written in the target language (intra-language explicitation), with no translational relation between the two texts. Human activities including translating and interpreting are always context-dependent and context-forming. They cannot be systematically studied or judged independently of their contexts. Any attempt to offer exhaustive descriptions and viable explanations for explicitation features of interpreting learners in C-E CI would require a proper contextualization, which is always specific to a given case and never adequately evident (Toury 2012: 23). It is rather important to contextualize learner's interpretation by situating it within the socio-cultural space in which it is used and by relating it to the human agents who manipulate it in power-oriented encounters. In addition, unlike written translation, TT of interpreting takes place in the same temporal and spatial setting as the ST and the major participants are all present in the communication. Therefore, while analyzing interpreting features, it is critically important to consider spatial settings and other aspects related to interpreting discourse, and these factors that influence interpreters' choice in C-E CI.

## 3.2 Three Meta-functions of SFL

SFL is concerned with actual application of language. Halliday's functional grammar is "designated to account for how the language is used" and "each element in a language is explained by reference to its function in the total linguistic system" (1994: 39-40). As SFL equates meaning of a sentence with its function, Halliday also labels three meta-functions, namely ideational metafunction, interpersonal metafunction and textual metafunction respectively. As Halliday illustrates the basics of three metafunctions:

> All languages are organized around two main kinds of meaning, the "ideational" or reflective, and the "interpersonal" or active. These components, called "metafunctions" in the terminology of the present theory, are the manifestations in the linguistic system of the two very general purposes which underlie all uses of language: (i) to understand the environment (ideational), and (ii) to act on the others in it (interpersonal). Combined with these is a third metafunctional component, the "textual", which breathes the relevance into the other two (Halliday 1994; 2000).

Halliday's grammar is full-fledged, which enriches the interpretation of meaning and function with specific realizations at the lexico-grammatical level. In other words, the ideational meaning can be manifested by the system of transitivity, interpersonal meaning by Mood & Modality, and textual meaning by Theme-Rheme analysis as well as cohesion. The following sections briefly introduce the realization of these meanings.

### 3.2.1 Ideational Meaning and Its Lexico–grammatical Realization

Ideational meaning, introduced by Halliday, refers to "a way to express speaker's experience of the world, and of his own internal world" (Halliday 1978: 45). This meaning is achieved by Transitivity System in the lexico-grammatical level, which "construes the world of experience into manageable set of process types" (Halliday 1994: 107).

The basic constituents of the system are the process (verb and verbal group), participants (noun and noun groups) of the process and the environment in which the process takes place. There are three basic functional labels in the Transitivity System: Process, Participant and Circumstance. These "semantic categories" explain "how phenomena of the real world are represented as linguistic structure" (ibid: 109).

As is known to us, Halliday identifies six major processes types in total, which comprise material process, mental process, relational process, behavioral process, verbal process and existential process. This categorization depends on meaning and former three are principal types as they represent "majority of all clauses in a text" and "balanced in frequency over the language as a whole" (ibid: 138).

The material process more often than not involves physical action of doing and happening; the verbs in the material process are relevant to physical activities. For instance, in the sentence, "Alice broke the window yesterday", the verb "broke" is a physical action, and hence it is a material process.

The mental process is concerned with our cognition, perception and affection that relates to our experience of inner world; the verbs are involved in perception, reaction and cognition as well. For instance, in the clause, "she likes the gift very much", the verb "likes" reveals the participant's inner feeling, and thus it is a mental process.

The third major process, the relational process basically refers to the process of "being", "attributing" and "identifying"; for instance, in the clause "Sarah is the beautiful woman", the verb "is" indicates the identical relation between "Sarah" and "the beautiful woman", hence it is considered a relational process. Table 3.1 presents other processes along with three main processes mentioned above.

**Table 3.1 Process types and their respective participants**

| Process types | Process meaning | Participants |
|---|---|---|
| Material | Doing: doing, happening | Actor, goal |
| Mental | Sensing: seeing, feeling, thinking | Senser, phenomenon |
| Relational | Being, attributing, identifying | Carrier, attribute, identified, identifier/ token, value |
| Verbal | Saying | Sayer, target |
| Behavior | Behaving | Behaver |
| Existential | Existing | Existent |

Table 3.1 is a summary of the processes and their respective participants. Within each process, the participants are labeled based on the role they play in the clause. For instance, in a mental process, it is very feasible to call the initiator of the process "senser" and what being sensed as "phenomenon". Participants of other processes are also called for accordingly.

As to the circumstances, which "encode the background against which the process takes place" (Thompson 1996: 104), while Halliday specifies nine major types, consisting of the extent which describes distance and duration, location, manner, cause, contingency, accompaniment, role, matter and angle. Circumstance is regarded a category that stands on its own; for instance, in the clause "I will be in the US for the summer", the phrase indicates that duration "for the summer" is a typical circumstance. Other circumstances would not be elaborated here.

Transitivity analysis is applicable to explicating the meaning within the single clauses, however, it does not fully account for the relation and meaning in the composite clauses. Therefore, the ideational component falls into the experiential function mentioned above and logical function when it comes to multi-clauses in a certain text, with the latter expounding the relation between ideas. Specifically speaking, the logical function "relates to the connections between messages and to the ways in which we signal these connections" (ibid: 35).

The logical function developed by Halliday is complex with dozens of terms involved, which is beyond the scope of current research. Therefore, the common types of logical relations are touched upon, when it comes to the analysis of logical relations between compound clauses. The major types of logical relations cover additive relation, concessional relation, causal relation, adversative relation, conditional relation, proportional relation and summarizing relation.

### 3.2.2 Interpersonal Meaning and Its Lexico-grammatical Realization

The previous section presents the ways that ideational meaning realizes in a clause, especially concerning experiential function. This section elaborates another aspect of the clause meaning as an exchange. This chain of meaning is recognized as interpersonal as it reflects how the "interaction" and "transaction" are going on involving speakers or writers and audience (Halliday 1994: 34).The interpersonal meaning is achieved in terms of speech functions by means of Mood system, of the attitude of speaker by Modality, and of the relations between interaction parties.

According to Halliday, "in the act of speaking", the speaker "adopts for himself a speech role" and hence assigns a complementary role to the listener (ibid: 68). He identifies four primary speech functions including statement, question, offer and command. These functions rely on the fundamental types of speech role of either giving or demanding, and on the nature of commodity exchanged in the form of either "goods and services" or "information". Table 3.2 gives a summary of four speech functions, with their respective realization patterns and examples.

**Table 3.2 Primary speech functions realized by the Mood System** (Halliday 2014: 136)

| Commodities exchanged role in exchange | (a) goods and services | (b) information |
|---|---|---|
| (i) Giving | Offer<br>*Would you like this teapot?*<br>Realized by interrogative | Statement<br>*He's giving her the teapot.*<br>Realized by declarative |
| (ii) Demanding | Command<br>*Give me that teapot!*<br>Realized by imperative | Question<br>*What is he giving her?*<br>Realized by Wh-question |

It can been seen from Table 3.2 that speech functions are realized by different sentence patterns, which are actually known as Mood System that is the aspect of grammar meaning carries interpersonal meaning. The Mood System is the combination of "Subject", "Finite" and "Modal Adjunct" as well. Subject is usually realized by nominal group, and "Finite", as an essential part of a verbal group, is the verbal operator expressing primary tense (is, has, had), polarity (yes or no) and modality (can, might). Figure 3.1 demonstrates the relevant information about Mood System.

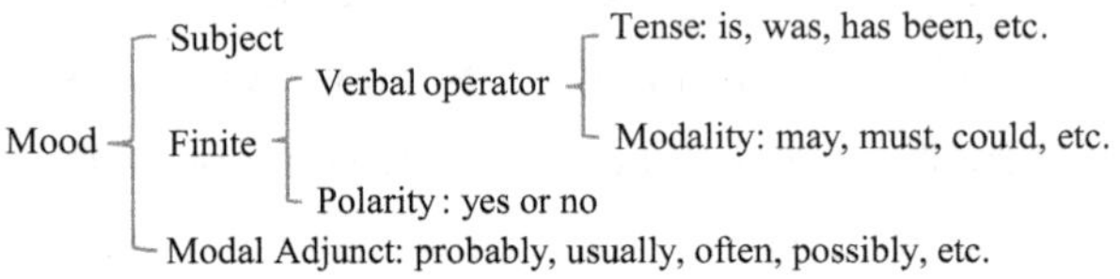


**Figure 3.1 Composition of Mood elements**

Subject is possessed with interpersonal significance as it is "something by reference to which the proposition can be affirmed or denied" (Halliday 1994: 76). That is to say, the Subject is responsible for the validity of the clause. On the other hand, Finite relates "the proposition to its context" in three ways. First, the tense operator relates the proposition to the time of speaking; second, Modality relates to "the speaker's judgment of the probabilities, or the obligations, involved in what he is saying"; third, Polarity, the "choice between positive and negative", makes a clause arguable between the speaker and the listener (ibid: 75).

Apart from the finite modal operator (FMO) in Mood like "can", "must", modal adjuncts reflect the Modality of a clause, which indicate the attitude of the speaker. Modality is defined as the "intermediate degrees between positive and negative poles" (ibid: 88). It refers to "the area of meaning that lies between yes and no — the intermediate ground between the positive and negative polarity" (ibid: 356).

Modality is realized through different linguistic devices, including finite modal operator, modal adjunct, passive verb predicator, and adjective predicator and appraisal words. Table 3.3 below shows a summary of modality and its different realizations.

Table 3.3 presents a brief summary of modality system and typical realizations in terms of speech functions in the form of a proposition or a proposal, as well as of intermediacy including modalization and modulation. In addition, one of the main purposes of verbal communicating is to establish and maintain harmonious social links among people. Therefore, analysis of social relations between interacting parties also performs a significant role in the interpersonal metafunction.

**Table 3.3 Review of Modality and its relations** (cited from Halliday 1994: 91)

| Commodity exchanged | Speech function | | Types of intermediacy | | Typical realization | Example |
|---|---|---|---|---|---|---|
| Information | Proposition | Statement | Modalization | Probability (possible/ probable/ certain) | Finite-modal-operator, modal adjunct and both | They *must* have known.<br>They *certainly* knew.<br>They *certainly must* have known. |
| | | Question | | Usuality (usually/ always/ often) | Finite-modal-operator, modal adjunct and both | It *must* happen.<br>It *always* happens.<br>It *must always* happen. |
| Goods & services | Proposal | Command | Modulation | Obligation (allowed/ supposed/ required) | Finite-modal-operator, passive verb predicator | You *must* be patient.<br>You're *required* to be patient! |
| | | Offer | | Inclination (willing/ keen/ determined) | Finite-modal-operator, adjective predicator | I *must* win!<br>I am *determined* to win. |

The social relations in language use are achieved not only by means of Mood & Modality and sometimes also by word choices. For instance, the choice of speech function partly reflects the power relationship between interactants. In general, those in the superordinate position are inclined to give command. Demanding or requesting somebody to do something is itself an exercising of power, as Fairclough (1989:55) puts it, "there is obviously a close connection between requests and power". The selection of Subject also reflects the power relations between interacting parties, as Subject is responsible for the "validity" of a clause. For instance, proposing a question can start with "Can you give me..." or "Could I ask you..." The second one is more polite in the way that speaker himself as the Subject shoulders the responsibility of the clause and lowes the obligation of the addressee.

### 3.2.3 Textual Meaning and Its Lexico-grammatical Realization

Up to date, an introduction is given about lexico-grammatical realization of the ideational meaning and interpersonal meaning, which are the utilization of language potential to signify those outside of language. This section deals with lexico-grammatical realization of the textual meaning, which refers to resources that realize the inward working metafunction of the language.

Textual meaning relates to construction of text. It means "being able to build up sequences of discourse, organizing the discursive flow and creating cohesion and continuity as the text moves along" (Halliday, 1994: 29). There are usually two systems through which this stream of meaning flow, namely system of Theme and system of Cohesion. This section presents a brief introduction to Theme and much detailed information about Cohesion.

From the textual perspective, a clause is composed of two parts: Theme and Rheme. Theme is described "the point of departure for the clauses as message" (Halliday 1967: 212). It "extends from the beginning of the clause up to (and including) the first element that has a function in transitivity" (Halliday 1994: 53). In addition, this "first element" is called "topical Theme" (ibid: 53), while words such as "well", "and", "so", etc., which naturally appear at the beginning of a clause, are categorized as textual Theme (ibid: 53). Rheme commonly refers to the given information in a clause, which is about the Theme.

Theme is the starting point of a message and the particular element that "organizes the clause as a message" (ibid: 38). The Theme-Rheme distinction can reveal how a text unveils and develops. As Baker illustrates, the element selected at the Theme position has two functions:

> It acts as point of orientation by connecting back to previous stretches of discourse and thereby maintaining a coherence point of view and it acts as a point of departure by connecting forward and contributing to the development of latter stretches. (Baker 1992: 121)

For a well-organized text, the Theme-Rheme distinction can show clearly how a text unveils and develops. Baker (1992), for example, adopts the Theme-Rheme analysis to explain why some translations are well-formed grammatically yet still has an air of awkwardness. She suggests that this kind of awkwardness is mostly a result of ill-formed thematic progression (1992: 124-125).

The thematic progression is realized by "configuration of structural functions" as Theme and Rheme are assigned with particular position in a clause, while cohesion refers to the "non-structural resources for discourse" (Halliday 1994: 308-309), and "relations of meaning that exist within the text" (Halliday & Hasan 1976: 4). The term "cohesion" covers "the linguistic devices by which the speaker can signal the experiential and interpersonal coherence of the text" (Thompson 1996: 147).

In general, there are four primary types of cohesion, including reference, substitution or ellipsis, conjunction and lexical cohesion.

Reference is "a relationship between things, or facts" (Halliday 1994: 309). It is "the set of grammatical resources which allow the speaker to indicate whether something is being repeated from somewhere else in the text" (Thompson 1996: 148). Typically, this cohesive device is mostly realized by personal pronouns (e.g. she/her, he/him, etc.), demonstratives (e.g. this/these, here/there, etc.) and comparatives (e.g. similar, such, another, etc.).

Substitution involves the process of the replacement of one item by another (e.g., nominal substitutes one/ones and verbal substitutes do/does). The substituted item has the same structural function and meaning as that for which it substitutes (Halliday & Hasan 1976: 89).

It is worth mentioning that it is rather important to distinguish reference from substitution. Substitution is a relation between linguistic items, such as words and phrases; whereas reference is a relation between meanings. In terms of linguistic system, reference is a relation on the semantic level, whereas substitution is a relation on the lexico-grammatical level, the level of grammar and vocabulary, or linguistic "form" (ibid). Ellipsis is very similar to substitution, which is in this respect simply "substitution by zero". It "presupposes something by means of what is left out" (Halliday 1994: 316).

Conjunction refers to "the combining of any two textual elements into a potentially coherent complex semantic unit" (Thompson 1996: 156). It is the most significant means through which the logical relations in a text are realized. Those most common logical connecters can be in the form of words (e.g. and, but, therefore), word groups and phrases (e.g. in addition, on the contrary) as well as minor clauses (e.g. what is more, in other words, that is to say).

Lexical cohesion is described as the selection of lexical items that are "related in some way to those that have gone before" (Halliday 1994: 330). Halliday and Hasan (1976) classify it into two main categories: lexical reiteration and collocation. The former includes lexical repetition, synonym/antonym and superordinate/hyponym. The latter refers to association of lexical items that have the "co-occurrence tendency" (ibid: 333).

The system of cohesion, one of the important Hallidayan theories, is later introduced to China. Some Chinese scholars categorize the four types of cohesive devices into two broad classes: grammatical cohesion comprising of reference, substitution, ellipsis and conjunction reviewed above, and lexical cohesion.

Figure 3.2 is an overview of cohesive devices. The application of various cohesive devices builds up a cohesive chain of a text that contributes to its overall texture.

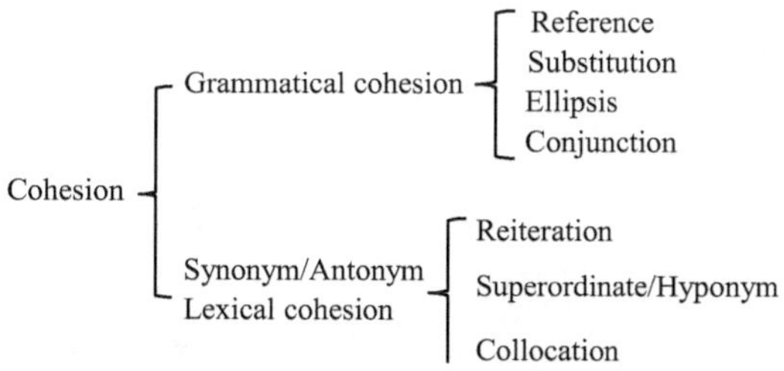


**Figure 3.2 Composition of cohesive device**

The present study concentrates on explicitation features of textual meaning, and of cohesive devices in particular. It does not mean that ideational meaning and interpersonal meaning are not as important as the textual meaning, and three metafunctions in SFL are equally significant. The main reasons why this research focuses on explicitation features of textual meaning are as follows.

In the first place, the framework of Systemic Functional Linguistics (Halliday & Matthiessen 2004) has incredibly enriched the scope of linguistic research with a significantly functional and multi-dimensional perspective on language. However, it is hard to find objective criteria for keeping the three categories apart. While identifying linguistic items, it is hard to distinguish whether they belong to the "ideational", "interpersonal", or "textual" metafunction of language. For instance, linguistic items such as *still* or *entirely* carry with the interpersonal metafunction of language (2004: 128), but they also have ideational function too.

Moreover, given the fundamental problem that corpus methodology relies on observing large amounts of data, it is much likely to conduct a research on textual meaning, cohesive device in particular, as cohesive markers are comparatively easy to identify.

Finally yet importantly, the corpus data employed in the study are Chinese EFL learner's C-E interpreted texts, and there are more errors and lexical repetitions as compared with professional interpreting corpus. This makes it impossible to concentrate on all three metafunctions expressed by linguistic items.

To sum up, based on the reasons noted above, the current research focuses on explicitation features of textual meaning, of cohesive devises in particular, in C-E CI by Chinese EFL students. This will make the results more objective and reliable, but incomplete in the sense that it does not aim to identify all explicitation instances concerning three metafunctional together.

Taking account of the cohesive devices introduced above, the present study also investigates-*that* as a subordinator. According to Rohdenburg (1996:161), the subordinator "*that* generally happens to have triggered the boundary signal, which signifies the relationship between the main clause and the subordinate clause so as to avoid the ambiguity". Therefore, the current study adopts the following analytic framework for textual explicitation with specific subcategorization in Figure 3.3.

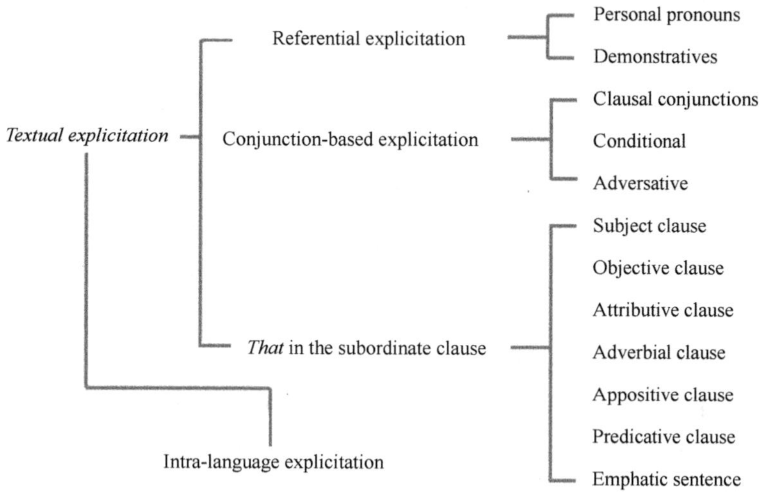


**Figure 3.3 Analytic framework of textual explicitation**

## 3.3 The Effort Model of Interpreting

The most common factors researchers often resort to consider as motivations for explicitation that include linguistic difference between SL and TL, cultural discrepancies that SL and TL reflect, and stylistic preference in text-building strategies. In addition to these motivations, this study also attempts to explore reasons that account for explicitation from the cognitive effort involved in interpreting process.

Cognitive issues were absent from mainstream interpreting for a long time, but became the point of interest from the 1990s on (Pöchhacker & Shlesinger 2001; Pöchhacker 2004). Different from written translation, the cognitive factors involved in interpreting, such as processing capacity and working memory, as well as processing capacity limitations, have been central to cognitive effort required in interpreting over the past decades (Gile 2009: 253). Cognitive effort during the interpreting process includes "listening and analysis component, a speech production component, and a short-term memory component" (ibid: 160). Gile (ibid) named these components "efforts" to emphasize their effortful nature, as they call for deliberate action that requires decisions and resources.

The Effort Models involved in interpreting stem from "two intuitive ideas based on observation and introspection" (Gile 2009: 159):

① Interpreting requires some sort of "mental energy" that is only available in limited supply.

② Interpreting takes up almost all of this mental energy, and sometimes requires more than is available, at which times performance deteriorates.

As mentioned earlier, in general, the core efforts required in interpreting cover Listening and Analysis Effort, Production Effort and Memory Effort. The Listening and Analysis Effort consists of all comprehension-oriented operations involved in interpreting, from "the subconscious analysis of the sound waves carrying the source-language speech which reach the interpreter's ears through the identification of words to the final decisions about the meaning of the utterance" (Gile 2009: 160).

Production Effort includes a set of operations, which range from "the mental representation of the message to be delivered to speech planning and the performance of the speech plan" (Gile 2009: 163). It also covers self-monitoring and self-correction when necessary during the interpreting.

As to Memory Effort, psychologists traditionally draw a general distinction between long-term memory, which viewed as "memory" in daily life, and short-term memory, referred to as the ability to keep information and process it over a short period. Short-term memory, which is also called working memory, is viewed an important determinant of cognitive operations involved in interpreting. There is a consensus about the following points of working memory (Gile 2009: 167):

> ① Working memory is a set of mechanisms or processes involved in the control, regulation and active maintenance of task-relevant information in the service of complex cognition; it operates primarily on currently "activated" information from long-term memory.
>
> ② Working memory requires processing capacity.
>
> ③ Working memory has a small storage capacity.

Working memory is necessarily a part of the language-comprehension process and of the speech-production process. Working memory is apparently an important part of Memory Effort, which refers to "a step in the interpreting process that involves memory and memory operations, not as a conceptual entity from cognitive psychology" (Gile 2009: 167).

Consecutive interpreting consists of two phases: comprehension phase and target-speech productions phase (Gile 2009: 175). In terms of Effort Model, the comprehension phase mainly involves Listening and Analysis Effort and Memory Effort. The effort in the first phase is associated with "the time between the moment it is heard and processed mentally and sent on to (long-term) memory" (Gile 2009: 175-176). The production phase involves a set of mental operations devoted to recalling the successive parts of the original speech from long-term memory and produce target speech. Furthermore, phase one is mainly influenced by the speaker, while in phase two the interpreter is free to exert the three Efforts and allocate processing capacity to produce the natural target speech as much as possible.

In summary, owing to cognitive operations related to Memory Effort, what the interpreter can grasp in CI is the general idea of the source speech, not the original linguistic forms. Therefore, interpreters often employ interpretive methods to interpret the original speech and to help the target audience understand the logical relations and information flow of the original speech. In addition, interpreting constraints that force "interpreters to deviate from their habitual speech production patterns may account for the poor quality of language output in students' interpreting exercises" (Gile 2009: 165). It is because student interpreters tend to use source-language words and structures to construct their own target-language speech, which leads to speech production more vulnerable. It will make the student interpreters' speech more hesitant, less idiomatic, less clear, and less pleasant to listen to, compared with professional interpreters (Gile 2009: 164-166).

## 3.4 Summary

So far, we have discussed the theoretical foundation for the present study bases upon, including explicitation within the scope of Descriptive Translation Studies, Systematic Functional Grammar, and Effort Model of interpreting. The working definition of inter-language explicitation and intra-language explicitation for the present research is also given. Based on theoretical insights, there is a tentative working model for descriptive-explanatory analysis of corpus-based learners' interpreting studies, which will guide the present study. Figure 3.4 demonstrates the working model used in this study.

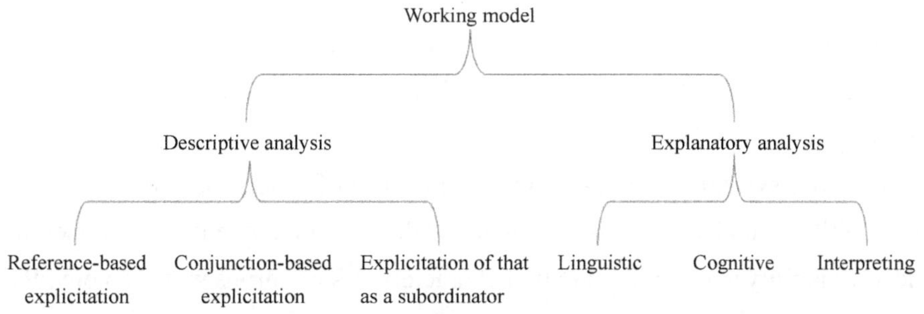


**Figure 3. 4 The working model of the study**

# Chapter Four Research Design

The former chapter puts forward the theoretical basis upon which the current study is grounded and analytic framework for textual explicitation in brief. This chapter deals with methodological issues. It will start with introducing corpus as a major methodology for empirical research. To address the research questions mentioned in 1.4, the current study adopts the combination of a quantitative analysis and a qualitative analysis. For the quantitative analysis, this study conducts a statistical data for the explicitation of textual meaning based on multilayered categorization. This research also makes the qualitative analysis for the description of explicitation features and explanation for reasons that trigger such features found in Chinese EFL students' C-E CI. Then, it elaborates upon the corpora adopted in the current study. Finally, the study outlines the procedure for conducting the research. In addition, it also pinpoints the lexico-grammatical features related to explicitation of textual meaning.

## 4.1 Corpus Methodology

The current study is conducted under the framework of CTS, and corpus linguistics is a well-established methodology in translation studies and empirical in nature. A corpus approach to the investigation of naturally occurring language is empirical in nature (Neumann & Hansen-Schirra 2012: 21), and the "empiricist approach" is "dominated by the observation of naturally occurring data, typically through the medium of the corpus" (McEnery & Wilson 2001:5).

Corpus methodology depends on the observation of actual and authentic translation and interpreting data. In this sense, the information, knowledge and understanding are gained through actual experience and direct data collection (Black 1999:3). In general, corpus methodology exhibits several characteristics of the following.

Firstly, it allows systematic observations with an aim of producing replicable studies (Black 1999: 4), and it follows logically consistent methods that rely on authentic-data observation.

Secondly, reliability and validity are two characteristics of corpus methodology. Reliability is "concerned with the exactitude of the measuring instrument or method", and useful tools which "do not change their interpretation of a given element" (Neumann & Hansen-Schirra 2012: 22). Validity refers to "whether the choice of method is appropriate to the phenomenon under investigation and whether the chosen indicators actually measure the concept under investigation" (ibid).

Finally, the result of the research by using a corpus is verifiable. Popper argues that theories are hard to verify absolutely and forever; however, they can be falsified, i.e. they can be proven wrong (1959, 2002).

In a word, considered an empirical method, corpus-based approaches to translation and interpretation focus on "how translation and interpretation patterns differ from their source texts or from the original texts written in target language" (Zanettin, Bernardini & Stewart 2003: 2). A corpus-based analysis can identify the textual explicitation features in C-E CI found in the Corpus of Chinese EFL Students. In addition, this study makes a comparison between the corpora of Chinese EFL students and Professional Interpreters with regard to explicitation features of textual meaning in C-E CI through using corpus statistics in particular.

The analysis of corpus data belongs to quantitative research, while the description and explanation of statistical results call for qualitative study. The large-scale corpus of translation or interpretation can provide rich data for translation or interpreting studies, from which the frequency of translation universals is statistically calculated. On the other hand, the determination of the research object, the choice of corpus data, the description of the statistical data, and the analysis and the explanation for such results all require for qualitative approach. The statistical data reflects one part of the empirical research while the factors outside the data comprise the other part. The former part is an objective description and the latter is more subjective; and the combination of the two constitutes the overall research.

It is noteworthy that the quantitative approach alone does not exactly improve the objectivity of translation studies, so researchers should avoid exaggerating the role that statistical data plays in CTS. As Tymoczko (1998:3) pointes out: "behind the establishment of corpora, as behind the design of any experiment or research program or survey, lies intuition and human judgment". Corpora in CTS are products of actual human beings, and thus reflecting the expectations, views and restrictions of those actual human beings. Therefore, it is advisable not to place too much emphasis on the importance of quantitative data while ignoring the qualitative one. Thus, the combination of quantitative and qualitative approaches makes the CTS more reliable and well-established branch of translation studies.

## 4.2 Corpora Used in the Present Study

The current study adopts three subcorpora: the parallel corpus of Chinese EFL students in C-E CI, the parallel corpus of C-E Conference Interpreting, and the original English corpus of press conferences. The first one is the Chinese EFL Learners Corpus (CEL), which is regarded a main source of observation; the second is Professional Interpreters Corpus (PIC) regarded as a reference corpus; and the last one is the Original English Corpus (OEC), which can be used for intra-language comparison with the interpreted English of Chinese EFL students.

Specifically, the CEL is composed of C-E transcriptions of CI done by Chinese students majoring in English between the year 2003 and 2007. The PIC and the OEC comprise a number of press conferences held by the Chinese and US governments from the year of 2003 to 2014. Table 4.1 shows the specific structure and size of the three subcorpora.

**Table 4.1 The composition of the corpus data**

| Subcorpus | STs | TTs | Total | Percentage |
|---|---|---|---|---|
| Chinese EFL Learners Corpus (CEL) | 176,599 | 154,902 | 331,501 | 40.95% |
| Professional Interpreting Corpus (PIC) | 182,796 | 143,143 | 325,939 | 40.26% |
| Original English Corpus (OEC) | | 152,145 | | 18.79% |

As displayed in Table 4.1, three subcorpora employed in this study are designed to ensure as much comparability as possible between the target texts in the students' and professional corpora and the original English texts. For inter-language explicitation, both CEL and PIC parallel subcorpora, not only have similar corpus size, but also use Chinese as the source language and English as the target language in CI setting. Most importantly, three subcorpora contain similar topics under discussion, which cover similar domain. These features make it possible to compare explicitation features between CEL and PIC parallel subcorpora. For intra-language explicitation, the target texts of CEL and that of OEC subcorpora have roughly the same corpus size and the similar subjects under discussion, which cover economy, diplomatic policy and related issues. In addition, these texts are close enough as measured by total word count. Baker (1995: 234) advises that two corpora are comparable in the sense that they "should cover a similar domain, variety of language and be of comparable length." Three subcorpora cover similar topics under discussion, and of comparable length in similar interpreting setting. Therefore, three subcorpora used in this study meet this criterion. The following sections introduce the detailed description of three subcorpora.

### 4.2.1 Chinese EFL Learner Corpus

The data in this corpus consist of the interpreted texts in C-E CI done by English major students from 18 different colleges in China between the year 2003 and 2007. The corpus size is composed of approximately 34 thousand tokens (each Chinese character or English word is counted as one token). Table 4.2 presents the overall size of CEL with specific number of speech files and transcribed texts.

**Table 4.2 Overview of the CEL interpreting corpus**

| Year | The number of speech files | The number of transcribed texts | Chinese (characters) | English (words) | C-E overall size (token) |
|---|---|---|---|---|---|
| 2003 | 366 | 366 | 30 212 | 27 371 | 57 583 |
| 2004 | 382 | 378 | 34 209 | 30 533 | 64 742 |
| 2005 | 382 | 380 | 38 367 | 33 264 | 71 631 |
| 2006 | 354 | 348 | 32 364 | 33 010 | 65 374 |
| 2007 | 380 | 382 | 41 447 | 30 724 | 72 171 |
| Total | 1 864 | 1 854 | 176 599 | 154 902 | 331 501 |

The interpreted materials all involve hot issues both at home and abroad, which are closely relevant to general foreign affairs. It includes speeches given by officials and leaders at the conference such as the exhibition conference, seminar opening and closing ceremony.

The content in the speech was delivered distinctly and logically in Mandarin Chinese. Therefore, it posed no difficulty for Chinese students to comprehend the original speech. After listening to the Chinese speech, the Chinese students were required to interpret the part of or the whole speech into English.

### 4.2.2 Professional Interpreters Corpus

The interpreting data used for professional interpreters in this paper comes from the subcorpus of C-E Conference Interpreting Corpus (CECIC 4.0) constructed by the research team at Shanghai Jiao Tong University. The CECIC 4.0 consists of three subcorpora: namely the Original English Corpus of Press Conferences by US government, the C-E Parallel Corpus of Press Conference Interpreting and the C-E Parallel Corpus of Chinese Government's Work Report done by Chinese government. In order to match the corpus size and make it comparable to the students' corpus, the present study applies the subcorpus, C-E Parallel Corpus of Press Conference Interpreting from 2003-2014. Table 4.3 presents the detailed information about this Professional Interpreters Corpus (PIC).

As shown in Table 4.3, PIC comprises 15 C-E conference-interpreting events from 2003 to 2014, which are interpreted by top-level interpreting professionals in China. The STs and TTs are aligned at sentence level. The content in conference interpreting is also closely relevant to general foreign affairs covering the subjects of economy, diplomatic policy and related issues, thus CEL could be comparable to PIC in terms of explicitation features in C-E CI.

**Table 4.3 Overview of PIC**

| Year | Primary speakers | STs | TTs | C-E overall size |
|---|---|---|---|---|
| 2003 | Tang Jiaxuan, Wen Jiabao | 4 590+7 911 | 2 852+6 322 | 21 675 |
| 2004 | Li Zhaoxing, Wen Jiabao | 9 637+7 199 | 7 776+6 056 | 30 668 |
| 2005 | Li Zhaoxing, Wen Jiabao | 6 907+7 060 | 5 403+5 211 | 24 581 |
| 2006 | Li Zhaoxing, Wen Jiabao | 9 209+7 654 | 7 326+7 290 | 31 479 |
| 2007 | Zhou Xiaochuan, Li Zhaoxing, Wen Jiabao | 15 891+11 192 +6 564 | 11 008+8 188 +6 624 | 59 467 |
| 2008 | Wen Jiabao, Yang Jiechi | 7 862 +10 140 | 7 742+6 290 | 32 034 |
| 2009 | Wen Jiabao, Yang Jiechi | 8 181+9 422 | 7 360+6 626 | 31 589 |
| 2010 | Wen Jiabao, Yang Jiechi | 8 148+9 096 | 6 895+6 570 | 30 709 |
| 2011 | Yang Jiechi | 9 744 | 6703 | 16 447 |
| 2012 | Wen Jiabao | 9 311 | 7707 | 17 018 |
| 2013 | Li Keqiang | 8 200 | 6362 | 14 562 |
| 2014 | Li Keqiang | 8 878 | 6832 | 15 710 |
| Total | 6 speakers | 182 796 | 143 143 | 325 939 |

It is also worth mentioning that with regard to compilation of both corpora mentioned above, especially at the stage of transcribing the recordings into written texts, the available transcriptions on line are not primary source of written forms, as those transcriptions are generally approximate representations of the interpretations. Therefore, while doing transcription, the research team members resort to their ears to write the transcription, and take down fluent speeches, repetitions, and even paralinguistic features such as hesitations, pauses and revisions. As a result, the transcribed texts faithfully represent the original speeches by both professional interpreters and Chinese EFL learners. The paralinguistic features are marked with special annotation, such as interruptions, pauses, repetitions and revisions. They are regarded relatively important sources for investigation of paralinguistic features found in C-E consecutive interpretation by both professional interpreters and Chinese EFL students, even though they are not the scope of the present study.

After finishing transcription and annotation of Chinese STs as well, Chinese STs and English TTs are aligned manually at the sentence level. In fact, the students’ corpus contains consecutive interpretation from Chinese to English or English to Chinese, both done by Chinese EFL students. However, for the current study, only Chinese-to-English interpretating is within the scope of investigation.

As to the comparability of the two corpora mentioned above for inter-language comparison, firstly, both of the parallel corpora contain Chinese-English consecutive setting. Secondly, the corpora share topics in common, which are closely relevant to general foreign affairs activities, including economy, politics, diplomatic policy and related issues. Lastly, the sizes of the two corpora are close enough as measured by total word count. Therefore, it is feasible to make a comparison between CEL corpus and PIC regarding textual explicitation in C-E CI.

### 4.2.3 Original English Corpus

The study explores not only inter-language textual explicitation, which makes a contrastive analysis between the source text and the target text, but also intra-language explicitation, which conducts a comparative analysis between the translated text and the original (non-translated) text. Therefore, it is necessary to find an appropriate original English corpus that is comparable with the interpreted texts of Chinese EFL learners. The original English corpus is the subcorpus of the CECIC 4.0 mentioned in 4.2.2 covering the year of 2003 to 2014. The subjects of original English corpus are similar to that of Chinese EFL learners, which are relevant to general foreign affairs. Table 4.4 demonstrates the detailed information of the original English corpus (OEC).

**Table 4.4 Overview of OEC**

| Year | Primary speakers | The number of words | Overall size |
|---|---|---|---|
| 2003 | McClellan, Boucher | 8 563+7 145 | 15 708 |
| 2004 | Bush, Boucher | 7 035+6 767 | 13 802 |
| 2005 | Bush, Ereli | 6 039+9 886 | 15 925 |
| 2006 | Bush, McCormack | 9 633+6 121 | 15 754 |
| 2007 | Rice, Snow, Perino | 5 683+5 685+7 914 | 19 282 |
| 2008 | Rice, Hadley, Lazear | 5 672+5 043 | 10 715 |
| 2009 | Bush, Obama | 7 108+8 842 | 15 950 |
| 2010 | Obama | 5 224+9 287 | 14 511 |
| 2011 | Obama | 9 772 | 9 772 |
| 2012 | Obama | 4 905 | 4 905 |
| 2013 | Obama | 7 040 | 7 040 |
| 2014 | Jay Carney | 8 781 | 8 781 |
| total | 13 speakers | 152 145 | 152 145 |

As shown in Table 4.4, the original English corpus (OEC) used in this study consist of transcriptions of a number of press conferences held by the US government from 2003 to 2014. The corpus has roughly similar size and topics under discussion with students' corpus so as to ensure as much comparability as possible between the interpreted English texts of students and the original English texts.

## 4.3 Data Collection

### 4.3.1 Subjects

Research subjects include Chinese EFL students majoring in English and professional interpreters. These students are in the last year of English major, and do not have interpreting working experience except attending an interpreting course. They all have Chinese as their mother tongue and English as their foreign language, and come from 18 different colleges in China.

The professional interpreters are of top level and highly qualified, who are compared as "national team of Chinese interpreters" (Zong 2012). The interpreters provide services for press conferences and are "all from Foreign Ministry because interpreters from Department of Translation and Interpretation are the best of China" (Guo 2013). They are usually appraised for their accurate and flexible interpreting performance, but they may also receive some criticism for minor errors occasionally.

### 4.3.2 The Comparability of Texts

As described in Table 4.1, the three subcorpora used in this study, CEL, PIC and OEC have roughly similar size and topics under discussion, which cover similar domain. In addition, all the texts are either official speeches or reports form Chinese or American governments, covering economy, culture, diplomatic policy and related issues. These features make it possible to compare explicitation features between CEL and PIC parallel subcorpora for inter-language explicitation, and between the interpreted texts of CEL and that of OEC subcorpora for intra-language explicitation.

In this way, the three subcorpora are comparable in terms of corpus size and topic of discussion. Such design meets the criteria for the comparability of texts proposed by Baker (1995: 234), who advises that two corpora are comparable in the sense that they "should cover a similar domain, variety of language and be of comparable length". We believe that such design of three subcorpora will serve as a good starting point for us to investigate inter-language explicitation of Chinese EFL students as compared with that of professional interpreters, and intra-language explicitation of interpreted English texts of students in relation to that of original English texts respectively.

### 4.3.3 Procedure for Data Collection

The research objects, Chinese EFL students who are majoring in English, were familiar with the topic of the speech and whole procedure of the interpreting test. The length of material that requested students to interpret was about three minute's speech. Students were allowed to listen to the whole speech once so as to familiarize themselves with the background of the material that was heard in the speech. Then they were required to interpret the part of or the entire Chinese speech into English. The content of interpreted speech fell into four passages in 2003 interpreting test and five passages in the remaining years and each passage contained several sentences. The length of pause was determined according to the content and level of difficulty between a pause. "Ding Dong" served as an alert tone both at the beginning and ending of the pause during which students were required to interpret the Chinese speech into English immediately. As students heard first "Ding Dong" sound, they were supposed to interpret promptly what they just heard into English. When the second alert tone rang, they were required to stop interpreting and prepared to listen to next passage. The Chinese students majoring in English could make some notes while listening to the passage.

The interpretations of the Chinese EFL students were recorded in cassettes, but for the purpose of convenient storage in the computer, tape recordings were converted into electronic audio files MP3. This procedure ensured that not only the file size was moderate, but also maintained the quality of the transcription in the tape recording. The audio files were stored in accordance with the year, the group and serial numbers; for instance, 03-20-1 stood for first audio file of 20th group in the 2003 year. Finally, the content of audio files was transferred into transcribed texts, so that it could be stored as *.txt files* in the computer and lend support to conduct a research on interpreted texts of Chinese students majoring in English.

In addition, while transcribing the audio files into interpreted texts, there was an <CE serial number> in the beginning of each sentence in C-E CI, thus facilitating the alignment at sentence level. For example, <CE1> referred to the first sentence in C-E CI done by Chinese students. Great effort was made to accurately reproduce the information of the C-E CI as it was recorded, both at the linguistic and paralinguistic levels.

As to the linguistic level, all the words uttered by Chinese EFL students were transcribed as much as possible. The punctuation used to signal sentence boundaries relied on the duration of pause, intonation, syntactic function of a word in the sentence. At paralinguistic level, great endeavors were made to mark the disfluency pauses, false starts, pause fillers and grammatical mistakes, which included mispronounced and unintelligible words. Besides, there were also several annotations used to reveal the head information and other paralinguistic features. Table 4.5 illustrates the detailed information.

**Table 4.5 Annotation of CEL corpus**

| Type | Annotation symbols | Explanations |
|---|---|---|
| Type of the test | <SPOKEN> | Spoken |
| Rank of the test | <TEM8> | Test for English majors Band Eight |
| Grade | <GRADE4> | Fourth Grade |
| Year | <YEAR03> | Year 2003 |
| Group | <GROUP5> | Group 5 |
| Gender | <SEX=F >,<SEX=M > | Sex=Female, Sex=Male |
| Score | <SCORE=54 > | Score= 54 points |
| Within-group rank | <LEVEL=2 > | Within-group rank = 2 |
| Sentence number | <CE2 > | Chinese to English sentence 2 |
| Grammatical mistake | <> | Lives <life > ; are < were> |
| Mispronunciation | <> | Make < meek> |
| Pause | … | Disfluency pauses |
| Oral features | Er, oh, en, um, well | Pause fillers |

The snapshot below in Figure 4.1 illustrates the specific demonstration of the markup text in the students' corpus. The picture indicates that it is the interpreted text of a female Chinese student in C-E CI with the score of 80, which equals to first level within group 5 in the year of 2003.

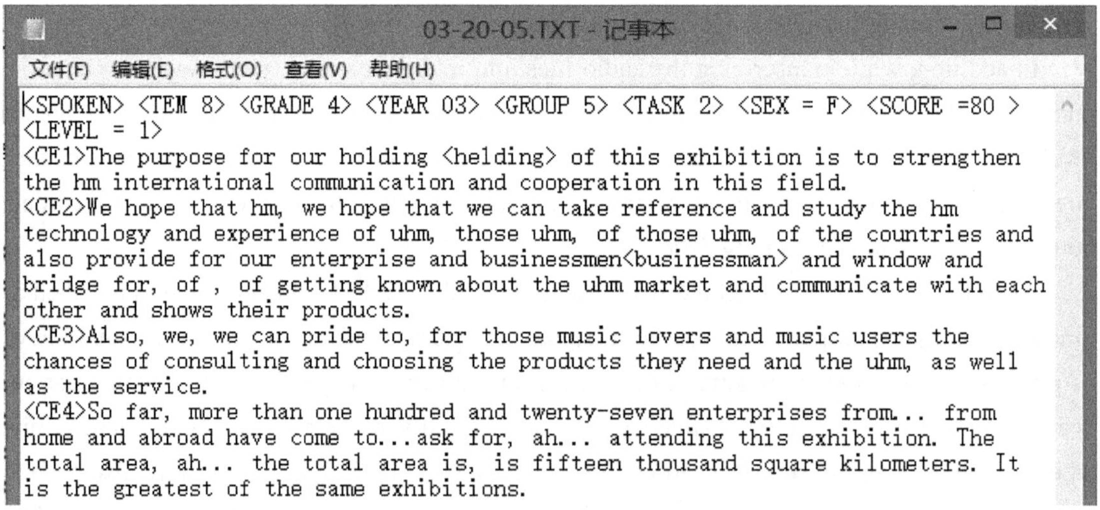
03-20-05.TXT - 记事本
文件(F) 编辑(E) 格式(O) 查看(V) 帮助(H)
<SPOKEN> <TEM 8> <GRADE 4> <YEAR 03> <GROUP 5> <TASK 2> <SEX = F> <SCORE =80 >
<LEVEL = 1>
<CE1>The purpose for our holding <helding> of this exhibition is to strengthen the hm international communication and cooperation in this field.
<CE2>We hope that hm, we hope that we can take reference and study the hm technology and experience of uhm, those uhm, of those uhm, of the countries and also provide for our enterprise and businessmen<businessman> and window and bridge for, of , of getting known about the uhm market and communicate with each other and shows their products.
<CE3>Also, we, we can pride to, for those music lovers and music users the chances of consulting and choosing the products they need and the uhm, as well as the service.
<CE4>So far, more than one hundred and twenty-seven enterprises from... from home and abroad have come to...ask for, ah... attending this exhibition. The total area, ah... the total area is, is fifteen thousand square kilometers. It is the greatest of the same exhibitions.

**Figure 4.1 Snapshot of annotation in CEL corpus**

## 4.4 Research Procedure

The ways in which Chinese EFL students exhibit inter-language explicitation and intra-language explicitation of textual meaning in C-E consecutive interpretation are probed along three dimensions. Those dimensions consist of Reference-based Explicitation, Conjunction-based Explicitation and explicitation of *that* in subordinate clauses in the current study respectively. More importantly, the explicitation features of textual meaning in C-E CI by Chinese EFL students are compared with that of professional interpreters based on multilayered dimensions.

The present study deals with explicitation features of textual meaning in C-E CI. In general, textual meaning in a discourse is achieved by two systems: System of Theme and System of Cohesion demonstrated in 3.2.3. The current research primarily focuses on explicitation of cohesion in C-E CI by Chinese EFL students in particular. The specific procedures for the analysis of the data in the present study are as follows:

**First step: selecting linguistic devices related to explicitation of textual meaning.**

Since different lexico-grammatical forms can help achieve the textual meaning in a discourse, it would be impractical to conduct a full-fledged research about corpus-based explicitation of all linguistic resources in a corpus. Therefore, prior to exploring all the linguistic devices relating to the textual meaning, cohesion in particular for the study, a careful and informed decision should be made as to which major cohesive devices to be focused upon.

The identification of cohesive devices relies on the following three criteria: (i) they belong to the most frequently used cohesive devices concerning textual meaning (Halliday and Hasan 1976). (ii) Moreover, they are relatively frequent in three subcorpora: students' corpus, professional corpus and the original English corpus respectively. (iii) The number of instances is big enough for analysis, and most of the cohesive devices selected for study belong to a closed category such as pronouns, demonstratives and conjunctions as well.

The potential cohesive devices fall into three main categories based upon the criteria mentioned above. These are the category of reference, substitution and conjunction as well. Owing to the fact that no significant difference exists between students and professionals with regard to the occurrence of substitution, thus the study excludes substitution from investigations. In general, the personal pronoun reference and the demonstrative reference are selected acknowledged referential types (Halliday & Hasan 1976: 37). As for conjunctions, adversative, causal, conditional and other conjunctions are regarded frequently used cohesive devices for a close investigation. As to intra-language explicitation, *that* as a subordinator in multiple subordinating clauses is also a consideration besides cohesive devises mentioned above.

As far as the personal reference concerned, personal pronouns with subjective and objective case forms are selected as searching items for explicitation of cohesive devices in C-E CI. As to demonstrative reference, singular demonstratives *this* and *that*, plural demonstratives *these* and *those* on the part of participant, and circumstantial demonstratives *here* and *there* are regarded as subjects of investigation for explicitation of cohesive devices in C-E consecutive interpretation as well.

With regard to conjunctions, causal conjunctions of *because, since, therefore, thus and so,* adversative conjunctions of *but, however, though, yet,* and *although*; conditional and other conjunctions *if, in order to, so as to* and *so that* etc. are considered the objects for the present study. The following Table 4.6 shows the detailed information.

**Table 4.6 Cohesive devices investigated in the corpora**

| Subtypes types | Subjective case | Objective case | Demonstratives |
|---|---|---|---|
| Reference | Speaker: I, we<br>Addressee: you<br>Third person: he, she, they | Speaker: me, us<br>Addressee: you<br>Third person: his, her, them | Singular: this, that<br>Plural: these, those<br>Place: here, there |
| Conjunctions | Adversative conjunctions:<br>yet, although, though,<br>however, but | Causal conjunctions:<br>because, so, since,<br>thus, therefore | Conditional & other:<br>if, so that, in order to,<br>so as to |

Table 4.6 illustrates the linguistic devices identified as the research objects for inter-language explicitation of textual meaning, especially cohesive devices in C-E CI in the current study. It is worth mentioning that the searching items in operation might not be fully consistent with the criteria by which they are identified in the research as listed above. This is because some of them are not highly frequent in terms of instances found in the corpora.

In addition, as for intra-language textual explicitation, *that* as a leading word in multiple subordinating clauses is regarded the focus of investigation besides linguistic resources mentioned above, based on the comparison between Chinese EFL learners' corpus and the original English corpus.

**Second step: Extracting language-pair segments for explicitation analysis**

Since the present study deals with inter-language and intra-language explicitation patterns of Chinese EFL students in C-E CI through an integrated corpus approach, it is worthwhile to mention those software packages used to assist searching items in the corpus.

The ICTCLAS (Institute of Computing Technology, Chinese Lexical Analysis System) and CLAWS (Constituent Likelihood Automatic Word-tagging System) are employed as word segmentation software for Chinese and word-tagging software for English. In other words, the Chinese STs are word segmented with the help of ICTCLAS, and the TTs are annotated in terms of part of speech, using the system CLAWS (developed by UCREL at Lancaster), which is the latest version of the POS tagging software for English text. Both software packages can achieve over 95% accuracy on average with even higher rate for segmentation of Chinese words and major categories of English words respectively. The purpose of segmentation of the Chinese STs and tagging the English TTs with part-of-speech information is to facilitate the searching in later stage of research, thus making it possible to capture the picture of differences in word usage through grammatical information when it is necessary. The following pictures (Figure 4.2 and Figure 4.3) vividly demonstrate students' STs and TTs at sentence level after using ICTCLAS software for Chinese word segmentation and CLAWS for English tagging.

```
<SPOKEN><TEM8><GRADE4><YEAR05><GROUP><TASK2>
<CE1> 今天_t 是_v 辞旧迎新_l 的_u 时刻_n ，_w 也_d 是_v 我们_r 回顾_v 与_p
展望_v 的_u 时刻_n 。_w
<CE2> 在_p 过去_t 的_u 一_m 年_q 里_f ，_w 我们_r 向_p 世界_n 报道_v 了_u
中国_ns 在_p 现代化_vn 进程_n 中_f 取得_v 的_u 成就_n ，_w 向_p 世界_n 展现_v
了_u 一个_m 大踏步_d 前进_v 的_u 中国_ns 。_w
<CE3> 同时_n ，_w 我们_r 关注_v 着_u 变化_vn 中_f 的_u 世界_n ，_w 关注_v 着
_u 整个_b 世界_n 在_p 经济_n 、_w 社会_n 、_w 文化_n 等_u 各个_r 方面_n 取得
_v 的_u 发展_vn 与_c 进步_vn 。_w
<CE4> 我们_r 也_d 报道_v 了_u 一些_m 令_v 人_n 遗憾_a 的_u 冲突_vn 、_w 动荡
_an 和_c 灾难_n ，_w 但_c 和平_n 与_c 发展_v 始终_d 是_v 我们_r 报道_v 的_u
主线_n 。_w
<CE5> 在_p 过去_t 的_u 一_m 年_q 中_f ，_w 我们_r 还_d 努力_ad 建立_v 、_w
增进_v 与_p 听众_n 朋友_n 们_k 的_u 友谊_n ，_w 来自_v 世界_n 各地_r 的_u 听
众_n 来信_n 数量_n 达到_v 130万_m 封_q 。_w
```

**Figure 4.2 Student's ST excerpt for Chinese word tagging**

For CTS, the most frequently used software packages to assist search in the corpus are ParaConc and AntConc tools. As it known to us, the well-established and widely applied translationconcordancer, ParaConc can perform a bunch of such searching tasks as simple word search, regular expression search, tag search and parallel search. The last mode of search is especially crucial for the parallel corpus in the present study in that it enables the co-occurrence of fragments from both source and target texts, and it also facilitates the mapping of the target text onto the source text.

```
<SPOKEN> <TEM8> <GRADE4> <YEAR05> <GROUP108> <TASK1> <SEX=F> <SCORE=84>
<LEVEL=1>
<CE1> Now_RT it_PPH1 is_VBZ a_AT1 time_NNT1 to_TO we_PPIS2 go_VV0 back_RP to_II
a_AT1 ,_, to_II a_AT1 last_MD year_NNT1 and_CC ,_, the_AT arrival_NN1 of_IO
the_AT million_NNO and_CC also_RR it_PPH1 is_VBZ a_AT1 time_NNT1 for_IF us_PPIO2
to_II ..._... look_VV0 back_RP on_II the_AT past_JJ year_NNT1 and_CC at_II
the_AT same_DA time_NNT1 look_VV0 forward_RL to_II the_AT new_JJ year_NNT1 ._.
<CE2> In_II the_AT past_JJ year_NNT1 ,_, we_PPIS2 had_VHD recalled_VVN our_APPGE
province_NN1 in_II Chinese_JJ province_NN1 in_II its_APPGE modernization_NN1
<nobyzation> and_CC also_RR show_VV0 ..._... fast_RR developing_JJ China_NN1
to_II the_AT whole_JJ world_NN1 ._.
<CE3> Meanwhile_RR we_PPIS2 have_VH0 pay_NN1 attention_NN1 to_II the_AT
changing_NN1 of_IO the_AT world_NN1 ,_, we_PPIS2 focus_VV0 ,_, focus_VV0 on_II
the_AT development_NN1 and_CC progress_NN1 of_IO the_AT world_NN1 ..._... ,_,
economic_JJ ..._... we_PPIS2 would_VM change_VVI <changes> in_II development_NN1
and_CC progress_NN1 of_IO the_AT world_NN1 in_II the_AT development_NN1 of_IO
economic_JJ ,_, society_NN1 and_CC culture_NN1 ._.
<CE4> However_RR ,_, we_PPIS2 had_VHD great_JJ ,_, we_PPIS2 had_VHD great_RR
some_DD conflicts_NN2 and_CC disasters_NN2 ,_, we_PPIS2 also_RR reputed_VVN
the_AT ,_, piece_NN1 of_IO development_NN1 are_VBR always_RR our_APPGE main_JJ
fame_NN1 ._.
```

**Figure 4.3 Student's TT excerpt for English tagging**

Here comes detailed information about the extracting procedures used in this study: first, all Chinese STs and their corresponding English TTs are uploaded into ParaConc, and then, with the aid of parallel search in the software, the language-pair segments that contain all the cohesive devices demonstrated in Table 4.6 are extracted from the corpus. Second, all the "coupled pair" instances extracted from the corpus are made manual identification of whether they belong to explicitation or not. The following Figure 4.4 vividly shows the example of personal pronoun "we" in coupled pair that extracted from the ParaConc.

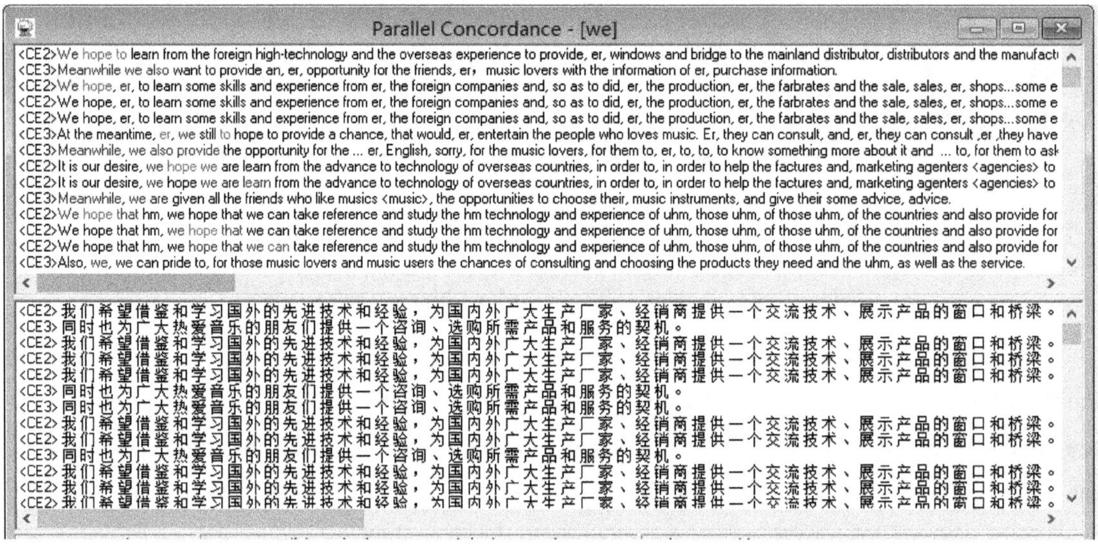


**Figure 4.4 Snapshot of student's language pair segments in ParaConc**

As to intra-language explicitation, AntConc is applicable to extract language segments that contain those cohesive devices selected for the present study in Table 4.6 and *that*-clauses in the original English. AntConc is free downloaded software that documents concordance and patterns with the ability to sift through a large corpus of documents in a given language. As a powerful suite of lexical analysis tool, AntConc can generate frequency lists, concordances, collocations, keywords in selected texts. For instance, there are seven main toolbars on the screen of AntConc, such as Concordance, Collocates, Keywords, and Wordlist. After typing into the linguistic resources in Search Term, the toolbars Concordance and File View are employed to generate concordance lines and the context in which those linguistic resources appear.

The following Figure 4.5 is a snapshot of Concordance lines of *because* taken from AntConc in the original English.

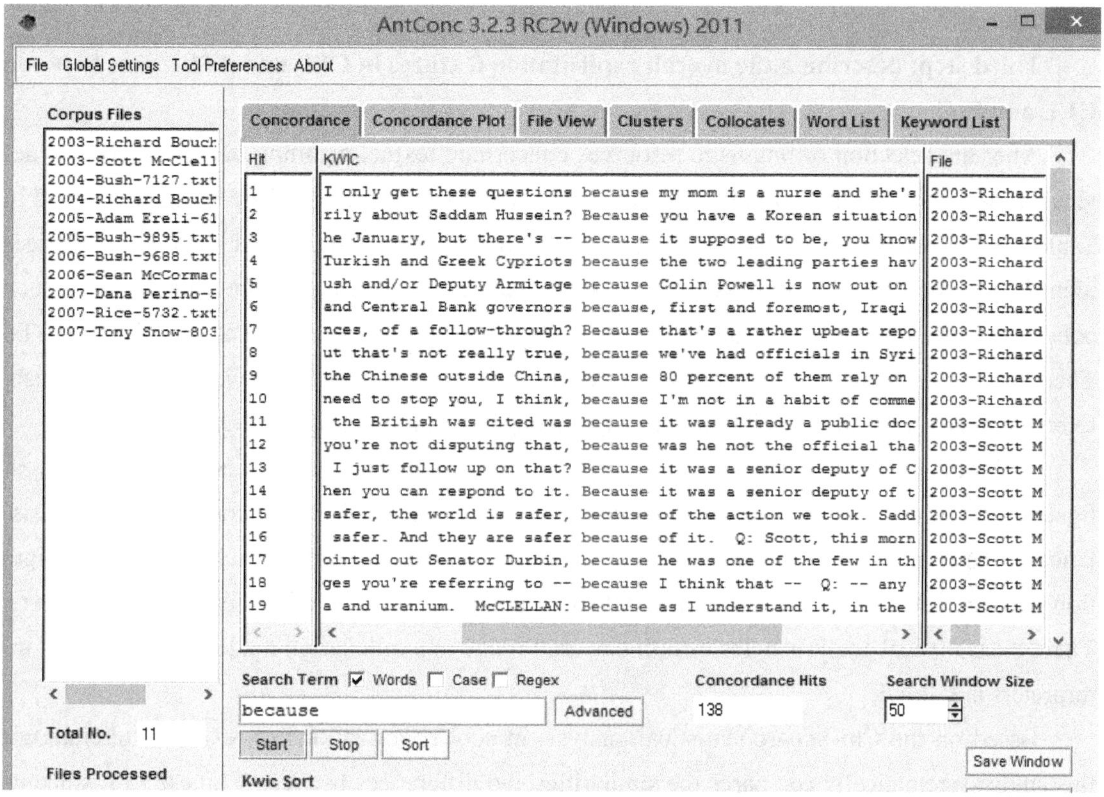


**Figure 4.5 Snapshot of Concordance lines in AntConc**

This step is primarily concerned with identifying explicitations in different subtypes of cohesive devices demonstrated in Table 4.6. In practice, as for inter-language explicitation, I have to first determine whether the investigated cohesive devices in TTs has a corresponding form in its Chinese STs, if so, it is not counted as an explicitation instance. While looking at parallel concordances between the ST-TT "coupled pair" in terms of multiple subtypes concerning personal pronouns, demonstratives and conjunctions, those instances may be regarded explicitation, in which additions or clarifications are made by the interpreter when she/he offers additional textual information that can be inferrable from the co-text or situation. As to intra-language explicitation, after extracting those instances from AntConc, this research makes a comparison between students' interpreted English and the original English with respect to the frequency of cohesive devices selected for the study and of *that* as subordinator in multiple subordinating clauses where *that* can be optional.

It is also worth mentioning that the most important fact to be considered in the process of analysis is that source and target text sentences were not compared in a word-by-word or phrase-by-phrase manner, but taking into account the whole of the sentence. Therefore, the instances which contain different cohesive devices are extracted from the corpus in sentence level not in phrase level.

**Third step: describing the overall explicitation features in CEL and differences between CEL and PIC**

After the selection of linguistic resources concerning textual meaning, namely, cohesive devices in particular, all the parallel concordance lines containing the linguistic forms mentioned in Table 4.6 are extracted from the corpus through the help of ParaConc. Based on cohesive devices identified in the English TTs, this study makes an analysis regarding whether the usage of such cohesive devices belongs to explicitation or not by tracing back to corresponding Chinese STs. Then, the statistical analysis helps observe overall frequency of cohesive devices used in English, to reveal major types of explicitation while excluding pure addition, not applicable instances.

As for the professional interpreters' corpus, the parallel concordance lines of the same investigated linguistic forms as in students' corpus are also extracted from the corpus with the assistance of ParaConc. The explicitation features are also identified based on multilayered investigation of linguistic resources concerning textual meaning on the part of professional interpreters. Then, the statistical analysis helps examine overall usage of explicitation made by professional interpreters in C-E CI.

Based on the Chi-Square statistical analysis in subcategorizations of textual explicitations, this study systematically compares the similarities and differences between Chinese EFL students and professional interpreters with regard to inter-language explicitation. This research also examines multiple situations in which Chinese EFL students and professional interpreters employ diverse textual explicitations.

This study also tries to compare findings about textual explicitation features of Chinese EFL students with those of professionals, thus examining the differences between Chinese EFL students and professional interpreters concerning inter-language textual explicitation. These results would have some implications for interpreter training in the future. By doing so, this study hopes to shed some new light on the scope of explicitation done by Chinese EFL students.

**Fourth step: exploring motivational factors that trigger such patterns and differences**

A great deal of research has investigated explicitation in translation and interpreting through different methods. However, few discuss possible reasons for such explicitations. In order to fill the gap, this research attempts to put forward some potential motivations that might triggerinter-language explicitations made by both professional interpreters and Chinese EFL students, and possible explanations for intra-language explicitationand for the differences between Chinese EFL students and professional interpreters.

Explicitation in translation and interpretation results mostly from linguistic and non-linguistic factors. As is known to us, meaning obviously does not belong to a consistent and stable category that simply made explicit or implicit. Therefore, translators and interpreters are inclined to act as mediator, facilitating the communication as much as possible by handling linguistic differences such as lexical and syntactic differences between language pairs, and by non-linguistic ones like translation norms and cognitive factors. The whole process seems to be an act of explanation performed by interpreters, in accordance with their experience and the criteria adopted during the translation or interpretation.

While discussing potential motivations that trigger explicitation, it is hard to pinpoint the exact factor that triggers the given explicitation. A certain shift in interpretation might involve register consideration or potential target audience expectation, or different levels of interpreting experience of professional interpreters and learners. It is without doubt that spotting the exact motivations for given interpreting shifts would be better to involve a process-based study, which could elicit unknown factors that might be remain hidden in a product-based investigation.

The interpreters usually are more inclined to add implied information in a given sentence in order to minimize the risk of an undesired interpretation for audience. By doing so, the interpreters try to avoid the risk of leaving the audience entirely in the dark. To some extent, explicitation could be regarded a "risk-management" strategy on the part of a translator or an interpreter.

Other motivational factors for explicitation may involve constituents that are more psychological or cognitive in nature. It is a general acknowledgement that translators and interpreters are not merely doing the task of translating and interpreting, in the mean time they are both readers and writers (or audience and speakers in the case of interpreting). This kind of double identity might lead them to make the following potential decisions in their mind: they are trying their best to get the target text made clear to readers as much as possible, as they are especially aware of the difficulties of constructing meaning. Alternatively, they choose to solve those ambiguous and difficult problems in an explicit way by explicitating implied markers for everything they have just construed, and making implied information in the source text explicit in the target text when the construction process is rather fresh in their mind. More bluntly, translators and interpreters would try their best to help readers and audience as well in that they, translators and interpreters, are also readers (Chesterman 2004).

In a word, the study attempts not only to capture the inter-language and intra-language explicitation features of Chinese EFL students in C-E CI, but also to explain the potential factors that elicit such features. The possible motivations are most likely from those factors mentioned above including linguistic ones such as lexico-grammatical and syntactic differences and non-linguistic ones like translation norms, psychological and cognitive constituents. The potential motivational factors are taken into consideration based on explicitation features of textual meaning found in this study. Here comes the final step of the research procedure in the following paragraph.

**Last step: discussingimplications for interpreters' training**

The vast majority of CTS mainly investigates written translation, a few about professional interpretation, and fewer studies deal with students' interpretation. In order to fill in the gap, this study attempts to explore explicitation features of textual meaning by Chinese EFL students in C-E CI and touches upon motivational factor that may trigger such features. This research also makes a comparison between professional interpreters and Chinese EFL students with respect to explicitation features of textual meaning in C-E CI. Thus, this study has implications for interpretation training.

It is an acknowledgement that corpus-based analysis of students' translations will inform us about both translation process and product (Olohan 2004: 39). Learner Corpora (LC) is quite significant for translation and interpreting studies, translator/interpreter training in particular. LC refers to corpora that include systematic electronic collections of texts produced by language learners. The LC is widely applied in the research fields such as Second Language Acquisition (SLA) and foreign language teaching (Granger 2002; 2004; 2008; 2009), Contrastive Linguistics (LC) (Aston et al 2004; Gilquin et al 2005) and translator and interpreter training (Peter, 2008).

In view of this, the current study attempts to detect textual explicitations in LC interpreting data, their patterns and motivations may distinguish from those found in professional interpretations. Specifically, interpreters perform their task under certain constraints inherent in this mode of language mediation, including the time constraint, limited short-term memory capacity and the background knowledge constraint. In addition, interpreting learners are less confident because of lack of interpreting experience.

In this background, the study also attempts to compare findings of Chinese EFL students with those of professionals, and to discuss implications for interpreter training in the future. By doing so, this study expects to shed some new light on the scope of explicitation by Chinese EFL students.

# Chapter Five Comparison of Inter-language Textual Explicitation between Chinese EFL Students and Professional Interpreters in C-E CI

The current chapter analyzes inter-language textual explicitation, which depends on the comparison between source texts and their corresponding target texts. Primary focus is on explicitations of cohesive devices in C-E CI made by both Chinese EFL students and professional interpreters. The first part will present overall statistics of cohesive devices that appear in the Chinese EFL Learner Corpus (CEL) and Professional Interpreters Corpus (PIC) respectively. The second part will concentrate upon the explicitation features of textual meaning along with the multiple dimensions of cohesive devices, mainly Personal pronoun-based Explicitation, Demonstrative-based Explicitation and Conjunction-based Explicitation by Chinese EFL Learners and professional interpreters respectively. The second part will also identify similarities and differences between Chinese EFL learners and professional interpreters in terms of multiple subcategories of textual explicitation. The last part presents a summary of explicitation features in each subcategory.

## 5.1 Overall Statistics

Before digging into specific types of explicitation features, let's look at the overall distribution of linguistic devices, cohesive devices selected for this study in particular, both in the Chinese EFL Learner Corpus (CEL) and Professional Interpreters Corpus (PIC) respectively. The software ParaConc automatically yields the instances of cohesive devices through uploading two corpora mentioned above. The overall statistics are calculated by manual addition of each subcategory of cohesive devices. The frequency (per thousand words) is measured by this formula: counts. Table 5.1 demonstrates the total occurrence and frequency (per thousand words) of cohesive devices chosen for the present study.

**Table 5.1 Global statistics of cohesive devices in students' and professional corpora**

| Cohesive device | Specifications | CEL (students) count/frequency[①] | | PIC (professionals) | |
|---|---|---|---|---|---|
| Reference | Personal nominative case | 3 557 | 22.96‰ | 3 969 | 27.73‰ |
| | Personal objective case | 819 | 5.29‰ | 1 144 | 7.99‰ |
| | Demonstratives | 2 283 | 14.75‰ | 1 991 | 13.91‰ |
| Total | | 6 659 | 43‰ | 7 104 | 49.63‰ |
| Conjunctions | Causal conjunctions | 308 | 1.99‰ | 503 | 3.51‰ |
| | Adversative conjunctions | 274 | 1.77‰ | 365 | 2.55‰ |
| | Conditional and others | 48 | 0.31‰ | 252 | 1.76‰ |
| Total | | 630 | 4.07‰ | 1 120 | 7.82‰ |
| *That* as a subordinator (total) | | 610 | 3.94‰ | 1 253 | 8.75‰ |

As shown in Table 5.1, in terms of word count, professional interpreters used more cohesive devices than Chinese EFL students did, particularly regarding conjunctions. Among them, the usage of nominative case of personal pronouns and demonstratives, and causal conjunctions ranks the top three cohesive devices with respect to professional interpreters and student interpreters alike. As far as the students' corpus is concerned, the occurrence of nominative case of personal pronouns is the highest. For both corpora, regarding the type of cohesive devices, the use of reference is far higher than the other two types, then the conjunctions, finally comes the use of *that* as a subordinator.

With regard to the frequency of cohesive devices in both students' and professional corpora, the frequency of reference is the highest, and then of conjunctions, the last one is *that* as a subordinator. Specifically, as to the students' corpus, the total frequency of reference ranks the highest, which appears 43 times per thousand words with the nominative case of personal pronouns as the most frequent one. The conjunctions hold the second place with the 4.07‰ frequency and *that* as a subordinator is the last one with 3.94‰ frequency respectively. As far as the professional interpreters are concerned, the similar rank goes to the frequency of cohesive devices with reference in the first place, *that* as subordinator comes next and the conjunctions as the last one with the frequency rate of 49.63‰ , 8.75‰ and 7.82‰ respectively.

In order to get better visual perception, based on the statistical figures attained from Table 5.1, the overall occurrence and standardized frequency of different cohesive devices are generated in chart forms for both students' and professional corpora. Figure 5.1 and Figure 5.2 display the overall occurrence and the specific frequency of different cohesive devices separately.

① Here frequency refers to the occurrence of words among per thousand words, which in the table uses the symbol ‰ .

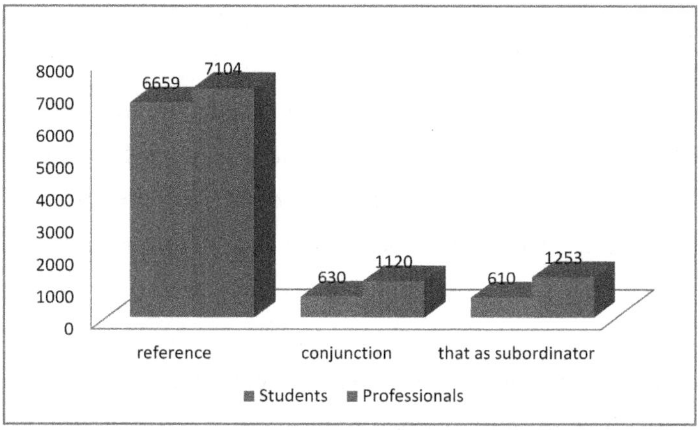


**Figure 5.1 Overall occurrence of cohesive devices in students' and professional corpora**

As shown in Figure 5.1 above, it is apparent that the overall occurrence of reference and of conjunctions is much higher in the professional corpus than in the student corpus. The Chinese EFL students use a few more demonstratives than professional interpreters do, though. In other words, it is likely that professional interpreters tend to use more conjunctions and *that* as subordinator in their interpreting than Chinese EFL students, while demonstratives are less likely to appearin professional interpreters' corpus compared with Chinese EFL students'. Overall, there are far more instances of cohesive devices in the professional corpus than in students' corpus.

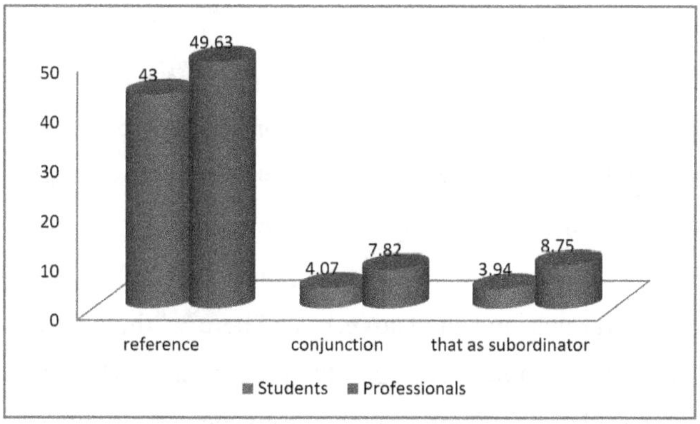


**Figure 5.2 Standardized frequency of cohesive devices (per thousand words) in students' and professional corpora**

As shown in Figure 5.2, with respect to the frequency of cohesive devices that appear every thousand words, professional interpreters far more frequently employ cohesive devices than Chinese EFL students do in every subcategory. In terms of subcategories, the most frequently used one is the reference with the frequency of 49.63‰ for professionals while only 43‰ for students. The second frequent one is *that* as a subordinator for professionals, whereas for students is the conjunction with the frequency of 8.75‰ and 4.07‰ respectively. The least frequently used one is the conjunction for professionals and *that* as a subordinator for students with the frequency of 7.82 ‰ and 3.94‰ respectively.

In a nutshell, according to those descriptive statistics mentioned above, professional interpreters are inclined to use far more cohesive devices than Chinese EFL students based on the total occurrence of cohesive devices in Table 5.1 and Figure 5.1. Accordingly, with respect to the frequent usage of the reference, the conjunctions and *that* as a subordinator, it seems that professionals tend to employ more frequently those cohesive devices selected for the study than students in accordance with Figure 5.2.

The general description about overall statistics of cohesive devices in professional and students' corpora is stated with regard to overall occurrence of the reference, the conjunctions and *that* as a subordinator, and their standardized frequency per thousand words in this section. Yet it is hard to claim anything about the explicitation instances of cohesive devices in the two corpora (PIC and CEL) on account of limited information about the overall usage of cohesive devices alone. Therefore, the following sections analyze the specific features of explicitation in terms of the reference, conjunction and *that* as a subordinator in both professional and students' corpora. The following section presents the detailed statistics about each cohesive device selected for this research.

## 5.2 Reference-based Explicitation

According to Halliday and Hasan (1976: 31), reference is a property in which an item in a text (a presupposing element), "instead of being interpreted semantically in [its] own right," requires recourse to another item (a presupposed element) (ibid). It is "the most applied cohesive device in texts" (Koch 2001: 6). That is why the explicitation of reference is the most important cohesive device to take a close look at in the first place. In English, the reference is achieved through pronouns, demonstratives, and such adverbs as "here", "there", "now", and "then".

Based on the framework of categorization in the present study (Figure 3.3), two main subcategories under reference-based explicitation are taken into account. In this section, we will give detailed description and analysis of subcategories under reference-based explicitation in both students' and professional corpora.

### 5.2.1 Personal Pronoun–based Explicitation

Halliday and Hasan (1976:37) further classify reference into personal pronouns, demonstratives, or comparatives. Personal reference is "reference by means of function in the speech situation" (ibid) and is realized with the help of personal pronouns, possessive determiners, and possessive pronouns.

The nominative and objective cases of personal pronouns are included in the scope of the research with the view to observing the most frequent personal pronominal reference both in students and professional corpora. This section deals with the usage and explicitation of each personal pronoun. Table 5.2 presents overall occurrences of nominative and objective case of personal pronouns in students' and professional corpora, which gives an overall picture of differences in the application of personal pronouns between professional interpreters and students in C-E CI.

**Table 5.2 Occurrence of personal pronouns in students' and professional corpora**

| Nominative case | Students frequency | Professionals frequency | Chi-Square | Significance (*p*) | |
|---|---|---|---|---|---|
| First person | 171.40 | 196.94 | 26.910 4 | 0.000***① | - |
| Second person | 4.26 | 53.79 | 652.537 6 | 0.000*** | - |
| Third person | 53.97 | 26.55 | 137.686 2 | 0.000*** | + |
| Total | 229.63 | 277.28 | 68.616 0 | 0.000*** | - |
| Objective case | Students frequency | Professionals frequency | Chi-Square | Significance (*p*) | |
| First person | 35.51 | 18.09 | 83.326 4 | 0.000*** | + |
| Second person | 4.26 | 53.79 | 652.537 6 | 0.000*** | - |
| Third person | 13.11 | 8.03 | 17.950 4 | 0.000*** | + |
| Total | 52.87 | 79.92 | 83.185 0 | 0.000*** | - |

Based on Table 5.2, according to the results of significance ($p$), there exists a statistically significant difference ($p < .05$) between students and professionals in terms of usage of personal pronouns. In other words, there are more personal pronouns in the form of both nominative and objective case in the professional corpus than in students' corpus. However, whether it is the nominative case or objective case, students tend to employ more third personal pronouns than professional interpreters do in C-E CI.

As to the nominative case of personal pronouns, there is not a striking difference found between students and professionals with respect to the frequency of the first person. Nevertheless, students tend to employ more third person pronouns and fewer second person pronouns than professionals. As for the objective case of personal pronouns, students use more first person and third person pronouns and fewer second person pronouns than professionals. The following two Figures 5.3 and 5.4 vividly show the specific information.

After extracting all the instances of nominative and objective case of personal pronouns with the help of ParaConc, the analysis of each instance falls into four subcategories: mistake, repetition, correspondence and explicitation. The personal pronoun that is misused in the sentence is regarded a mistake; and the examples can be seen in the following sentences.

① The asterisk (*) indicates significance level, and the "+" and "-" signs on the right side indicate "overuse" and "underuse".

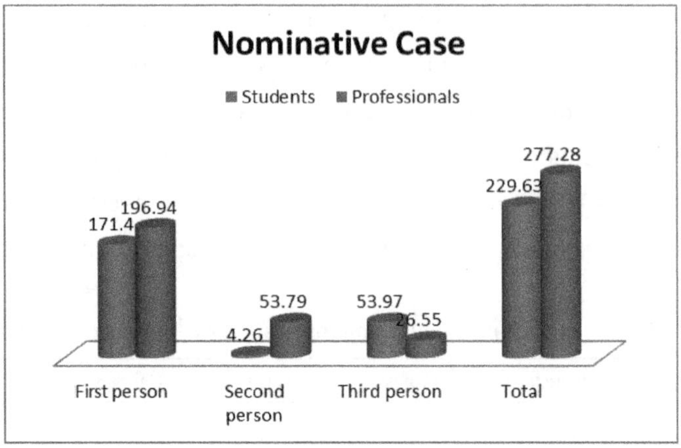


**Figure 5.3 Frequency of nominative case in students' and professional corpora**

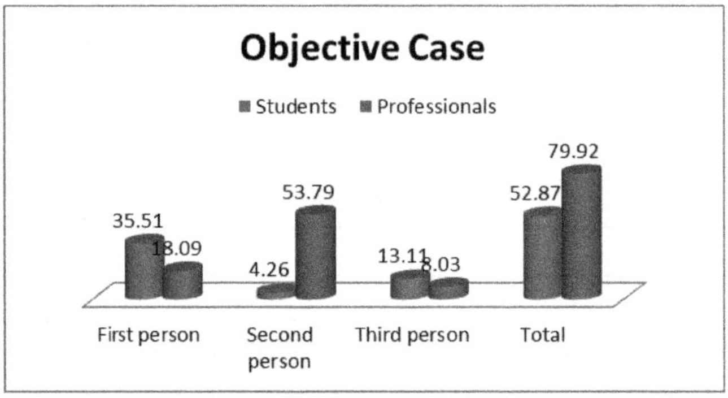


**Figure 5.4 Frequency of objective case in students' and professional corpora**

1 ) Mistake

**Example 5.1**

ST: 我还想提出一点，加强农业和农村建设。

TT: [[We]], I would also like to say that we need to strengthen the development of the countryside and agriculture. (Professional)

Here, *we* in the square bracket is wrongly used, then the interpreter found that it should be *I* instead of *we* in the target text. The sentence below is the example of a student who misused the personal pronoun *we* in the following C-E CI.

**Example 5.2**

ST：这座城市最大的特色在于它有丰厚的文化内涵，其中精髓在老城。

TT: Er the greatest characteristic of this city is its er gr..., is its strong er culture er [[we]] whose, whose and the most attractive parts lies on it's... (Student)

In the target text above, *we* in the square bracket is applied wrongly by a student in the C-E CI. Therefore, it is categorized a mistake in the analysis.

2) Repetition

Similarly, as to repetition, the personal pronoun that is repetitive in the interpreted English of C-E CI is regarded a repetition in both students' and professional corpora. The specific examples are as follows:

**Example 5.3**

ST: 同时也为广大热爱音乐的朋友们提供一个咨询、选购所需产品和服务的契机。

TT: Meanwhile, this exhibition will provide, will provide you a, uhm, will provide [[you]] a chance for these, er, English fans to, er, consult and choose their, uhm, musical instruments. (Student)

In C-E CI above done by a student, the second pronoun *you* in the square bracket together with *will provide* is repetitive in the interpreted English, therefore, it is regarded a repetition. The following example illustrates the instance of the repetition done by a professional interpreter.

3) Correspondence

As for correspondence, if the personal pronoun in the target text corresponds to the interpretation of the personal pronoun in the source text, then it is categorized as *correspondence* in the analysis. In Example 5.4, it is obvious that the objective case *us* in the target text corresponds to "我们" (us) in the source text, so it is labeled as correspondence in the analysis of personal pronouns.

**Example 5.4**

ST: 这是前人留给我们的遗产，是一笔宝贵的资源，它属于龙城、属于中国、属于世界。

TT: It is a pre, precious, precious heritage that our ancestor has left [[us]]. Er It is very precious, it belongs to the Longcheng, it also belongs to China, belongs to the world. (Student)

Here is another example of correspondence of the personal pronoun interpreted by a professional in C-E CI.

**Example 5.5**

ST: 前人给我们奠定了很好的基础。

TT: So our predecessors have already laid a very good foundation for [[us]]. (Professional)

The objective case of personal pronoun *us* in the square bracket corresponds to the Chinese personal pronoun "我们" (us) in the source text, so it is considered a correspondence in the analysis.

4) Explicitation

According to the working definition in this study, explicitation points to additions or clarifications found in interpreted texts, which can be derivable from the co-text and situation through contextualization in C-E CI. In example 5.6, the personal pronoun *I* in the square bracket along with the verb *think* in the target text is added so as to clarify the subject that is hidden in the source text, so it is taken as the explicitation of the personal pronoun in C-E interpreting done by a student.

**Example 5.6**

ST: 本届展览会已有 270 多家中外企业报名参展，展出总面积 15 000 平方米，是目前国内同类乐器展览会中规模最大的。

TT: Er, by now there are 217 companies in this exhibition, and the exhibition er, contains 15,000 square meters at all. Er, [[I]] think it is biggest exhibition in the same kind of er, exhibition all over the country. (Student)

There is another instance of explicitation found in the professional corpus below, where the professional interpreter added the personal pronoun *I* together with the verb *believe* as an insertion in the target text compared with the source text.

**Example 5.7**

ST: 实际上我刚才已经回答了你所有的问题。

TT: Actually [[I]] believe I have addressed both of your questions. (Professional)

Based on the four subcategorization of the selected item under analysis, Table 5.3 shows the quantitative analysis of the pronoun-based explicitation detected in both students' and professional corpora in detail.

**Table 5.3 Explicitation of personal pronouns in students' and professional corpora**

| Nominative case | Students frequency | Professionals frequency | Chi-Square | Significance ($p$) | |
|---|---|---|---|---|---|
| First person | 52.94 | 91.59 | 156.552 5 | 0.000*** | - |
| Second person | 1.29 | 12.78 | 144.382 6 | 0.000*** | - |
| Third person | 23.24 | 14.67 | 28.624 0 | 0.000*** | + |
| Total | 77.47 | 119.04 | 133.264 7 | 0.000*** | - |
| Objective case | Students frequency | Professionals frequency | Chi-Square | Significance ($p$) | |
| First person | 9.81 | 5.52 | 17.709 9 | 0.000*** | + |
| Second person | 1.29 | 12.78 | 144.382 6 | 0.000*** | - |
| Third person | 5.16 | 3.21 | 6.701 1 | 0.010** | + |
| Total | 16.27 | 21.52 | 10.928 0 | 0.001*** | - |

With respect to the explicitation observed in the nominative case of personal pronouns, the results show that there is a statistically significant difference ($p < .05$) between students and professional interpreters. In other words, professionals tend to explicitate personal pronouns more than students do regarding the first person and second person pronouns in particular. For professionals, the explicitation found in the form of the first and second person is two times higher than that in the students' corpus. However, there is an exception for this tendency in the explicitation of the third person. There are more explicitations observed in the students' corpus than in the professional corpus. Figure 5.5 demonstrates the specific information.

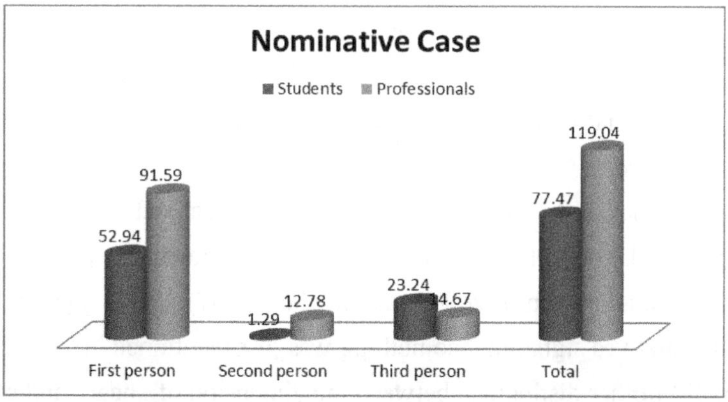


**Figure 5.5 Explicitation of nominative case in students' and professional corpora**

As to the explicitation detected in the objective case of personal pronouns, the findings suggest that professionals are inclined to explicitate more than students do in terms of total explicitations. However, specifically, there are more explicitations of the first person and third person in the students' corpus than in the professional corpus. Putting it differently, students tend to explicitate the objective case of the first and third person pronouns while professionals do not. The differences can be more clearly in Figure 5.6.

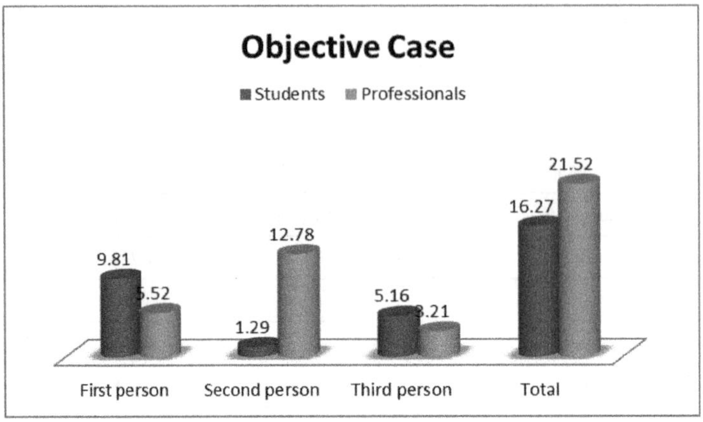


**Figure 5.6 Explicitation of objective case in students' and professional corpora**

Overall, based on the findings mentioned above, professional interpreters tend to explicitate-personal pronouns more than students do in C-E CI, although there are exceptions to both tendencies. To be specific, the explicitation found either in the subjective case or in the objective case of personal pronouns shows, students also tend to explicitate more compared with professionals with respect to third person pronouns.

### 5.2.2 Demonstrative–based Explicitation

Three types of reference exist in English: (i) personal (personal pronouns such as *he*, *they*, *her*); (ii) demonstrative (demonstrative pronouns such as *this*, *that*, *these*, *those*, *here*, *there*); (iii) comparative (adjectives and adverbs expressing identity, similarity, difference, such as *the same*, *similar*, *different*) (Halliday & Matthiessen 2004). This section deals with the explicitation of demonstrative reference.

According to Halliday and Hasan, the demonstrative is realized "by means of location, on a scale of proximity" in relation to the speaker (space) or the moment of speech (time) (Halliday & Hasan 1976: 37-38) and is "a form of verbal pointing" (ibid: 57). While, judging from what Koch mentioned, "Demonstratives signal that something was just mentioned" (koch 2001: 5). Halliday and Hasan (1976: 38) further distinguish between the dimension of "near" and of "not near" with regard to semantics of demonstrative reference. It is worth mentioning that the adverbial demonstratives of place (here and there) typically function as adjuncts in a clause and occur outside of a noun phrase, while nominal demonstratives ("this", "these", "that", "those") tend to occur as elements of a nominal group (ibid: 57-58).

This section elaborates upon the occurrence and explicitation of both nominal demonstratives and adverbial demonstratives of place found in students' and professional corpora. First, we look at the quantitative analysis of demonstratives in both students' and professional corpora in Table 5.4.

**Table 5.4 Occurrence of demonstratives in students' and professional corpora**

| Demonstratives | Students frequency | Professionals total count | Chi-square | Significance ($p$) | |
|---|---|---|---|---|---|
| Here | 13.88 | 4.54 | 69.129 3 | 0.000*** | + |
| There | 12.39 | 22.49 | 44.082 0 | 0.000*** | - |
| This | 93.74 | 71.40 | 45.102 1 | 0.000*** | + |
| That | 13.17 | 18.09 | 11.630 2 | 0.001*** | - |
| These | 6.71 | 12.71 | 27.943 0 | 0.000*** | - |
| Those | 7.49 | 9.85 | 4.816 3 | 0.028* | - |
| Total | 147.38 | 139.09 | 3.618 8 | 0.057 | + |

Based on Table 5.4 above, unlike the personal pronouns, it shows that there is no significant difference ($p$ >.05) between students and professional interpreters in terms of total demonstratives occurring in both students' and professional corpora. However, there is a statistically significant difference ($p$ < .05) in the usage of adverbial demonstratives *here* and *there*, and nominal demonstratives *this*, *that* and *these*. In other words, students are inclined to employ the adverbial demonstrative *here* and the nominal demonstrative *this*, while they are less likely to use the adverbial demonstrative *there* and nominal demonstratives *that* and *these* compared with professional interpreters.

The instance of demonstratives also falls into four subcategories such as mistake, repetition, correspondence and explicitation. The specific examples are as follows.

1 ) Mistake

**Example 5.8**

ST：我们举办这个展览会的目的是，加强在这一领域的国际交流与合作。

TT：The purpose, the purpose of this exhibition is to strengthen communication and cooperation on [[these]]〈this〉areas. (Student)

The demonstrative *these* with square bracket in the target text is a wrong useage by a student in C-E CI. It is a grammatical mistake and should be the form in the angle bracket in accordance with the annotation of students' corpus in Table 4.3. The following is an example of mistake taken from the professional corpus.

**Example 5.9**

ST: 这个规划将有利于发挥三地的优势，加强合作，优势互补。

TT: And in accordance with this plan, [[that]] we will be able to give full scope to the advantages of the three areas and further strengthen their cooperation and enable these three areas to draw on each other's strength. (Professional)

The demonstrative *that* in the square bracket in the target text is redundant or unnecessary since *that* does not function as a subordinator here. Therefore, it is regarded a mistake made by a professional.

2 ) Repetition

**Example 5.10**

ST: 同时也为广大热爱音乐的朋友们提供一个咨询、选购所需产品和服务的契机。

TT: At the same time, we hope that this exhibition will uhm, give those [[those]] who like uhm, music, a a good chance to con con consult and··· buy er, the product they want to buy. (Student)

It is apparent that the second *those* with the square bracket is a repetition in the interpreted texts produced by students in Example 5.10. The example below is a repetition done by a professional in the professional corpus.

**Example 5.11**

ST: 但是，这是由于我，由我们自己决定的，任何国家不能对人民币升值或贬值施加压力。

TT: At the end of the day, this, [[this]] decision is for China itself to make. No country is in a position to pressure, pressurize the Chinese side to appreciate or depreciate the RMB. (Professional)

It is apparent that the second *this* with square bracket in the target text is a repetitive demonstrative in the professional corpus. It gives the specific example of correspondence with regard to demonstratives found in both students' and professional corpora below.

3 ) Correspondence

**Example 5.12**

ST：我们举办这个展览会的目的是，加强在这一领域的国际交流与合作。

TT: The purpose of our holding the exhibition is to strength, strength the international cooperation in [[this]] field. (Student)

The nominal demonstrative *this* with the square bracket in the target text corresponds to the demonstrative in the source text "这" (this) found in a student's C-E CI. The example below is a correspondence found in the professional corpus.

**Example 5.13**

ST：关于个人的风格，我想中国的历任外长各人都有各人的这个，呃，风格，但是有一点是共同的，那就是忠于国家，忠于人民，广交天下的朋友，促进和平发展事业。

TT：Talking about personal style, I think each of the successive foreign ministers of China has his own personal style, but they all share a commonality, [[that]] is, loyalty to the country, loyalty to the people, and a commitment to make as many friends as possible in order to promote world peace and development. (Professional)

It is easy to notice that the nominal demonstrative *that* in the square bracket is equivalent to the interpretation of the nominal demonstrative "那" (that) appeared in the source text of the professional corpus. Therefore, it is regarded a correspondence of the demonstrative *that* found in the professional corpus. The sentence below is the specific example of explicitation found in students' and professional corpora in C-E CI.

4) Explicitation

**Example 5.14**

ST: 本届展览会已有 270 多家中外企业报名参展，展出总面积 15 000 平方米，是目前国内同类乐器展览会中规模最大的。

TT: So this exhibition, er, fair has got , er, 270 companies signed to exhibit [[here]]. The total exhibition, er, exhibition area is 1,500 kilometers, er, square kilometers. It is the largest one of the same kind, er, musical instrument exhibition fair, er, at present. (Student)

The adverbial demonstrative *here* with square bracket in the target text is added to clarify the place where the exhibition is held. Therefore, the adverbial demonstrative of place *that* is taken an instance of explicitation in line with the working definition given in section 3.3. The interpretation below is an example of explicitation found in the professional corpus.

**Example 5.15**

ST: 我想世界上绝大部分将要参加奥运会的各国运动员，对于北京的空气质量、环境、运动设施，啊，都是满意的，都是有信心的。

TT: I believe most athletes who are going to take part in the Olympic Games in Beijing are satisfied with the air quality, environment and sports facilities in Beijing. They have full confidence in [[these]] conditions. (Professional)

It is apparent that the subject plus the object complement is omitted in the last clause of the source text in Chinese, while in the target text, not only the subject *they* but also the object compliment *these conditions* are explicitated in order to clarify the aspects in which *they* have full confidence in. Therefore, the nominal demonstrative *these* in the square bracket is regarded an explicitation found in the professional corpus. Table 5.5 presents the elaborate quantitative analysis of explicitations that statistically measured in students' and the professional corpora in detail.

**Table 5.5 Explicitation of demonstratives in students' and professional corpora**

| Demonstratives | Students count/ frequency | | Professionals count/ frequency | | Chi-Square | Significance ($p$) | |
|---|---|---|---|---|---|---|---|
| Here | 74 | 4.78 | 35 | 2.45 | 11.067 7 | 0.001*** | + |
| There | 1 | 0.06 | 64 | 4.47 | 66.251 4 | 0.000*** | - |
| This | 220 | 14.20 | 302 | 21.10 | 20.231 1 | 0.000*** | - |
| That | 21 | 1.36 | 117 | 8.17 | 74.723 4 | 0.000*** | - |
| These | 36 | 2.32 | 61 | 4.26 | 8.583 1 | 0.003** | - |
| Those | 3 | 0.19 | 41 | 2.86 | 35.946 4 | 0.000*** | - |
| Total | 355 | 22.92 | 620 | 43.31 | 94.911 6 | 0.000*** | - |

Based on Table 5.5, there is a statistically significant difference ($p < .05$) between students and professional interpreters in terms of total explicitations. Students are less likely to explicitate both nominal and adverbial demonstratives compared with professional interpreters, although students employ more demonstratives than professional interpreters do according to Table 5.4. The explicitations (620 in total) found in professional corpus are almost two times higher than those appeared in students' corpus (355 in total). However, there is an exception in the students' corpus in terms of the explicitation of adverbial demonstrative *here*. In other words, students are more likely to explicitate the adverbial demonstrative of place *here* (74 explicitations) compared with professional interpreters (35 explicitations). The explicitation of adverbial demonstrative *here* in the students' corpus is two times higher than the explicitation found in the professional corpus.

In order to present clearly the fact that professional interpreters tend to explicitate both nominal and adverbial demonstratives more than students, although students are likely to use more demonstratives in C-E CI compared with professionals, the following bar chart explicitly shows the explicitation of each demonstrative found in students' and professional corpora.

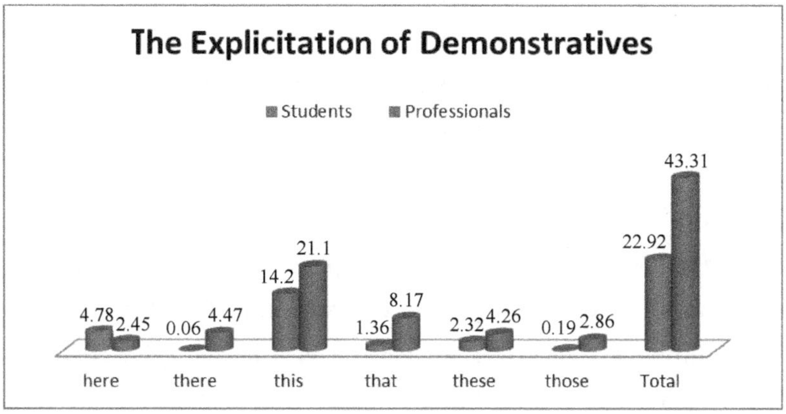


**Figure 5.7 Explicitation of demonstratives in students' and professional corpora**

Although there are more demonstratives found in the students' corpus than in the professional corpus, we can identify the ways in which students and professional interpreters might employ demonstratives in both similar and different ways. As to the similarity, both students and professional interpreters are inclined to interpret the demonstratives in Chinese (ST) into the corresponding demonstratives in English (TT). As for the difference, there are more mistakes and repetitions detected in the use of demonstratives in the students' corpus compared with demonstratives found in the professional corpus. The following pie charts clearly demonstrates these similarities and differences of adverbial demonstratives *here* in both students' and professional corpora.

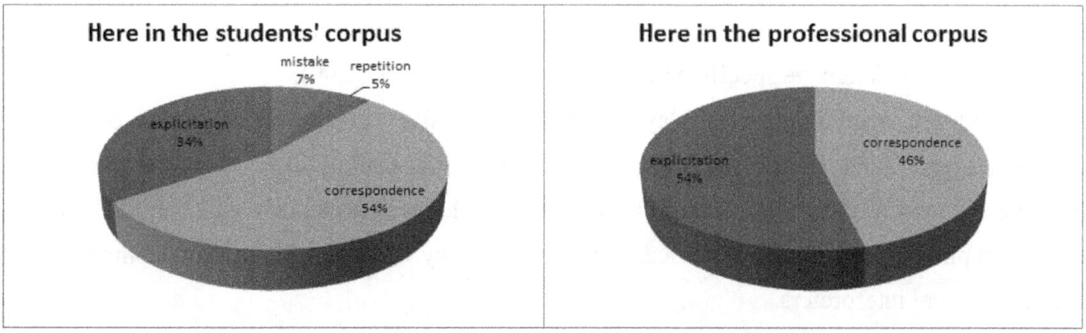


**Figure 5.8 Proportion of *here* used in students' and professional corpora**

The pie chart above vividly illustrates that half of the adverbial demonstrative *here* in English is equivalent to the corresponding demonstrative in Chinese for both students and professional interpreters. Nevertheless, there is almost no mistake and repetition in the professional corpus while mistakes and repetitions are frequent in the students' corpus. Students explicitate only one-third of the adverbial demonstrative *here*, whereas over a half is explicitation for professional interpreters. This partly explains why there are more instances of explicitations found in professional corpus even though there are more demonstratives in students' corpus.

In line with the differentiation of reference by Halliday and Hasan, the last referential cohesive device is comparatives. In general, comparative reference is realized with the help of identity, similarity, difference (in the case of general comparison), or enumerative and epithetic expressions (in the case of particular comparison) (Halliday & Hasan 1976: 76-77). According to Thompson (1996: 149), any comparison "includes two things that are being compared; and any comparative attached to one entity or concept thus implies the existence of the other entity or concept". Typical examples in the case of general comparison include the use of "same", "such", "similar", "other", "different", etc. The comparison is achieved with additionof enumerative comparative devices including "more", "fewer", "less" or epithetical comparatives, that is, comparative adjectives, such as "better", "worse", "more difficult", "less difficult", etc.

As to comparatives found in the students' and professional corpora, there is no statistically-significant difference ($p > .05$) not only in the usage of comparatives, but also in the explicitation of comparatives for both students and professional interpreters. Therefore, the detailed analysis of referential comparatives is not in the scope of this study. The following subsection gives a summary of occurrence and explicitation of referential cohesive devices in students' corpus in relation to the professional corpus.

### 5.2.3 Summary of Reference–based Explicitation

Cohesion refers to "the grammatical and lexical elements on the surface of a text which can form connections between parts of the text" (Tanskanen 2006: 7). Blum-Kulka also offers a similar explanation of cohesion, which is defined "an overt relationship holding between parts of the text, expressed by language specific markers" (Blum-kulka 2001: 299).

In addition, according to Halliday and Hasan, cohesive devices are of vital importance to connect all parts in a text and they play an active part in successfully interpreting the message for the audience and readers alike. Therefore, the present chapter particularly concentrates upon the use and explicitation of cohesive devices in C-E CI done by Chinese EFL students compared with the professional interpreters.

The current research employs Halliday and Hasan's categorization about cohesion, which is tested by time and practice. Since Halliday and Hasan describe cohesion based on English language writing, and the present study deals with the interpreted English texts or the original English, the choice of Halliday's categorization about cohesion is relatively appropriate.

Halliday and Hasan break down the cohesive devices into two main categories: grammatical and lexical cohesion. The current section focuses on one of the important subcategories of grammatical cohesion — reference that is achieved through pronouns, demonstratives and comparatives. Since there is no significant difference between students and professional interpreters in terms of the use of comparatives, this section only concentrates upon the occurrence and explicitation of personal pronouns with nominative and objective case forms, and of demonstrative pronouns and adverbials in students' corpus in relation to the professional corpus.

As to the personal pronouns, overall nominative and objective cases of personal pronouns are much more frequent in the professional corpus than in students' corpus. However, there is an exception to it, that is, third person pronouns are more likely to occur in students' corpus than in the professional corpus in C-E CI whether they are in the nominative case or objective case form. Likewise, similar results yield regarding the explicitation of personal pronouns; that is to say, professional interpreters tend to explicitate more personal pronouns than Chinese EFL students do in C-E CI.

Unlike personal pronouns, no statistically significant difference ($p > .05$) exists between students and professional interpreters with respect to the total occurrence of demonstratives in their respective corpus. Nevertheless, except the occurrence of nominal demonstrative *those*, there is a statistically significant difference ($p < .05$) in other nominal and adverbial demonstratives found in students' and professional corpora respectively. Similarly, Chinese EFL students are far less likely to explicitate pronominal and adverbial demonstratives in comparison with professional interpreters even though there are more occurrences of total demonstratives in students' corpus than in the professional corpus.

In a word, based on the findings mentioned above, whether they are personal pronouns or demonstratives, Chinese EFL students make far fewer explicitations than professional interpreters do with respect to referential cohesive devices in C-E CI. The following section introduces another important cohesive device — the conjunction and its explicitations in detail.

## 5.3 Conjunction-based Explicitation

As is known to all, conjunction is yet another important cohesive device discussed by Halliday and Hasan, and is quite different in nature from reference. Based on what Halliday and Hasan (1976: 226) have suggested, the cohesive function of conjunctions is indirect and is realized "by virtue of their specific meanings", which "presupposes the presence of other components in the discourse". In other words, conjunctions relate "linguistic elements that occur together in succession", thus creating logical and coherent ties between segments of text (ibid: 227). According to Thompson (1996: 156), conjunctions combine "any two textual elements into a potentially coherent complex semantic unit".

With conjunctions, we will achieve a specification of the way in which segments of a text systematically and coherently connected to each other. Therefore, the conjunction is regarded a significant part of textual organization to be included in the analysis of the study, and may yield interesting results.

In addition, previous studies also investigated the usage of conjunctions in translation and interpreting and yielded some general results. Just as Gumul (2006) notes an increase in conjunctive devices in the work of interpreters between English and Polish, so does Becher (2011) in a corpus-based study of English to German translations. Therefore, it would be more meaningful to take a closer look at the use of conjunctions in students' interpreted texts compared with professional interpreters in C-E CI.

In light of the categorization about conjunctions made by Halliday and Hasan in *Cohesion in English,* this study examines three types of conjunctions: causal, adversative, and conditional conjunctions. The following section elaborates upon the occurrence and explicitation of causal conjunctions detected in students' and professional corpora as well.

### 5.3.1 Causal Conjunction-based Explicitation

Conjunctions are considerably significant cohesive devices in both English and Chinese. Conjunctions broadly refer to "the combining of any two textual elements into a potentially coherent complex semantic unit" (Thompson 2014: 225). Therefore, it is necessary to conduct an analysis of the usage and the explicitation of conjunctions by students and professional interpreters.

Causal conjunctions indicate a cause-effect relation (of reason, result, or purpose) and includes such connectives as "so", "thus", "because", "therefore", etc. (Halliday & Hasan 1976: 256). This section statistically analyzes the major causal conjunctions in terms of their occurrences and explicitations found in students' and professional corpora. Table 5.6 presents detailed information about the occurrence of specific causal conjunctions employed by students and professional interpreters respectively.

**Table 5.6 Occurrence of causal conjunctions in students' and professional corpora**

| Causal conjunctions | Students frequency | Professionals frequency | Chi-square | Significance (*p*) | |
|---|---|---|---|---|---|
| Because | 2.00 | 6.64 | 37.829 0 | 0.000*** | - |
| Since | 1.16 | 4.33 | 27.847 3 | 0.000*** | - |
| Therefore | 0.06 | 2.51 | 35.987 9 | 0.000*** | - |
| Thus | 0.45 | 0.07 | 4.045 4 | 0.044* | + |
| So | 16.20 | 21.52 | 11.494 9 | 0.001*** | - |
| Total | 19.88 | 35.07 | 63.808 6 | 0.000*** | - |

As shown in Table 5.6, there is a statistically significant difference ($p < .05$) between students and professional interpreters in terms of total causal conjunctions. Similarly, almost every causal conjunction analyzed in this study is also statistically significant in students' and professional corpora. However, there is an exception, that is, there is no statistically significant difference ($p > .05$) found in the use of the conjunction *thus* between students and professional interpreters. In other words, professional interpreters tend to employ more causal conjunctions compared with students except the causal conjunction *thus*. Students are inclined to use more causal conjunction *thus* than professional interpreters.

Causal conjunctions that appear in students' and professional corpora fall into four different subcategories: mistake, repetition, correspondence and explicitation. Here are the typical examples extracted from the interpreted texts of students and professional interpreters.

1) Mistake

Mistake refers to those instances in which the conjunctions are wrongly used or cannot be regarded as a causal conjunction in that example. There are more instances of mistakes found in students' corpus than in professional corpus. The examples are as follows:

**Example 5.16**

ST: 本届展览会已有 270 多家中外企业报名参展，展出总面积 15 000 平方米，是目前国内同类乐器展览会中规模最大的。

TT: [[So]] far, there are more than two hundred and seventy companies both at home and abroad have applied for... the... fair. The total area has covered... one thousand and five hundred... kilometers... square meters. This is the largest scale of the fa-instrmu- instrument fair in the domestic market. (Student)

**Example 5.17**

ST: 但是他们想抹黑中国，请注意，我讲的是中国，啊，这是办不到的。因为他们这么做是得到了，是遭到了中国人民、世界人民反对的，他们是站在中国人民和世界人民的对立面，他们这样抹黑，想办法抹黑中国，只能证明他们自己本身是一种什么颜色。

TT: However, for those people who want to tarnish the image of China. I'm talking about China. If they want to tarnish the image of China, they will never get their way because what they are doing is opposed by people in China and people around the world. By [[so]] doing, they are putting themselves against the Chinese people and the world's people. For those people who want to tarnish China's image, they will only tarnish their own image. (Professional)

In Examples 5.16 and 5.17, the conjunction *so* with the square bracket appeared respectively. However, they are not considered in the sense of causal conjunctions for the fact that the *so* along with *far* does not function as a causal conjunction in Example 5.16. While *so* in Example 5.17 indicates what has just been stated in the previous clause rather than in the sense of cause-effect relationship. Therefore, *so* in Examples 5.16 and 5.17 are regarded a mistake in our analysis.

In addition, it is better to mention the situations in which the use of *so* is considered a mistake instead in the sense of a casual conjunction. Two types of situations are omitted from the study of explicitation: the one refers to those clauses in which *that* is preceded by *so* and an adjective, and here *so* indicates the degree rather than the cause-effect, for example:

**Example 5.18**

ST: 我想先说明一个事实,台湾与大陆的经济联系十分紧密, 可以说到了不可分割的地步。

TT: I would like to share with you the following facts. The Taiwan and Mainland of China already have very close economic ties. It is fair to say that our ties are [[so]] close that actually such ties are indivisible. (Professional)

Another example refers to the conditional result introduced by *so that* in the adverbial clause, for instance:

**Example 5.19**

ST: 我们愿意同美方进一步加强磋商与合作,这个推动呢,战略经济对话和其他的机制啊,发挥更多的积极的作用,使两国的经贸合作关系啊,为两国人民带来更多的实惠。

TT: We would like to strengthen consultation and cooperation with United States, strengthen our strategic economic dialogue and other mechanisms, [[so that]] they can play a more positive role in promoting our ties. We should also vigorously develop our economic cooperation and trade [[so that]] they can bring more real benefits to peoples of the two countries. (Professional)

The examples of repetition are illustrated in the following subsection.

2 ) Repetition

**Example 5.20**

ST: 其规模之大、人数之多、范围之广、技术之新都是前所未有的。

TT: This serving the, this servingness near appear, appeared in the world because er... because of the, because of the huge... [[because]] the, because the huge, er, the amount of people and the technology is so modern. (Student)

**Example 5.21**

ST: 对个人投资者来讲呢,随着我们这个国民经济的增长、人均收入的提高,个人财富的增长。

TT: For, for the individual investors, as the Chinese economy further develops, and as the personal income grows further, so, [[so]] does the wealth of the average citizens in China. (Professional)

It is easy to notice that the causal conjunction *because* with square bracket in Example 5.20 and *so* with square bracket in Example 5.21 becomes repetitive occurrence for both students and professional interpreters. So the causal conjunctions *because* and *so* in the square bracket are regarded as repetitions. The specific instances serve to expound the correspondence of causal conjunctions in the following subsection.

3) Correspondence

The correspondence of causal conjunctions refers to those instances in which conjunctions in the target text correspond to their counterparts in the source text. The specific examples in the students' and professional corpora are as follows:

**Example 5.22**

ST: 所以我们大家都存在着一个如何来调焦距啊、对光圈的这么一个任务。

TT: [[Therefore]], we all have the task of adjusting the focus and apertures. (Professional)

**Example 5.23**

ST: 我们希望借鉴和学习国外的先进技术和经验,为国内外广大生产厂家、经销商提供一个交流技术、展示产品的窗口和桥梁。

TT: We hope, er, to learn some skills and experience from er, the foreign companies and, [[so]] as to did, er, the production, er, the farbrates and the sale, sales, er, shops... some experience to improve their abilities. So our role is... we play, er, we have to bridge them and give them some experience and help. (Student)

The causal conjunction *therefore* with square bracket in Example 5.22 corresponds to the corresponding causal conjunction "所以" in Chinese, and the other causal conjunction *so* along with *as to* in Example 5.23 can be traced back to "为" that indicates the reason in the source text. Therefore, both causal conjunctions *therefore* and *so* are analyzed as a correspondence.

4) Explicitation

The following examples illustrate the instances of explicitations in students' and professional corpora respectively.

**Example 5.24**

ST: 在过去的一年中,我们还努力建立、增进与听众朋友们的友谊,来自世界各地的听众来信数量达到 130 万封。

TT: In the past, in the past year we work hard to establish and improve the friendship with audience of from the, er, from various countries. [[Thus]] we have already received more than one point, one point three million letters from the audience of the, of various parts of the world. (Student)

**Example 5.25**

ST: 应该尽力避免战争,战争的爆发是不符合世界各国的利益的。

TT: Every effort has to be made to avoid war [[because]] war does not serve the interest of any country in the world. (Professional)

In Example 5.24, the causal conjunction *thus* with square bracket is added in the target text to clarify the causal-effect relationship with the previous clause which is hidden in the source text. Similarly, the causal conjunction *because* in Example 5.25 is added in the target text to state clearly the reason why "the war should be avoided with every effort" in the source text. The logical relationship which is hidden between two clauses in Chinese comes to the surface with the addition of the causal conjunction *because* in English, so that the audience of English have a clear understanding of logical relationship between two clauses spoken in Chinese. Therefore, both causal conjunctions *thus* and *because* are regarded as explicitations in the analysis.

The following pie charts in Figure 5.9 present the percentage of casual conjunctions in terms of mistake, repetition, correspondence and explicitation found in students' and professional corpora respectively.

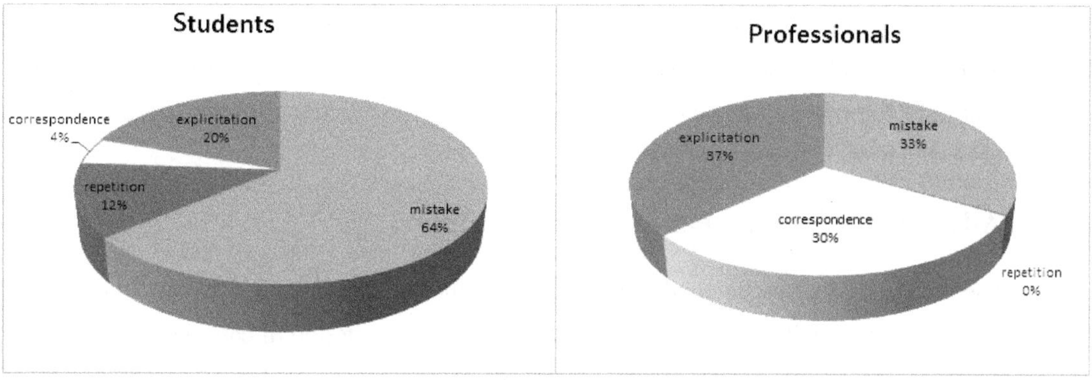


**Figure 5.9 Proportion of causal conjunctions used in students' and professional corpora**

As shown clearly in Figure 5.9, 64% of conjunctions are wrongly used or do not perform cause-effect relationship in the students' corpus, while mistakes only account for 33% in the professional corpus. There is only one repetition found in the professional corpus, which takes up zero percentage in the proportion of causal conjunctions.

With regard to professionals, the largest proportion is explicitation that accounts for 37%, whereas the explicitation takes up only 20% in the students' corpus. Overall, students are less likely not only to use conjunctions that denote cause-effect relationship, but also to explicitate causal conjunctions compared with professional interpreters.

Table 5.7 presents a detailed statistical analysis of explicitations detected in students' and professional corpora so that we have a complete picture of the differences regarding explicitationsof causal conjunctions between students and professional interpreters.

**Table 5.7 Explicitation of causal conjunctions in students' and professional corpora**

| Causal conjunctions | Students count/frequency | | Professionals count/frequency | | Chi-square | Significance ($p$) | |
|---|---|---|---|---|---|---|---|
| Because | 25 | 1.61 | 53 | 3.70 | 12.404 7 | 0.000*** | - |
| Since | 6 | 0.39 | 19 | 1.33 | 7.837 6 | 0.005** | - |
| Therefore | 1 | 0.06 | 20 | 1.40 | 18.752 9 | 0.000*** | - |
| Thus | 3 | 0.19 | 0 | 0.00 | 2.772 3 | 0.096 | + |
| So | 24 | 1.55 | 93 | 6.50 | 46.409 5 | 0.000*** | - |
| Total | 59 | 3.81 | 185 | 12.92 | 75.567 1 | 0.000*** | - |

As shown in Table 5.7, there is a statistically significant difference ($p$ <.05) in terms of the total explicitation of causal conjunctions between students and professional interpreters in C-E CI. Overall, professionals have the tendency to explicitate more conjunctions that indicate causal-effect relationship between clauses than students in C-E CI. In other words, the explicitations found in professional corpus (185 in total) reach to three times higher than those occurred in students' corpus (59 in total) with respect to causal conjunctions. However, there is one exception, that is, students not only use more causal conjunction *thus*, but also explicitate it more than professional interpreters explicitate.

### 5.3.2 Adversative Conjunction-based Explicitation

The section above gives detailed quantitative account of differences between students and professional interpreters with respect to the occurrence and explicitation of causal conjunctions.

This section deals with adversative conjunctions which express a relation used as "contrary to expectation" (Halliday & Hasan 1976: 250). The expectation "might be derived from the content of what is being said, or from the communication process, the speaker-hearer situation" (ibid). Some examples of adversative conjunctions include "but", "yet", "however", "(al) though", etc. This kind of conjunctions is concerned with transitions between messages, managing progression as the text unfolds.

**Table 5.8 Occurrence of adversative conjunctions in students' and professional corpora**

| Adversative conjunctions | Students frequency | Professionals frequency | Chi-square | Significance ($p$) | |
|---|---|---|---|---|---|
| But | 13.82 | 18.44 | 9.951 0 | 0.002** | - |
| However | 3.03 | 3.14 | 0.028 9 | 0.865 | + |
| Though | 0.19 | 0.28 | 0.233 0 | 0.629 | - |
| Yet | 0.19 | 2.03 | 23.265 1 | 0.000*** | - |
| Although | 0.45 | 1.61 | 9.858 9 | 0.002** | - |
| Total | 17.69 | 25.50 | 21.213 0 | 0.000*** | - |

The above statistical analysis shows that there is a statistically significant difference ($p < .05$) between students and professional interpreters with respect to the total number of adversative conjunctions found. Professional interpreters are more likely to employ adversative conjunctions compared with students, to be specific, there are 365 adversative conjunctions in the professional corpus while 274 adversative conjunctions discovered in the students' corpus. Nevertheless, there is an exception to this tendency, that is, the adversative conjunction *however* is found to be more in the students' corpus (47) than in the professional corpus (45).

As causal conjunctions depicted in the previous section, the adversative conjunctions that found in students' and professional corpora are further classified into four different subcategories: mistake, repetition, correspondence and explicitation. In general, the mistake and the repetition are easy to identify, here comes the typical examples of the correspondence and explicitation extracted from the interpreted texts of students and professional interpreters.

1) Correspondence

Here illustrates the specific instances of adversative conjunctions in ST that correspond to those in TT interpreted by both students and professionals.

**Example 5.26**

ST: 我们也报道了一些令人遗憾的冲突、动荡和灾难，但和平与发展始终是我们报道的主线。

TT: We also cover some regretful conflicts and disasters. [[However]], peace and development is as the main, the main key of our reports. (Student)

**Example 5.27**

ST: 我在这里想讲一段话。中华人民共和国成立以来，在党和政府的领导下，我国的现代化建设事业取得了巨大的成就，但是我们也走过弯路，有过教训。

TT: Since the founding of the People's Republic of China, under the leadership of our Party and the central, and the government, remarkable achievements have been made in advancing China's modernization drive, [[yet]] at the same time, we have taken some detours and learned hard lessons. (Professional)

In Example 5.26, it is apparent that, in the students' corpus, the adversative conjunction *however* in English is the exact interpretation of the conjunction "但" in Chinese. Likewise, in Example 5.27, a professional interpreter interpreted the adversative conjunction "但" in Chinese into its corresponding adversative conjunction *yet* in English. So both *however* and *yet* in the square bracket are taken as correspondence of the adversative conjunction "但" in the study.

2 ) Explicitation

The following are the classic examples of explicitations with respect to adversative conjunctions found in the students' corpus and professional corpus respectively.

**Example 5.28**

ST: 我想强调呢，和平和发展仍然是时代的主题，那么国际力量的对比呢，是朝着有利于维护世界和平方向发展的，世界总体的形势呢，是稳定的。

TT: I wish to stress that peace and development remain the general trend of our times. The international balance of power has changed in favor of world peace and development. The world situation is on the whole stable, [[but]] the world is not entirely peaceful. (Professional)

**Example 5.29**

ST: 这是前人留给我们的遗产，是一笔宝贵的资源，它属于龙城、属于中国、属于世界。

TT: This is the heritage by our ancient per..., people, [[but]], but it is also the resources belong to Long Cheng; belong to China; belong to the world as well. (Student)

In Example 5.28, the adversative conjunction *but* is added to clarify the impliciations of last clause in Chinese. With the addition of the adversative conjunction *but*, the audience are easy to associate the logical relation of the last clause with the previous one so that they can get a clear picture.

Similarly, in Example 5.29, the adversative conjunction *but* with the square bracket in English is added to clarify the logical relationship between the first clause and the second one that is hidden in Chinese. Therefore, *but* in the square bracket is considered an instance of explicitation made by a student and a professional interpreter.

Based on the analysis mentioned above, Table 5.9 shows a specific statistical analysis of explicitations performed by students and professiona linterpreters in C-E CI. As a result, we can get a complete picture of the differences between students and professional interpreters with regard to explicitations of adversative conjunctions.

**Table 5.9 Explicitation of adversative conjunctions in students' and professional corpora**

| Adversative conjunctions | Students count/frequency | | Professionals count/frequency | | Chi-square | Significance ($p$) | |
|---|---|---|---|---|---|---|---|
| But | 13 | 0.84 | 89 | 6.22 | 62.902 6 | 0.000*** | - |
| However | 5 | 0.32 | 12 | 0.84 | 3.466 8 | 0.063 | - |
| Though | 3 | 0.19 | 2 | 0.14 | 0.129 1 | 0.719 | + |
| Yet | 0 | 0.00 | 10 | 0.70 | 10.821 8 | 0.001** | - |
| Although | 3 | 0.19 | 5 | 0.35 | 0.671 3 | 0.413 | - |
| Total | 24 | 1.55 | 118 | 8.24 | 70.006 0 | 0.000*** | - |

Based on Table 5.9, there exists a statistically significant difference ($p < .05$) between students and professional interpreters in terms of total explicitations. Professionals are more likely to explicitate the adversative logical relationships that are hidden in the source text compared with students. However, it is not the case regarding specific adversative conjunctions explored in this study. Statistically significant differences ($p < .05$) are only found between students and professional interpreters concerning the explicitation of *but* and *yet*. More specifically, there are 89 explicitations of *but* in the professional corpus while only 13 explicitations are found in students' corpus. In addition, there is no instance of explicitation about *yet* found in students' corpus, whereas there are 10 explicitations of *yet* in the professional corpus.

In order to know some motivational factors that account for such explicitation difference between students and professional interpreters, it is better to take a close look at the detailed information about the rest of adversative conjunctions used in C-E CI. The following chart explicitly presents the percentage of adversative conjunctions in terms of mistake, repetition, correspondence and explicitation respectively.

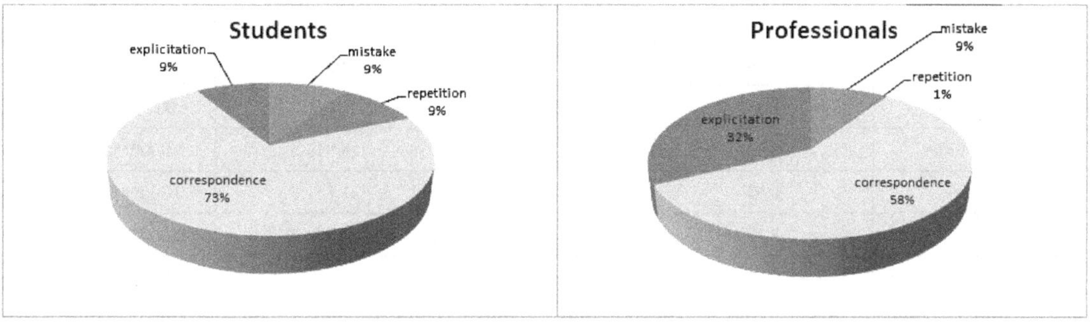


**Figure 5.10 Proportion of adversative conjunctions used in students' and professional corpora**

Based on the percentage shown in pie charts above, it is obvious that correspondence alone accounts for three quarters of the total adversative conjunctions, among which mistake, repetition and explicitation each takes up only one-tenth of the total, as far as students are concerned. With regard to professional interpreters, correspondence also accounts for the largest proportion, which takes up half of the total adversative conjunctions. However, explicitation alone accounts for one-third of the total adversative conjunctions in the professionals, which is over five times higher than those in students'corpus. Mistake plus repetition only takes up one-tenth of the total for professionals.

On the whole, for students, most of the adversative conjunctions (91%) they employed in the target text either can be traced back to corresponding adversative conjunctions in the source text, or wrongly and repetitively used in English. Explicitation only takes up less than one-tenth of the total adversative conjunctions in the students' corpus. However, as far as professional interpreters are concerned, explicitation accounts for one-thirds of all adversative conjunctions found in this study. These findings partly explain the reason why there are far more explicitations found in the professionals compared with students.

### 5.3.3 Conditional Conjunction–based Explicitation

The conjunction is an important feature of cohesive devices in creating coherence. In the current research, besides causal conjunctions and adversative conjunctions, conditional and other conjunctions will be included, since conjunction is still part of textual organization, and may yield interesting results. This section deals with conjunctions that indicate conditional, objective and consequential logical relationship between components of a sentence. Table 5.10 displays the quantitative analysis of occurrence of conditional conjunctions found in the students' and professional corpora.

**Table 5.10 Occurrence of conditional conjunctions in students' and professional corpora**

| Conditional & other conjunctions | Students frequency | Professionals frequency | Chi-square | Significance ($p$) | |
|---|---|---|---|---|---|
| If | 0.19 | 8.31 | 119.873 9 | 0.000*** | - |
| In order to | 1.55 | 2.86 | 5.899 2 | 0.015* | - |
| So as to | 0.32 | 2.03 | 18.919 5 | 0.000*** | - |
| So that | 1.03 | 4.40 | 31.851 7 | 0.000*** | - |
| Total | 3.10 | 17.60 | 155.682 9 | 0.000*** | - |

As seen in Table 5.10, there is a statistically significant difference ($p < .05$) between students and professional interpreters not only with regard to the total number of conditional conjunctions, but also with respect to every conditional conjunction analyzed in this study. In other words, compared with professional interpreters, students are far less likely to employ conditional conjunctions in C-E CI.

Similar to the way other conjunctions are subcategorized, the conditional conjunctions found in the students' and professional corpora are analyzed in terms of mistake, repetition, correspondence and explicitation. Since it is relatively easy to identify the instances of conditional conjunctions that are wrongly used or repetitively occurred, I will not go into them in this section any more. However, it is necessary to take specific examples of conditional conjunctions explicitated or correspond to respective conjunctions in the source text. Here are the typical instances of correspondence and explicitations about conditional conjunctions in both students' and professional corpora.

1) Correspondence

**Example 5.30**

ST: 更不用说我们全国各部门、各行业，都在进行着外交活动，为祖国交朋友，为人民办实事。

TT: On top of that, we know that different departments and industries across the country have also been actively engaged in other kinds of diplomatic activities [[so as to]] make friends for the motherland and do practical things for the people.

(Professional)

In Example 5.30, the conjunction *so as to* that indicates objective is also the interpretation of "为" in Chinese.

2 ) Explicitation

The specific examples of explicitations are illustrated in the following.

**Example 5.31**

ST: 我们希望借鉴和学习国外的先进技术和经验，为国内外广大生产厂家、经销商提供一个交流技术、展示产品的窗口和桥梁。

TT: We hope that the, this exhibition will borrow the, er, the advantages of the, of the international experiences, er, to, er, in order to, provide with the experience for our, for our enterprises and the sellers, er, [[so that]], so that to set up a bridge or a window for us to communicate the science and technologies... in China. (Student)

**Example 5.32**

ST: 调控得好，就可能保持中国这艘经济的大船平稳较快地航行。

TT: [[If]] we exercise the right macro-controls, we will be able to steer the big ship of the Chinese economy forward in a stable and relatively fast manner. (Professional)

In Example 5.31, the conjunction *so that* in the square bracket is added to clarify consequential relationship between the clauses in which *so that* appears with the previous clause. The conditional conjunction *if* in the target text, in Example 5.32, is also to explicitate the conditional relationship that is hidden between the first clause and the rest clause in the source text. Therefore, the conditional conjunction *if* and the conjunction *so that*, both of which indicate consequential relationship are considered explicitations. Table 5.11 below reveals elaborate statistical analysis on the explicitation of every conditional conjunction in the students' and professional corpora.

**Table 5.11 Explicitation of conditional conjunctions in students' and professional corpora**

| Conditional & other conjunctions | Students count/frequency | | Professionals count/frequency | | Chi-square | Significance ($p$) | |
|---|---|---|---|---|---|---|---|
| If | 0 | 0.00 | 48 | 3.35 | 51.951 5 | 0.000*** | - |
| In order to | 1 | 0.06 | 21 | 1.47 | 19.826 5 | 0.000*** | - |
| So as to | 0 | 0.00 | 19 | 1.33 | 20.562 1 | 0.000*** | - |
| So that | 2 | 0.13 | 27 | 1.89 | 23.608 6 | 0.000*** | - |
| Total | 3 | 0.19 | 115 | 8.03 | 115.552 0 | 0.000*** | - |

Based on the statistical analysis described in Table 5.11, admittedly, a statistically significant difference lies ($p < .05$) between students and professional interpreters in terms of explicitation of conditional conjunctions. In other words, students are far less likely to explicitate conditional and other conjunctions listed above compared with professional interpreters. According to the findings, there are only three explicitations discovered in students' corpus while there are 115 explicitations found in professional corpus in terms of total number of conditional and other conjunctions. More specifically, as for students, it is found that there is only one explicitation of *in order to* and two explicitations of *so that* in the students' corpus. As for professionals, the conditional conjunction *if* is the most explicitated one whose frequency is 48; the second one is *so that* with the explicitation of 27; the rest are conjunctions that imply objective meaning which are *in order to* and *so as to* with the explicitation of 21 and 19 respectively.

In order to have a complete picture of the distribution of conditional and other conjunctions in the students' and professional corpora, it is better to take a close look at those conjunctions within the subcategories of mistake, repetition, correspondence and explicitation. The following charts in Figure 5.11 presents the proportion of conditional and other conjunctions that are considered mistakes, repetitions, correspondence and explicitations in the students' and professional corpora.

**Figure 5.11 Proportion of conditional and other conjunctions used in students' and professional corpora**

The pie charts above show that a notable difference exists between students and professional interpreters with respect to the proportion of explicitation in the total number of conditional and other conjunctions. Although, for both students and professional interpreters, the percentage of correspondence takes up over half of the conditional and other conjunctions, a significant difference exists between students and professional interpreters with respect to explicitation. In other words, the percentage of explicitation employed by students merely occupy 6% which is less than one-tenth of total conjunctions, whereas the proportion of explicitation adopted by professional interpreters reaches to 46%, which is almost half of the total number of conjunctions found. In addition, in terms of mistake and repetition about conditional and other conjunctions, there is no mistake and repetition performed by professional interpreters, while mistake and repetition account for almost one-third of total conditional conjunctions in the students' corpus.

The findings that, students explicitate only 6% of total number of conditional conjunctions whereas professional interpreters explicitate 46% of the total conditional conjunctions, partly account for the fact that students are far less likely to explicitate than professional interpreters in terms of conditional conjunctions. In other words, as for students, correspondence, repetition and mistake altogether take up a strikingly large proportion of total conditional conjunctions; explicitation remains the smallest part. On the part of professional interpreters, correspondence and explicitation respectively account for half of the total number of conditional conjunctions.

The previous sections describe in detail the usage and explicitation of conditional and other conjunctions in both the students' and professional corpora. The following section will derive the conclusion from overall occurrence and explicitation of conjunctions.

### 5.3.4 Summary of Conjunction-based Explicitation

This section summarizes the usage and explicitation of total conjunctions found in students' and professional corpora respectively. Comparisons and statistical quantitative analyses are conducted with regard to different subcategories of conjunctions at lexico-grammatical level with respect to the interpretation of conjunctions in C-E CI. Table 5.12 demonstrates the total occurrence of conjunctions discovered in students' and professional corpora by comparison.

**Table 5.12 Occurrence of conjunctions in students' and professional corpora**

| Conjunctions | Students frequency | Professionals frequency | Chi-square | Significance ($p$) | |
|---|---|---|---|---|---|
| Causal conjunctions | 19.88 | 35.07 | 63.808 6 | 0.000*** | - |
| Adversative conjunctions | 17.69 | 25.50 | 21.213 0 | 0.000*** | - |
| Conditional & other conjunctions | 3.10 | 17.60 | 155.682 9 | 0.000*** | - |
| Total | 40.67 | 78.24 | 179.923 6 | 0.000*** | - |

Table 5.12 lists the total occurrence of conjunctions in terms of causal conjunctions, adversative conjunctions, and conditional and other conjunctions in students' and professional corpora respectively. Statistically significant difference ($p < .05$) exists between students and professional interpreters regarding total conjunctions. The total number of conjunctions in the professional corpus is almost two times higher than in the students' corpus. In addition, statistical differences also lie between students and professional interpreters with respect to the usage of causal, adversative, conditional and other conjunctions in C-E CI.

Students are not only less likely to employ conjunctions in total, but also less inclined to adopt causal, adversative and conditional conjunctions respectively compare with professionals.

However, the similarities exist concerning the frequency of conjunctions for students and professional interpreters. The most frequently used conjunction is the causal conjunction, then the adversative conjunction, the conditional, and other conjunctions are the least frequent one in both corpora.

A strikingly significant difference ($p < .05$) lies in the occurrence of conditional and other conjunctions between students and professional interpreters. With regard to students, the frequency of conditional conjunctions is merely three times per ten thousand words, whereas approximately 18 times per ten thousand words with respect to professional interpreters. This finding suggests that the frequency of conditional conjunction is over five times higher in the professional corpus than in the students' corpus. The significant difference between students and professional interpreters in terms of the occurrence of causal and adversative conjunctions is not as distinct as the occurrence of conditional and other conjunctions.

The total frequency of causal conjunctions, adversative conjunctions, conditional and other conjunctions is displayed above, while Table 5.13 allows us to take a close look at the frequency of explicitation in students' and professional corpora in terms of causal, adversative, conditional and other conjunctions respectively.

**Table 5.13 Explicitation of conjunctions in students' and professional corpora**

| Conjunctions | Students count/frequency | | Professionals count/frequency | | Chi-square | Significance ($p$) | |
|---|---|---|---|---|---|---|---|
| Causal conjunctions | 59 | 3.81 | 185 | 12.92 | 75.567 1 | 0.000*** | - |
| Adversative conjunctions | 24 | 1.55 | 118 | 8.24 | 70.006 0 | 0.000*** | - |
| Conditional & other conjunctions | 3 | 0.19 | 115 | 8.03 | 115.552 0 | 0.000*** | - |
| Total | 107 | 6.91 | 418 | 29.20 | 210.285 1 | 0.000*** | - |

As shown in Table 5.13, a statistically significant difference ($p < .05$) exists between students and professional interpreters in terms of the total frequency of explicitation, and each subcategory of conjunctions is listed. In other words, students are not merely less inclined to adopt conjunctions in their interpretations, and they have far less tendency to explicitate conjunctions in terms of every subcategory.

The most salient difference, between students and professional interpreters, lies in the explicitation of conditional and other conjunctions: there are only three occurrences of explicitation in the students' corpus whereas 115 explicitations in the professional corpus, which is almost 40 times of those in the students' corpus. The second distinct one exists in the explicitation of adversative conjunctions, that is, students only explicitate 24 instances of adversative conjunctions while the explicitations made by professionals are 118 by count, which are nearly 5 times of those adopted by students. The least notable difference lies in the explicitation of causal conjunctions, that being said, there are 59 explicitations in the students' corpus whereas 185 explicitations in the professional corpus, which is three times higher than in the students' corpus. Figure 5.13 demonstrates these differences more distinctly.

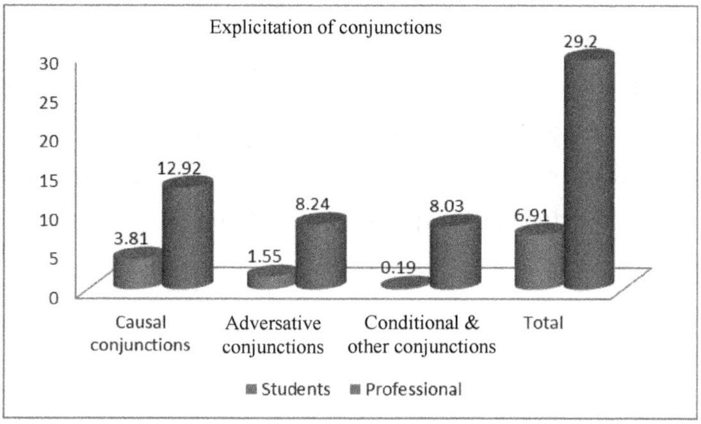


**Figure 5.12 Explicitation of conjunctions in students' and professional corpora**

As vividly reflected in Figure 5.12, a statistically significant difference ($p < .05$) lies, between students and professional interpreters, in terms of total explicitations as well as explicitations of causal, adversative, conditional and other conjunctions. However, for both students and professional interpreters, the most frequently explicitated conjunctions are causal conjunctions, then adversative conjunctions, finally the least frequent explicitations fall in conditional and other conjunctions.

It is necessary, other than explicitations, to take a close look at the proportion of mistake, repetition and correspondence of conjunctions, in order to situate the distribution of explicitation within the total percentage of conjunctions found in students' and professional corpora. The following pie charts in Figure 5.13 explicitly show the proportion of the mistake, repetition and correspondence and explicitation in the total number of conjunctions adopted by students' and professional interpreters respectively.

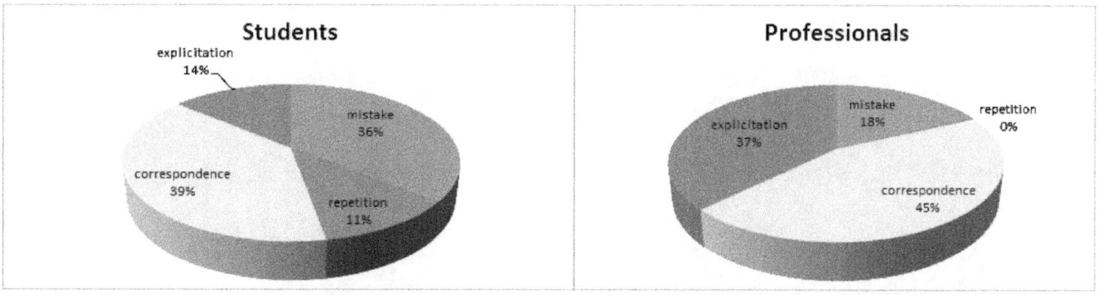


**Figure 5.13 Proportion of conjunctions used in students' and professional corpora**

As illustrated in the charts above, the correspondence takes up the largest proportion of conjunctions with the percentage of 39% and 45% for students and professional interprets respectively. Regarding students, the explicitation only accounts for 14% of the total conjunctions whereas the explicitation takes up 37% that is over one-third of total conjunctions adopted by professional interpreters. Concerning professional interpreters, mistakes and repetitions take up the least proportion of total conjunctions, while the mistake and repetition occupy half of the total conjunctions found in the students' corpus. These findings, with regard to students, suggest that the mistake, repetition and correspondence account for the strikingly largest proportion of total conjunctions compared with professional. This partly explains the reason why there are fewer explicitations discovered in the students' corpus than those in professional corpus by comparison.

# Chapter Six Intra-language Textual Explicitation by Chinese EFL students in C-E CI

This study does not merely focus on inter-language explicitation, which advocates the use of parallel corpora to discover the evidence of explicitated features; it also discusses the comparison of linguistic features between interpreted texts and original texts using comparable corpora.

After the Blum-Kulka's explicitation hypothesis, the previous explicitation studies using corpus-based approach predominately concentrate upon inter-language explicitation (Øverås 1998; Olohan 2004; Hu & Zhu 2008; Becher 2011; Károly 2014). In these studies, much of the analysis of explicitation has revolved around the comparison of target text with its source textas they facilitate investigation of the relationship between a translation and its source text. However, Baker (1995; 1996) proposes the novel way to examine the linguistic features of translated language, which employs corpora of original and translated language (in this case interpreted language) as another means with which to uncover evidence of explicitation in interpreting.

This chapter makes a comparison between students' interpreted English and the original English using a comparable corpus. Baker (1995: 234) introduces the notion of the comparable corpus as "two separate collections of texts in the same language. One corpus consists of original texts in the language in question and the other consists of translations in that language from a given source language or languages... both corpora should cover a similar domain, variety of language, and be of comparable length".

The comparable corpus consists of two subcorpora, namely the subcorpus of students' interpreted English texts translated from Chinese and the subcorpus of original English mentioned in 4.2.4. The students' interpreted English texts and the original English texts have almost the same corpus size and the similar subjects under discussion, which cover formal speeches, economy, diplomatic policy and related issues. That is to say, the comparable corpus applied in this study fits the criterion of Baker's definition about the comparable corpus.

The comparable corpus has provided a new angle from which the variations of translations or interpretations can be investigated in comparison with their original language. In this study, the application of comparable corpus allows us to investigate aspects of students' use of language in interpreted English compared with the original English. The primary focus is on the differences between students' interpreted texts and original English texts in terms of the use of cohesive devices. In other words, this study adopts the comparable corpus approach to identify the patterns of use of language, cohesive devices in particular, in students' interpreted text compared with the original English.

This chapter examines whether there exists intra-language textual explicitation, which focuses on the comparison between students' interpreted texts and its original texts in the same language. The main part of this chapter will respectively focus on the results of the language use along with the multi-layered dimensions of cohesive devices, namely Reference, Conjunction, and *that* as a subordinator in Subordinate Clause by Chinese EFL students. The first two sections look at reference and conjunction cohesive devices only, since they are most suitable for an automated corpus analysis. Statistical analyses help reveal the differences between students' interpreted texts and original texts in terms of the occurrence of cohesive devices. The following section is devoted to the statistical description of the reference in students' interpreted English in contrast with the original English along with the multiple dimensions of personal pronouns and conjunctions.

## 6.1 Reference

As an effective way to realize the textual meaning, cohesion is regarded an indispensable linguistic feature not only in discourse but also in translation and interpretation. The monumental work, *cohesion in English,* Halliday and Hasan (1976: 4) emphasize that cohesion "refers to relations of meaning that exist within the text, and that define it as a text". Cohesion occurs "where the interpretation of some element in the text is dependent on that of another" (Halliday & Hasan 1976: 4).

Cohesion, also defined as "the property of a text of being an interpretable whole rather than unconnected sentences" (Teich & Fankhauser 2004: 131), is an important element of texture since it helps the reader to relate phrases, sentences, and paragraphs within a meaningful whole of a text. As Koch puts it, cohesion is "the text-forming component of the linguistic system" (Koch 2001: 2).

Campbell also argues that cohesion is a unifying mechanism that ties textual segments, such as phrases, sentences, or paragraphs into a whole by "connections among the elements within thediscourse" (Campbell 1995: 5-6). In translation studies, Blum-Kulka regards cohesion as "an overt relationship holding between parts of the text, expressed by language specific markers"(Blum-kulka 2001: 299).Based on cohesion theory proposed by Halliday and Hasan (1976), the present study examines reference and conjunction cohesive devices with multiple subcategories, since they are most suitable for an automated corpus analysis.

Reference is the most apparent one in all cohesive devices. As Hadley puts it "reference is concerned with the identification of a thing, or specific group of things, by the use of certain reference items, such as personal pronouns. As these items appear in the text for the second or more times, they establish a network of meaning between the various sections of the discourse." (Hadley 1987) As an important component of cohesive devises, reference constitutes items in the English language which, "instead of being interpreted semantically in their own right, make reference to something else for their interpretation" (Halliday & Hasan 1976).

Halliday and Hasan (1976: 37) further differentiate reference as being personal, demonstrative, or comparative. Personal reference refers to using the pronouns to substitute the nouns that appear in the context. The present study focuses on the nominative and objective case of personal pronouns appeared in students' interpreted texts and in the original English, thus observing the similarities and differences in terms of using personal pronouns.

### 6.1.1 Personal Pronouns

Personal pronouns seem to be common cohesive devices in English. Most typically, personal pronouns "are used to refer to definite specific individuals identified in the speech situation (first and second person) or the preceding text (third person)" (Biber et al 1999: 328). Personal pronouns may be regarded as the most significant and central class of pronouns as they are most frequently used in English. This section takes a close look at the usage of personal pronouns not only in terms of number with singular or plural forms, but also with regard to case and person, in the students' interpreted texts and the original English corpus. Table 6.1 presents detailed information about personal pronouns with subjective and objective case forms.

**Table 6.1 Personal pronouns with subjective and objective case forms**

| | Person | Number | Subjective case | Objective case |
|---|---|---|---|---|
| Personal pronouns | First person | Singular | I | Me |
| | | Plural | We | Us |
| | Second person | Singular | You | You |
| | | Plural | You | You |
| | Third person | Singular | He, she, it | Him, her, it |
| | | Plural | They | Them |

According to Halliday and Hasan (1976: 31), personal pronouns belong to the group of referential cohesive devices and require a specific linguistic resourse to another item in the text. In addition, previous corpus findings reveal that "personal pronouns are by far most commonly employed in conversation" (Biber et al 1999: 333). Since the interpreted speech also involves a serious of conversations between a speaker and an addressee, the present study seeks to explore the use of personal pronouns in students' interpreted texts and in the original English.

Based on the subcategorization of personal pronouns given in Table 6.1 above, Table 6.2 provides the frequency of personal pronouns with subjective and objective case forms in the comparable corpus. The statistical analysis below shows that their use in English varies in the two subcorpora of the comparable corpus selected for the intra-language comparison.

**Table 6.2 Occurrence of personal pronouns in the students' interpreted English and the original English corpora**

| Subjective case | Students[1] count[2] | Frequency/ per 10 000[3] | Original[4] count | Frequency/ per 10 000 | Significance ($p$) | |
|---|---|---|---|---|---|---|
| First person | 2 655 | 171.398 6 | 5 652 | 371.487 7 | 0.000*** | - |
| Second person | 66 | 4.260 8 | 2 203 | 144.796 1 | 0.000*** | - |
| Third person | 836 | 53.969 6 | 1 694 | 111.341 2 | 0.000*** | - |
| Total | 3 557 | 229.241 6 | 9 549 | 627.625 0 | 0.000*** | - |
| Objective Case | | | | | | |
| First person | 550 | 35.506 3 | 405 | 26.619 4 | 0.000*** | + |
| Second person | 66 | 4.260 8 | 2 203 | 144.796 1 | 0.000*** | - |
| Third person | 203 | 13.105 1 | 436 | 28.656 9 | 0.000*** | - |
| Total | 819 | 52.872 1 | 3 044 | 200.072 3 | 0.000*** | - |

As shown in Table 6.2, there is obvious evidence of statistically significant difference ($p < .05$) between students' interpreted English and original English with respect to the occurrence of total personal pronouns with either subjective or objective case forms. That is to say, the personal pronouns in total are far less likely to occur in students' interpreted English compared with the original English, except the objective case of first person pronoun in the students' interpreted English. The specific result reports visually in the barcharts in Figure 6.1 in terms of each person pronoun frequency in students' interpreted English and the original English respectively.

As vividly shown in Figure 6.1, regarding the frequency[5] of subjective case of personal pronouns, a statistically significant difference ($p < .05$) lies between students' interpreted English and original English not only in terms of the total number, but also regarding every personal pronoun (i.e. first, second and third person). In other words, subjective case of personal pronouns is

① Students is the abbreviation of students' interpreted texts.

② Count by measurement is the sum of singular and plural pronouns.

③ Per 10 000 is the abbreviation for frequency of the personal pronoun per ten thousand words in the corpus.

④ Original refers to the Original English texts for the convenience of the space.

⑤ Frequency refers to the occurrence of personal pronouns every 10,000 words, and it is consistent across the sections in this chapter.

far less common in students' interpreted English compared with original English. Specifically, personal pronouns appear only 229 times① every 10,000 words in students' interpreted English while almost three times more (628 occurred in per 10,000 words) in the original English. However, with regard to students' interpreted English and the original English, the first person is the most frequently used pronoun with the frequency of 171 and 371 every 10,000 words respectively. The second person is the least in students' interpreted English with the frequency of only 4 times per 10,000 words, whereas third person is the least employed in the original English with the frequency of 111 every 10,000 words.

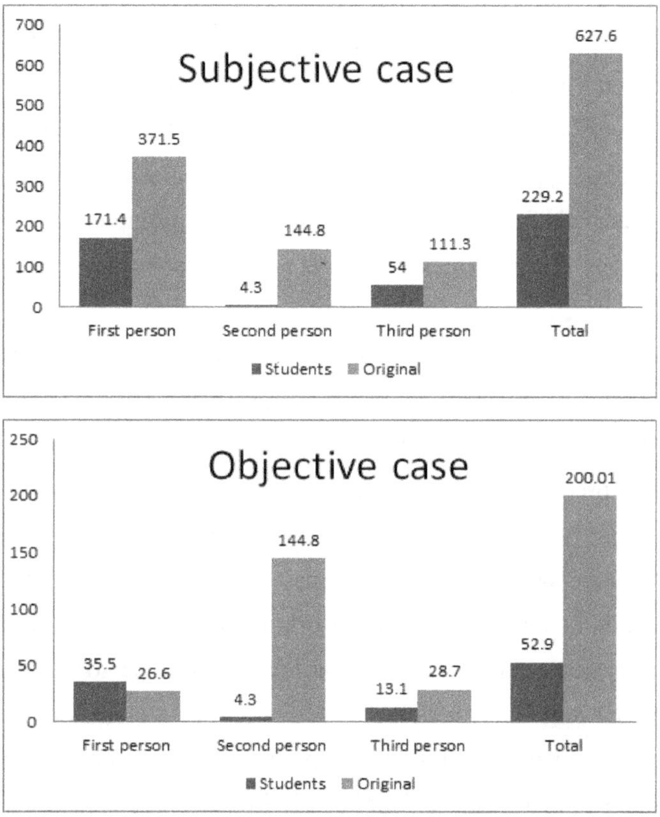


**Figure 6.1 Frequency of personal pronouns in the students' interpreted and the original English corpora**

As to the objective case of personal pronouns, there also exists a statistically significant difference ($p < .05$) between students' interpreted English and original English in terms of every category of personal pronouns. That is to say, the objective case of personal pronouns is more common in the original English than in students' interpreted English except the first person pronouns. The first person with objective case is more likely to appear in students' interpreted English com-

① It is the integer of the frequency in Table 6.2, and the process of integrating the frequency is consistent across the whole Chapter six.

pared with the original English. To be specific, objective case of personal pronouns in total occurs merely 53 times every 10,000 words in students' interpreted English whereas 200 per 10,000 words in the original English, which is roughly 4 times of pronouns in interpreted English. With regard to students' interpreted English, objective case of first person is most common, while second person is the least employed with the frequency of 36 and 4 times per 10,000 words respectively. In the case of original English, objective case of the second person is the most frequent with the frequency of 145 per 10,000 words, yet first person is the least used, which only appeared 27 times every 10,000 words respectively.

Whether in subjective case or in objective case forms, first person pronouns are most frequently used in both students' interpreted English and the original English. This result confirms the previous finding that "first and second person pronouns, referring to the speaker and the addressee, are naturally very common in conversation because both participants are in immediate contact, and the interaction typically focuses on matters of immediate concern" (Biber et al 1999: 333). It is the case that both first person and second person pronouns are more common in the original English, however, the frequency of second person pronouns are much lower in students' interpreted English.

Overall, subjective case of personal pronouns in total is far more common than objective case of personal pronouns in students' interpreted English and the original English respectively. However, personal pronouns, either in subjective case or in objective case, are far less likely to occur in students' interpreted English compared with the original English except with respect to the objective case of first person. These findings further imply that students are far less likely to employ not only inter-language explicitation compared with professional interpreters, but also intra-language explicitation in comparison with the original English in terms of personal pronouns.

In order to explain the reason why there is far fewer second person pronouns in the students' English than the original English, it is quite necessary to take a close look at second person pronouns in the source text. Indeed, it is found that there is no occurrence of corresponding Chinese second person pronoun singular form "你" or "你们" in the source text, which accordingly results in the fewer occurrence of their corresponding second person pronoun in the students' interpreted English compared with other pronouns.

The following section presents a detailed description of demonstrative reference detected in students' interpreted English compared with the original English, and descriptive statistical analysis shows the fundamental similarities and differences between students' interpreted English and the original English.

### 6.1.2 Demonstratives

Demonstrative pronouns such as "this", "that", "these", and "those", and adverbial demonstratives of place (here and there) belong to the important indicator of reference cohesive devices, and achieve textual cohesion "by means of location, on a scale of proximity" in relation to the speaker (space) or the moment of speech (time) (Halliday & Hasan 1976: 37-38).

Like the personal pronouns, the demonstratives have a deictic function and definite meaning. Demonstrative pronouns normally refer to things and "their reference depends on the context shared by speaker/writer and hearer/reader" (Quirk et al. 1995: 327). With demonstratives, we shall find it convenient to refer to an earlier part of discourse or a later part of discourse. The demonstrative pronouns are of great importance to the referential cohesion of the text as a whole, and they are the most common demonstratives, demonstrative pronoun *this* in particular, examined in the comparable corpus. Therefore, it is relatively significant to look at the occurrence of demonstrative pronouns and adverbial demonstrative of place in the students' interpreted English compared with original English. Table 6.3 provides descriptive statistics for demonstrative pronouns.

**Table 6.3 Occurrence of demonstratives in the students' interpreted English and the original English corpora**

| Demonstrative | Students count | Frequency/ per 10 000 | Original count | Frequency/ per 10 000 | Significance (*p*) | |
|---|---|---|---|---|---|---|
| Here | 215 | 13.879 7 | 227 | 14.920 0 | 0.447 | - |
| There | 192 | 12.394 9 | 1 009 | 66.318 3 | 0.000*** | - |
| This | 1 452 | 93.736 7 | 1 298 | 85.313 4 | 0.013 * | + |
| That | 204 | 13.169 6 | 1 445 | 94.975 2 | 0.000*** | - |
| These | 104 | 6.713 92 | 269 | 17.680 5 | 0.000*** | - |
| Those | 116 | 7.488 60 | 308 | 20.243 8 | 0.000*** | - |
| Total | 2 283 | 147.383 5 | 4 556 | 299.451 2 | 0.000*** | - |

As shown in Table 6.3, a statistically significant difference ($p < .05$) exists between students' interpreted English and the original English in terms of total number of demonstratives except the adverbial demonstrative *here*. In other words, the demonstratives in total are far less likely to occur in students' interpreted English, and their frequency is 147 times per 10,000 words, while the original English contains two times more of demonstrative pronouns and adverbials of place found in students' interpreted English with the frequency of 299 times every 10,000 words.

The frequency of every demonstrative in students' interpreted English and the original

English is given in the following bar chart for better visual perception in Figure 6.2.

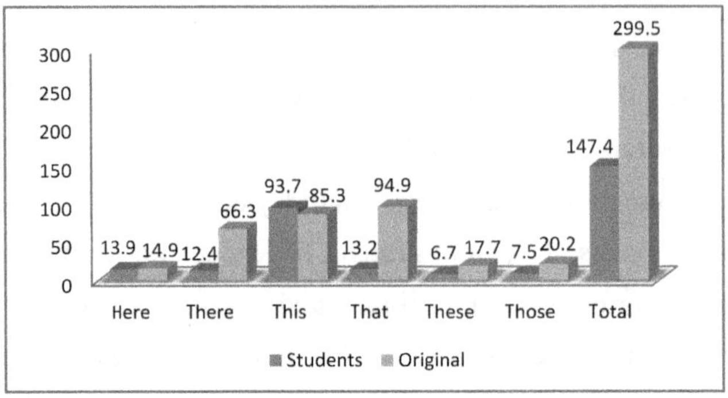


**Figure 6.2 Frequency of demonstratives in the students' interpreted and the original English corpora**

As shown in Figure 6.2, as to demonstrative pronouns, the frequency of singular form of demonstrative pronouns *this* and *that* is much frequent than their corresponding plural forms *these* and *those* both in students' interpreted English and original English. This preliminary result further supports the corpus findings that "the singular forms are more common than the plural forms in all registers" (Biber et al 1999: 349). Concerning adverbial demonstratives of place, *there* is much frequently used in the original English with the frequency of 66 times every 10,000 words, whereas the demonstrative adverbial *here* is more frequently employed in students' interpreted English with the frequency of 14 per 10,000 words.

As to students' interpreted English, the demonstrative *this* is the most frequently employed demonstrative pronoun with the frequency of 94 every 10,000 words, which is even slightly higher than the demonstrative *this* in the original English. Then follows the demonstratives *here*, *that*, *there* and *those* in turn with the frequency of about 14, 13, 12, and 8 times per 10,000 words respectively. The plural form of demonstrative pronoun *these* is the least frequently used in students' interpreted English with the frequency of about 7 times every 10,000 words.

In the case of original English, the demonstrative pronoun *that* is the most frequently used demonstrative with the frequency of 95 times per 10,000 words, which is as many as the most frequent demonstrative *this* in the students' interpreted English. Then comes the demonstratives *this*, *there*, *those*, and *these* in sequence with the frequency of 85, 66, 20, and 18 times every 10,000 words respectively. The adverbial demonstrative *here* is the least frequently used demonstrative in the original English with the frequency of only 14 times per 10,000 words.

It is worth noting that the demonstrative pronoun *that* is respectively more common in original English and students' interpreted English. It is most likely that "the reference of *that* in conversation is usually fairly vague and fits in with the use of other vague expressions in conversation" (Biber et al 1999: 350), even though the frequency of the demonstrative *that* is much higher in the original English than in the students' interpreted English.

This section gives the detailed statistical description of the frequency of demonstrative references used in the students' interpreted English compared with the original English. The following section will offer succinct summary of referential cohesive devices mentioned in students' interpreted English in intra-language comparison with the original English.

### 6.1.3 Summary of Reference

The previous subsections intend to reveal statistical analysis of referential cohesive devises in students' interpreted English compared with original English. The cohesive devices include subjective case and objective case of personal pronouns with singular and plural forms mentioned in Table 6.1, and demonstrative pronouns and adverbials of place depicted in Table 6.3.

According to the descriptive statistical analysis, there exists noticeable evidence of statistically significant difference ($p < .05$) between students' interpreted English and original English in terms of the frequency of personal pronouns with both subjective case and objective case forms. In other words, the personal pronouns with subjective and objective case forms are far less likely to occur in students' interpreted English compared with original English. The objective case of first person pronoun makes an exception with a slightly higher occurrence in students' interpreted English compared with original English.

The demonstrative reference, including demonstrative pronouns and adverbials of place, is also a consideration for the investigation of referential cohesive devices. Based on the statistical results in Table 6.3, the occurrence of demonstratives exhibits similar tendency as personal pronouns with subjective and objective case forms. That is to say, the demonstrative reference in total is far less likely to occur in students' interpreted English compared with original English. The demonstrative adverbial of place *here* is an exception with comparatively higher occurrence in students' interpreted English compared with the original English.

It is also noteworthy that the personal pronouns occur with much higher frequency by measurement than demonstratives in students' interpreted English and the original English. This finding confirms the preceding corpus finding based on statistical analysis of distribution, which is "demonstrative pronouns are rare compared with personal pronouns" (Biber et al 1999: 349).

These findings suggest that students' interpreted texts tend to contain fewer referential cohesive devices, including personal pronouns with subjective case and objective case forms and demonstrative pronouns and adverbials of place, compared with original English texts. This result, in turn, implies that students do not incline to adopt intra-language explicitation in C-E CI.

The following section will focus on another important indicator of cohesion and its occurrence in students' interpreted English compared with the original English, which may offer illuminating insight into intra-language explicitation.

## 6.2 Conjunctions

It is apparent that interpreting involves a shift from the source text concerning its structure or content. Since interpreters are dealing with two different systems of languages, they will certainly observe many differences between the lexical and grammatical systems of the languages involved, especially the way in which cohesion and coherence show themselves through cohesive markers in the interpreted text. Therefore, it is considerably important to spell out what has been stated implicitly in the source text in order to bring about textual cohesion, thus increasing he intelligibility of the interpreted text.

Cohesion is realized through cohesive markers which are the most important linguistic features of textual meaning. In addition, cohesion is potentially significant in any successful process of interpreting because a well-motivated selection of cohesive devices will help identify the semantic relations that exist within the text.

In general, cohesion is partly expressed through grammar and partly through vocabulary, and hence it has two types, that is, grammatical cohesion and lexical cohesion mentioned in 3.2.3. Among the cohesive relations, reference, substitution and ellipsis are grammatical, however, this study does not take substitution and ellipsis into account, because ellipsis is usually relevant to implicitation, and no significant difference exists regarding the occurrence of substitution. While lexical cohesion, as the name suggests, manifests itself through lexical items. Conjunction, which is the focus of this section, combines both grammatical and lexical features. In fact, as Halliday and Hasan (1976: 6) point out, conjunction is "mainly grammatical, but with a lexical component in it".

Conjunction, one of the important indicators of cohesive relations proposed by Halliday and Hasan, is "rather different in nature from the other cohesive relations" (Halliday & Hasan 1976: 226). Conjunction is a different type of semantic relation, which is "a specification of the way in which what is to follow is systematically connected to what has gone before" (ibid: 227).

Conjunctive relations refer to some "certain non-structural, text-forming relations" (ibid: 320), which indicate logical relationship between sentences in a text. The logical relationships include causal, adversative, conditional and other relations between and within sentences.

The conjunction is the focus of investigation in the current section, since it is still part of textual organization, and may yield interesting results. This section seeks to analyze the occurrence of conjunctions in students' interpreted English compared with the original English, and confined the investigation of conjunctions to Halliday and Hasan's (1976) classification about conjunctive relations which include causal, adversative, conditional and other types.

To be specific, Conjunction cohesive devices included in the study fall into three subcategore is:

(i) Causal conjunctions (e.g., because, therefore);
(ii) Adversative conjunctions (e.g., however, though);
(iii) Conditional & other conjunctions (e.g., if, in order to).

The following subsection deals with the occurrence of causal conjunctions in students' interpreted texts compared with the original English.

### 6.2.1 Causal Conjunctions

As Halliday and Hasan (1976: 226) state, the cohesive function of conjunctions is indirect and realized "by virtue of their specific meanings", which "presupposes the presence of other components in the discourse". Conjunctions relate "linguistic elements that occur together in succession," thus creating ties between segments of text (Halliday & Hasan 1976: 227). They combine "any two textual elements into a potentially coherent complex semantic unit" (Thompson 1996: 156).

Conjunctive relations express causal, adversative, conditional and temporal relationships "between related sentences and within sentences" (Dong & Lan 2010: 50). According to Halliday and Hasan (1976: 321), conjunctive relations represent "semantic links between the elements that are constitutive of text".

This subsection focuses on the occurrence of causal conjunctions in students's interpreted texts compared with the original English. Causal conjunction indicates a cause-effect relation between or within sentences and is expressed by such connectives as "so", "thus", "hence", and "therefore", etc. (Halliday & Hasan 1976: 256). Table 6.4 provides the occurrence of frequently used casual conjunctions in students' interpreted texts and the original English respectively.

**Table 6.4 Occurrence of causal conjunctions in the students' interpreted English and the original English corpora**

| Causal conjunctions | Students count | Frequency/ per 10 000 | Original count | Frequency/ per 10 000 | Significance ($p$) | |
|---|---|---|---|---|---|---|
| Because | 31 | 2.00 | 309 | 20.31 | 0.000*** | - |
| Since | 18 | 1.16 | 60 | 3.94 | 0.000*** | - |
| Therefore | 1 | 0.06 | 18 | 1.18 | 0.000*** | - |
| Thus | 7 | 0.45 | 2 | 0.13 | 0.121 | + |
| So | 251 | 16.20 | 731 | 48.05 | 0.000*** | - |
| Total | 308 | 19.88 | 1120 | 73.61 | 0.000*** | - |

As seen in Table 6.4, a statistically significant difference ($p < .05$) lies in the total number of causal conjunctions between students's interpreted English and the original English. Only by use of causal conjunction *thus*, no statistically significant difference ($p > .05$) exists between students' interpreted English and the original English. That is to say, there are far fewer occurrence of causal conjunctions occurred in the corpus of students' interpreted English compared with the original English except the occurrence of the casual conjunction *thus*. It seems that students have less striking tendency to adopt casual conjunctions in interpreted texts from Chinese. The original Englishtexts contain over three times more casual conjunctions (the occurrence of 1,120) than students' interpreted texts (the occurrence of 308). The specific result for the frequency of each causal conjunction is visually presented through the bar chart in Figure 6.3.

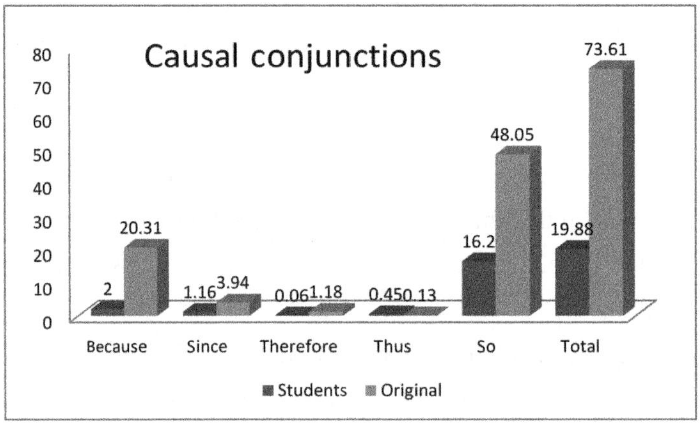


**Figure 6.3 Frequency of causal conjunctions in the students' interpreted and the original English corpora**

As shown in Figure 6.3, the total frequency of causal conjunctions in the original English (74/ per 10,000 words) is over three times more than in students' interpreted English (20/ per 10,000 words). Both for students' interpreted English and the original English, the most frequently used causal conjunction is *so*, with the frequency of 16 and 48 times per 10,000 words respectively. The least occurred in students' interpreted English is the causal conjunction *therefore*, which occurs only once in the corpus. While the least employed one in the original English is the causal conjunction *thus* where no statistically significant difference ($p > .05$) exists with students' interpreted English, with the occurrence of only two times.

In students' interpreted English, the most frequently used causal conjunction is *so* with the frequency of 16 times every 10,000 words. Then follows the occurrence of causal conjunctions *because*, *since*, and *thus* in turn with the frequency of two, one, and 0.5 times every 10,000 words respectively. Finally, the least frequently used causal conjunction is *therefore* with the frequency of about only 0.1 times per 10,000 words.

In the original English, the most frequently used is also the causal conjunction *so* with the

**Continued**

frequency of 48 time every 10,000 words. Subsequently comes the causal conjunctions *because*, *since*, and *therefore* in sequence with the frequency of 20, 4, and 1 times per 10,000 words respectively. Lastly, the least frequently used causal conjunctions is *thus* with the frequency of merely 0.1 times every 10,000 words in the corpus.

The finding is that, except the occurrence of causal conjunction *thus*, there are far fewer occurrences of causal conjunctions in students' interpreted English compared with the original English. This result, in turn, may suggest that students do not tend to make intra-language explicitation in their interpreted English. The following subsection presents the occurrence of adversative conjunctions in students' interpreted English compared with the original English as a whole.

### 6.2.2 Adversative Conjunctions

According to Halliday and Hasan (1976: 250), adversative conjunctions indicate a relation that is "contrary to expectation". In addition, this expectation "may be derived from the content of what is being said, or from the communication process, speaker-hearer situation" (ibid). This section presents the major conjunctions that indicate adversative relation between or within sentences in a text. Table 6.5 shows the frequency of adversative conjunctions found in students' interpreted English compared with original English.

**Table 6.5 Occurrence of adversative conjunctions in the students' interpreted English and the original English corpora**

| Adversative conjunctions | Students count | Frequency/ per 10 000 | Original count | Frequency/ per 10 000 | Significance ($p$) | |
|---|---|---|---|---|---|---|
| But | 214 | 13.82 | 853 | 56.06 | 0.000*** | - |
| However | 47 | 3.03 | 9 | 0.59 | 0.000*** | + |
| Though | 3 | 0.19 | 31 | 2.04 | 0.000*** | - |
| Yet | 3 | 0.19 | 52 | 3.42 | 0.000*** | - |
| Although | 7 | 0.45 | 24 | 1.58 | 0.001** | - |
| total | 274 | 17.69 | 969 | 63.69 | 0.000*** | - |

As described in Table 6.5, a statistically significant difference ($p<.05$) exists in students' interpreted English in comparison with the original English with respect to the total number of adversative conjunctions used. Likewise, the original English contains four times as many as adversative conjunctions (the frequency of 64 time every 10,000 words) in comparison with students' interpreted English (the frequency of 18 time per 10,000 words). In other words, the adversative conjunctions are far less likely to occur in the corpus of students' interpreted English compared with the original English. Nevertheless, the adversative conjunction *however* in students' interpreted English makes an exception with occurrence of 47 times, which is over 5 times more than in the original English with the occurrence of only 9 times. Figure 6.4 illustrates the specific result for every adversative conjunction in students' interpreted English with the original English by comparison for better visual perception.

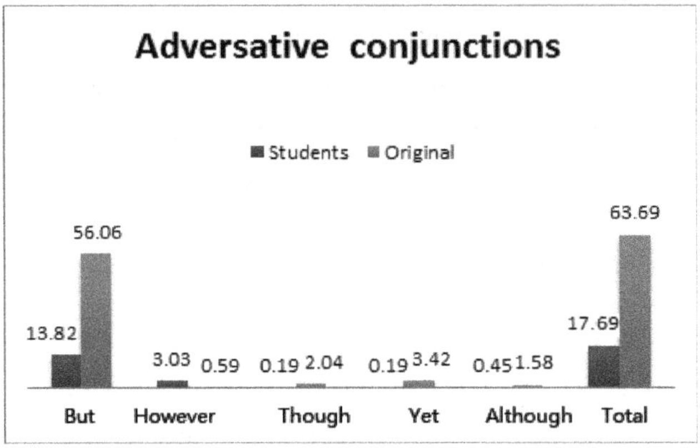


**Figure 6.4 Frequency of adversative conjunctions in the students' interpreted and the original English corpora**

As shown in Figure 6.4, the total frequency of adversative conjunctions (18 times per 10,000 words) in students' interpreted English reaches merely one-fourth of the adversative conjunctions (64 times per 10,000 words) in the original English. The adversative conjunction *but* is the most frequently used in both students' interpreted English and the original English, which confirms the corpus finding that "*but* is much likely to occur in the turn-initial position, which is considerably more common in conversation than in written registers" (Biber et al 1999: 83-84). The adversative conjunctions *though* and *yet* are the least frequently used in students' interpreted English, which only occurred 3 times, whereas the frequency of the conjunction *however* is the least in the original English with the occurrence of 9 times in the corpus.

In the students' interpreted English, the adversative conjunction *but* is the most commonly used one with the frequency of 14 times every 10,000 words. Subsequently follows the adversative conjunctions *however* and *although* in turn with the frequency of 3 and 0.5 times per 10,000 words. The least used adversative conjunctions are *though* and *yet* with the same frequency of 0.2 times every 10,000 words in the corpus of students' interpreted English.

On the contrary, in the subcorpus of original English, the most frequently adversative conjunction is also *but* with the frequency of 56 times every 10,000 words, which is 4 times as many as the corresponding conjunction in students' interpreted English. Then comes the adversative conjunctions *yet*, *though*, and *although* with the frequency of 3, 2, and 1.6 times every 10,000 words in the corpus of original English. The adversative conjunction *however* is the least common with the frequency of only 0.6 times every 10,000 words in the corpus.

In short, the finding is that, except the frequency of adversative conjunction *however*, students' interpreted English merely contains one-fourth of adversative conjunctions that occur in the corpus of original English. That is to say, students are far less likely to employ adversative conjunctions in their interpreted English compared with the original English. The result, in turn, may imply that intra-language explicitation is far less likely to occur in students' interpreted English compared with the original English in terms of adversative conjunctions.

### 6.2.3 Conditional and Other Conjunctions

The previous two subsections describe the frequency of causal and adversative conjunctions in students' interpreted English in comparison with the original English in detail. This section presents the occurrence and frequency of conditional or hypothetical (Trebit 2009) and other conjunctions which occur in students' interpreted English compared with the original English. Table 6.6 shows the quantitative statistical analysis of conditional and other conjunctions, which occur in students' interpreted English, by contrast with those corresponding counterparts appeared in the original English.

**Table 6.6 Occurrence of conditional & other conjunctions in the students' interpreted English and the original English corpora**

| Conditional conjunctions | Students count | Frequency/ per 10 000 | Original count | Frequency/ per 10 000 | Significance ($p$) | |
|---|---|---|---|---|---|---|
| If | 3 | 0.19 | 516 | 33.92 | 0.000*** | - |
| In order to | 24 | 1.55 | 42 | 2.76 | 0.011* | - |
| So as to | 5 | 0.32 | 1 | 0.07 | 0.124 | + |
| So that | 16 | 1.03 | 80 | 5.26 | 0.000*** | - |
| Total | 48 | 3.10 | 639 | 42.00 | 0.000*** | - |

As described in Table 6.6, there exists a statistically significant difference ($p < .05$) between students' interpreted English and the original English in terms of the total number of conditional and other conjunctions. However, the occurrence of *so as to*, which is used to express for achieving certain objective, no statistically significant difference ($p > .05$) is found between students' interpreted English and the original English. In other words, the conditional and other conjunctions are far less common in students' interpreted English in comparison with the original English except the linking adverbial *so as to*, which is 5 times more often in students' interpreted English than in the original English. Figure 6.5 visually presents the frequency of every conditional conjunction that appears in students' interpreted English and the original English corpora respectively.

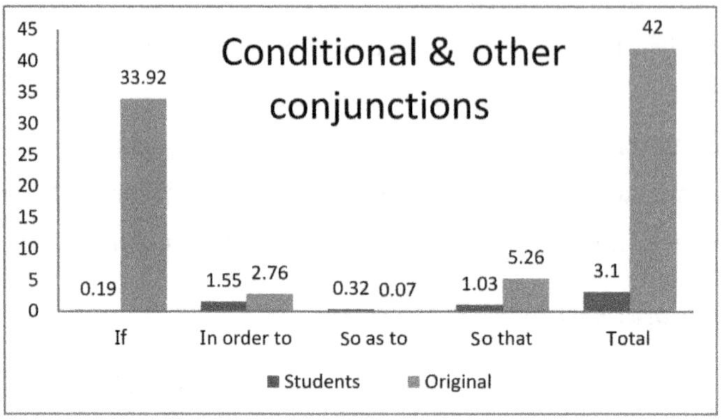


**Figure 6.5 Frequency of conditional and other conjunctions in the students' interpreted and the original English corpora**

As shown in Figure 6.5 above, a strikingly significant difference ($p < .05$) lies in the total frequency of conditional and other conjunctions observed in students' interpreted English and the original English respectively. On average, the frequency of conditional and other conjunctions in the original English (42/per 10,000 words) is approximately 14 times higher than those in the corpus of students' interpreted English (3/per 10,000 words). The discrepancy is striking in the frequency of the conditional conjunction *if* with the frequency of 34 times every 10,000 words in the original English while merely 0.2 times every 10,000 words in students' interpreted English. However, the conjunction *so as to* is the only exception that is much more frequent in the corpus of students' interpreted English compared with the original English.

In the corpus of original English, the most extremely frequent conditional conjunction is *if* with the frequency of 34 per 10,000 words, which is unexceptionally over 100 times higher than that occurring in students' interpreted English. Subsequently follows the conjunctions *so that*, *in order to* in sequence with the frequency of 5 and 3 times every 10,000 words respectively.The least frequently employed one is *so as to* with the frequency of merely 0.07 times per 10,000 words where no significant difference is found with the students' interpreted English by comparison.

On the contrary, in the subcorpus of students' interpreted English, the most frequently used one is the conjunction *in order to* with the frequency of approximately 2 times every 10,000 words. Then comes the conjunctions *so that* which indicates the result, and *so as to* which is used to express for reaching the objective, with the frequency of only 1 and 0.3 times every 10,000 words respectively. The least frequently employed one is the conditional conjunction *if* with the frequency of only 0.2 times every 10,000 words. It seems like the conditional conjunction *if* is far less likely to occur in the corpus of students' interpreted English compared with the original English.

Overall, the conditional and other conjunctions are far less likely to occur in the subcorpus of students' interpreted English than in the corpus of the original English by comparison. This finding, in turn, may suggest that intra-language explicitations are far less likely to occur in the subcorpus of students' interpreted English in comparison with the original English. The following subsection offers the comprehensive summary of all conjunctions in students' interpreted English compared with the original English with detailed descriptive statistical analysis.

### 6.2.4 Summary of Conjunctions

The previous sections concentrate upon the occurrence of conjunctive cohesive devices in the students' interpreted English in relation to the original English revolving along three major dimensions of conjunctions, namely, causal, adversative and conditional and other conjunctions. The current section offers a summary of conjunctive cohesive devices appeared in students' interpreted English in comparison with the original English.

Conjunctions are significant cohesive devices and the mastery of their use has a huge impact on students' textual competence (Bachman 1990) or discourse competence (Canale & Swain 1980), one of the major constituents of communicative competence. In addition, appropriate use of cohesive conjunctions enhances the rhetorical effectiveness of a text and facilitates text organization (Keen 2004: 88-94). That is to say, the use or misuse even overuse of conjunctive cohesive devices may exert considerable effect on the interpretation of a text. Therefore, the conjunctions are particularly of interest to some researchers.

Previous studies, as Verikaite analyzes, conjunctive discourse markers such as causal, adversative, and temporal conjunctions vary in the genres of textbooks and scientific research articles. Based on her findings, "the causal and temporal conjunctions were used more frequently in the research articles" (Verikaite 2005: 68).

Beikian et al (2013) also investigate the explicitation of conjunctive relations in the Persian translations from English. According to their results, "the most significant amount of added conjunctions in the TT is temporal type of relations, which covers about 42% of the total conjunctive relations, while the least number of explicitation is observed in the additive types of relations with a percentage of 9%" (Beikian 2013: 87).

The studies outlined above either focus on conjunctive discourse markers in different genres of English or conjunctive relations in translations. Other translation studies also reveal that conjunctions can contribute to the translation competence and naturalness of the translated text (Baker 1992: 112; Dong & Lan 2010; Hatim & Mason 1990: 206). The use of conjunctions helps the reader (or translator) make sense of the logical relationship (Hu 1994), which, in turn, informs the organization of linguistic resources in translation and interpreting. Thus, this section intends to summarize the conjunctive cohesive devices used in students' interpreted texts compared with naturally occurring texts in English and in similar genres. Table 6.7 briefly presents a statistical analysis of conjunctive devices centering around multi-layered dimensions in students' interpreted English in relation to the original English.

**Table 6.7 Occurrence of overall conjunctions in the students' interpreted English and the original English corpora**

| Conjunctions | Students count | Frequency/ per 10 000 | Original count | Frequency/ per 10 000 | Significance ($p$) | |
|---|---|---|---|---|---|---|
| Causal conjunctions | 308 | 19.88 | 1 120 | 73.61 | 0.000*** | - |
| Adversative conjunctions | 274 | 17.69 | 969 | 63.69 | 0.000*** | - |
| Conditional & other conjunctions | 48 | 3.1 | 639 | 42 | 0.000*** | - |
| Total | 630 | 40.67 | 2 728 | 179.30 | 0.000*** | - |

As shown in Table 6.7, there exists a statistically significant difference ($p < 0.05$) between students' interpreted English and the original English in not only the total number of conjunctions, but also every type of conjunctions. In other words, causal, adversative, conditional and other conjunctions are all far less likely to occur in students' interpreted English in relation to the original English. The most striking difference lies in the occurrence of conditional and other conjunctions, that is, the frequency of conditional and other conjunctions in the original English (42 times per 10,000 words) surprisingly reaches to approximately 14 times of corresponding conjunctions in students' interpreted English (3.1 times per 10,000 words). The students' interpreted English merely contains one-fourth of the total number of conjunctions including causal and adversative conjunctions found in the original English.

However, for both students' interpreted English and the original English, the most frequently employed one is the casual conjunctions, and then follows adversative conjunctions, while the least frequently used ones are conditional and other conjunctions. Figure 6.6 provides the specific results for the frequency of every subcategory of conjunctions for better visual perception.

As shown in Figure 6.6, a strikingly significant difference exists in the frequency of total conjunctions occurring in students' interpreted English and the original English. The frequency of conjunctions in the original English is 179 times every 10,000 words, which is over 4 times of conjunctions in students' interpreted English with the frequency of only about 41 times per 10,000 words. The marked difference exists in frequency of the conditional and other conjunctions, that is to say, conditional conjunctions in the original English are almost 14 times higher than in students' interpreted English.

In the subcorpus of students' interpreted English, the most frequently used conjunction is the casual conjunction with the frequency of approximately 20 times every 10,000 words. The frequently used ones are conditional conjunctions with the frequency of 18 and 3 times per 10,000 words respectively.

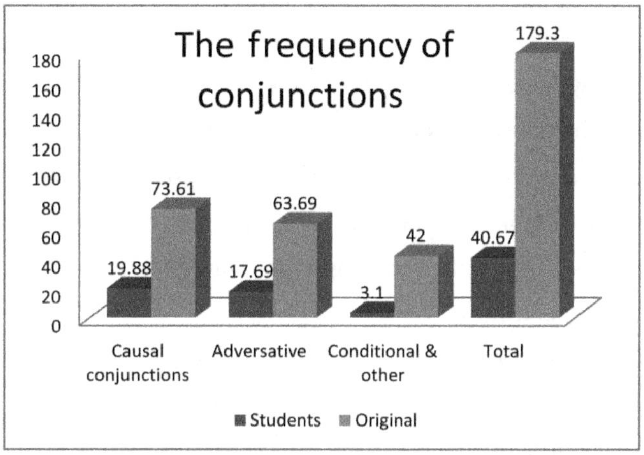


**Figure 6.6 Frequency of conjunctions in the students' interpreted and the original English corpora**

In the corpus of the original English, the causal conjunctions are also the most frequently used ones with the frequency of roughly 74 times every 10,000 words. Then follows the adversative conjunctions with the frequency of about 64 times per 10,000 words. Finally, the least frequently used ones are conditional and other conjunctions with the frequency of 42 times every 10,000 words.

In a word, the final finding is, that the conjunctive cohesive devices including causal, adversative, conditional and other conjunctions are less likely to occur in students' interpreted English in relation to the original English, in turn, may imply that students do not likely to adopt intra-language explicitations in C-E consecutive interpreted texts. The result also suggests that student interpreters tend to regard each clause or sentence in an isolated manner and fail to establish a logical relationship between or within sentences in their interpreted English texts compared with the original English.

## 6.3 Subordinate *That*-clauses

Subordinate clauses characteristically function as dependent component within the larger context. They often differ in their internal structure from main clauses (Huddleston 2005: 174). The following examples illustrate the typical differences:

(i) Alice is the best candidate for this position

(ii) I agree that Alice is the best candidate for this position

The sentence (i) itself is a main clause as a whole, whereas the same content in the sentence (ii) is a subordinate clause in the declarative sentence. The subordinate clause, a structure dependent in the clause, is marked as subordinate by its introductory word *that* in this case, which is generally regarded a subordinator. Subordinate clauses are not only led by the introductory word *that* but also introduced by *wh*-expressions as well. For instance, I could not think what it was. The underlined part with the *wh*-expression is also a subordinate clause.

However, for the research purpose, the subordinate clauses led by *that* as a subordinator are included in this study. Before making a statistical analysis of the occurrence of that as an introductory word, it is quite necessary to explain the important reasons why this study takes *that* as a subordinator into consideration as follows.

First, the reason is that according to Rohdenburg (1996: 161), the introductory word *that* generally happens to have triggered the boundary signal, which signifies the relationship between the main clause and the subordinate clause so as to avoid the ambiguity.

Secondly, the overall occurrence of *that* as a subordinator is comparatively high in the student's corpus and professional corpus respectively. The occurrence of *that* in the students' corpus is almost 900 times while the instance of *that* goes up to 1,253 times in the professional corpus. In other words, the frequency of *that* as an introductory word reaches 40 times per ten thousand words in the students' corpus, whereas 87 times per ten thousand words in the professional corpus.

Finally yet importantly, *that* clauses occurring in post-predicate positions perform functions of reporting the speech, thoughts, attitudes, or emotions of humans (Biber 1999: 660). And *that* is omitted when "the *that*–clause is direct object or complement, the introductory word *that* is frequently omitted except in formal use", otherwise that cannot be omitted in a subject clause, since without the subordinate marker the clause would be initially misinterpreted as a main clause (Quirk et al 1985: 1049). Therefore, it is of great necessity to explore *that*-clause adopted by students and professional interpreters in C-E CI.

The subordinate clauses led by the introductory word *that* may function as subject, object, complement, or adverbial in a superordinate clause. As the best-known and most comprehensive description of English grammar, *A Comprehensive Grammar of the English Language*, Quirk et al (1985: 1049) distinguish five categories of *that*-clause:

Subject: That the invading troops have been withdrawn has not affected our government's trade sanctions.

Direct object: I noticed that he spoke English with an American accent.

Subject complement: My assumption is that interest rates will soon fall.

Appositive: Your criticism, that no account has been taken of psychological factors, is fully justified.

Adjectival complementation: We are glad that you are able to join us on our wedding anniversary.

A subordinate clause plays a significant role in expanding ideas and thoughts in a discourse. The subordinate clause is usually introduced by a subordinating element such as a subordinating conjunction or a relative pronoun. It depends on the rest of the sentence for its meaning. It does not express a complete thought, so it does not stand alone. Thus, it is necessary to attach the subordinate clause to a main clause that completes its meaning. Subordinate clauses normally act as single part of speech, and they may function as subject, object, complement, or adverbial in a superordinate clause (Quirk et al 1985: 1047).

The present study only focuses on a variety of subordinate clauses led by *that* as a subordinator since *that* can introduce multiple subordinate clauses including subject clause, object clause, attributive clause, appositive and predicative clause. The following subsection presents the overall statistics of *that*-clause used in students' interpreted English compared with the original English.

### 6.3.1 Overall Statistics

The previous two sections 6.1 and 6.2 look at the reference and conjunctive cohesive devices that occurred in students' interpreted English in relation to the original English for intra-language comparison. This current section deals with the occurrence of subordinate clauses led by *that* as a subordinator in particular.

Subordinate clauses may perform a crucial role in extending the sentence structure and serve as an indicator for the degree of maturity in English. Just as Reid (1992: 93) reports, the use of subordinating structures indicates the development of writing maturity in English and is "indicative of a more sophisticated writer". In addition, to produce natural translations and interpretations, translators and interpreters may suggest adjusting certain ways of text organization in the source text in line with preferred ways of organizing the message in the target text. Other researchers (Adab 2000; Hatim & Mason 1990) make similar statements. The use of subordinate clauses to convey the complex and detailed message is one way of doing this.

Since the examples of subject clause, objective clause, and appositive are illustrated above, here follows the excerpts of attributive clause, adverbial clause, and predicative clause in which *that* as an introductory word. Here are some examples retrieved from students' corpus.

**Attributive Clause**

ST: 宏业公司的今天，得益于各级领导和有关部门的关心、客户的信任、供应商的默契配合和合作伙伴的鼎力相助。

TT: The great achievement [[that]] Hongye has achieved er... er are based on the... great... er... great concern of the leaders and the... er great... believe from our customers, the... the best cooperation from the er... from our partnerships. (Student)

It is a complete segment retrieved from the students' corpus in C-E interpreting, from which *that* clause "that Hongye has achieved" modifies the preceding noun "achievement". Thus, in our analysis, *that* clause is considered the attributive clause led by *that* as a subordinator.

**Predicative Clause**

ST: 我们举办这个展览会的目的是，加强在这一领域的国际交流与合作。

TT: The pursporous (purpose) of our hol, of having those er, those er exhibitions is [[that]], er, we want to intensified the, er, cooperation and communications, uhm, er, in this field with international, er, with the world. (Student)

In fact, in this study, the predicative clause is the same as the subject complement categorized by Quirk et al (1985: 1049). It refers to those clauses that come right after the be-verb in a sentence, so the clause, in the example above, led by *that* as a subordinator is regarded a predicative clause in short.

**Adverbial Clause**

ST: 我们愿意同美方进一步加强磋商与合作，这个推动呢，战略经济对话和其他的机制啊，发挥更多的积极的作用，使两国的经贸合作关系啊，为两国人民带来更多的实惠。

TT: We would like to strengthen consultation and cooperation with United States, strengthen our strategic economic dialogue and other mechanisms, so [[that]] they can play a more positive role in promoting our ties. We should also vigorously develop our economic cooperation and trade so that they can bring more real benefits to peoples of the two countries. (Professional)

This is also a whole sentence extracted from the professional corpus. In the target text, the clause introduced by *that* "they can play a more positive role in promoting our ties" is an adverbial clause that achieves the objective of previous main clause starts with "we". Here *that* is regarded a subordinator that introduces the adverbial clause mentioned above.

According to Quirk et al (1985: 1047), he and his colleagues differentiate the subordinate clauses into several major categories in accordance with their potential functions. The categories include "nominal, adverbial, relative, and comparative clauses". *That*-clauses or subordinate clauses led by *that* as a subordinator belong to one of the main subcategories of nominal clauses (Quirk et al 1985: 1048). Based on their potential functions, *that*-clauses may act as a subject, object, subject complementation, etc. Table 6.8 demonstrates the quantitative analysis of different subordinate clauses led by *that* as a subordinator in students' interpreted English compared with the original English.

**Table 6.8 Occurrence of *that* as a subordinator in the students' interpreted English and the original English corpora**

| That as a subordinator | Students count | Frequency/ per 10 000 | Original count | Frequency/ per 10 000 | Significance ($p$) | |
|---|---|---|---|---|---|---|
| Subject clause | 21 | 1.35 | 71 | 4.67 | 0.000*** | - |
| Objective clause | 240 | 15.49 | 1319 | 86.70 | 0.000*** | - |
| Attributive clause | 229 | 14.78 | 1314 | 86.37 | 0.000*** | - |
| Adverbial clause | 18 | 1.16 | 90 | 5.92 | 0.000*** | - |
| Appositive clause | 15 | 0.97 | 193 | 12.69 | 0.000*** | - |
| Predicative clause | 83 | 5.36 | 205 | 13.47 | 0.000*** | - |
| Total | 610 | 39.38 | 3196 | 210.07 | 0.000*** | - |

As shown in Table 6.8, a statistically salient difference lies in the use of *that* as a subordinator in a variety of subordinate clauses between students' interpreted texts and the original English texts. The subordinate clauses introduced by *that* as a subordinator are far less likely to occur in students' interpreted English in relation to the original English. The total frequency of *that*-clauses used in the original English is 210 times every 10,000 words, which is 5 times higher than in the students' interpreted English with the total frequency of merely 39 times per 10,000 words.

For both students' interpreted English and the original English, the objective clause led by *that* as a subordinator is most frequently employed with the frequency of approximately 16 and 87 times every 10,000 words respectively. However, the most strikingly salient difference exists in the occurrence of appositive clause led by *that* as a subordinator, namely, the original English contains over 13 times of appositives than in students' interpreted English. The least frequently used one is the subject clause in the original English with the frequency of about 5 times every 10,000 words, while in students' interpreted English, the appositive clause is the least frequently used one with frequency of only 1 time every 10,000 words.

In the original English, the most frequently used subordinate clause led by *that* as a subordinator are the objective clause and the attributive clause with the frequency of 87 and 86 times per 10,000 words. Subsequently follows the occurrence of predicative clause, appositive clause and the adverbial clause in turn with the frequency of 14, 13 and 6 times every 10,000 words respectively. The least employed one is the subject clause with the frequency of approximately 5 times every 10,000 words.

In the case of students' interpreted English, the objective clause and the attributive clause introduced by *that* as a subordinator are also most frequently employed ones with the frequency of 16 and 15 respectively. Then comes predicative clause, subject clause and adverbial clause with the frequency of approximately 5.4, 1.4, 1.2 times per 10,000 words. The appositive clause introduced by *that* as a subordinator has the least occurrence with the frequency of about 1 time every 10,000 words.

This section offers the overall statistical analysis of multiple subordinate clauses led by *that* as a subordinator in students' interpreted English compared with the original English. The following section concentrates upon the subordinate clauses where the introductory word or subordinator *that* can be frequently omitted.

### 6.3.2 *That* as a Subordinator

As mentioned earlier, the introductory word *that* may lead several subordinate clauses including subject clause, objective clause, attributive clause, appositive clause and the predicative clause. The previous section provides the specific examples of subordinate *that*-clauses, while this subsection only deals with the subordinate clauses in which *that* can be omitted.

Quirk et al (1985: 1049) further differentiate the situation in which *that* as a subordinator is likely to omit "when the that-clause is direct object or complement, the conjunction *that* is frequently omitted except in formal use, leaving a zero that-clause: I know it's late". In the old version of the book *Grammar* in 1972, Quirk and his collegues also concludes the motivational factors for *zero/that* clause by stating that:

> The zero *that*-clause is particularly common when the clause is brief and uncomplicated. In contrast, the need for clarity discourages or even forbids the omission of that in complex sentences loaded with adverbials and modifications. Any parenthetical material between the verb of the superordinate clause and the subject of the *that*-clause is especially likely to inhibit deletion. (Quirk et al 1972: 735)

In addition to the grammar books that offer information about what is grammatically acceptable, one of the practical reference works, Swan's *Practical English Usage* (1980) intends to guide non-native speakers of English in terms of usage of sentence structures, including *that*-clause constructions that include *that* as a subordinator and those which omit *that* by stating that:

> The conjunction *that* is used in several different ways. In certain kinds of sentence, it can be left out, especially in an informal style... That is used to introduce reported speech clauses. After the more common reporting verbs, that can be left out [examples are then given with said (*that*) and suggested (*that*)]... After more formal and less common verbs, *that* cannot be left out [with examples of *replied that* and *objected that*].

Considering the situations in which *that* as a subordinator can be omitted, the objective clause, subject complement (predicative clause) and subject *that*-clause (with anticipatory *it*) meet the criterion for intra-language explicitation. Table 6.9 gives statistical analysis of *that*-clauses where *that* as a subordinator can be frequently omitted, but explicitated instead in students' interpreted English compared with the original English.

**Table 6.9 Optional *that* as a subordinator in the students' interpreted English and the original English corpora**

| That as a subordinate | Students count | Frequency/ per 10 000 | Original count | Frequency/ per 10 000 | Significance ($p$) | |
|---|---|---|---|---|---|---|
| Subject clause (with anticipatory *it*) | 21 | 1.35 | 56 | 4.67 | 0.000*** | - |
| Objective clause | 240 | 15.49 | 1319 | 86.70 | 0.000*** | - |
| Predicative clause | 83 | 5.36 | 205 | 13.47 | 0.000*** | - |
| Total | 344 | 22.2 | 1580 | 104.87 | 0.000*** | - |

As described in Table 6.9, a statistically significant difference ($p < .05$) exists between students' interpreted English and the original English with respect to the optional *that* as a subordinator in objective clause, predicative clause and subject clause (with anticipatory *it*). Optional *that* as a subordinator in those three selected clauses is much more common in the original English than in students' interpreted English. That is to say, the instances of *that*-clause, in which *that* can be frequently omitted instead added in the clauses, are far less likely to occur in students' interpreted English in relation to the original English.

Nevertheless, for both students' interpreted English and the original English, optional *that* as a subordinator is most frequently to be added in objective clause, then in predicative clause, and finally least added in subject clause (with anticipatory *it* extraposed).

In a word, the overall occurrence of *that* as a subordinator is much more frequent in the original English where *that* can be optional while added instead than in students' interpreted English. This finding implies that students do not explicitate *that* as a subordinator in objective clause, predicate clause and subject clause (with anticipatory it extraposed) in their interpreted English in relation to the original English.

### 6.3.3 Summary of *That*–clause

Subordinate clause is imperative when a statement is too complex or detailed in a single clause. A subordinate clause merely complements a sentence's main clause, thereby adding to the whole unit of meaning. The subordinate clause is comparatively significant in developing a complex statement. Thus, subordinate clauses play an active role in expanding the statement that is complicated and long.

Some researchers (Adab 2000; Hatim & Mason 1990; Reid 1992) also suggest that the use of subordinating structures is the indication of "a more sophisticated writer" (Reid 1992: 93), and the subordinate clause is one of the favorable ways of organizing the complex message in English in order to produce natural translations and interpretations. Therefore, this whole section only focuses on overall occurrence of subordinate clauses led by *that* as a subordinator and optional *that* as a leading word in selected subordinate clauses, even though other subordinating conjunctions also introduce a variety of subordinate clauses.

Statistical analysis reveals the occurrence of subordinate clauses introduced by *that* in students' interpreted English compared with the original English. A statistically significant difference ($p < .05$) lies in the overall frequency of subordinate clauses led by *that* between students' interpreted English and the original English. *That* as a subordinator is much more frequent in the original English texts compared with students' interpreted English texts, and the overall frequency in the original English is approximately 5 times higher than in students' interpreted English.

As to both students' interpreted English and the original English, the objective clause and the attributive clause led by *that* are most frequently used; however, the frequency is far less common in students' interpreted English than in the original English. The appositive clause introduced by that is the least frequently used in students' interpreted English with the frequency of about 1 time every 10,000 words, whereas the least frequently used one in the original English is the subject clause with the frequency of approximately 5 times every 10,000 words. The specific statistical result for every subordinate clause led by *that* as a subordinator may refer back to Table 6.8.

With respect to the optional *that* as a subordinator, according to Quirk and his colleagues, the subordinator *that* is frequently omitted in the subject *that*-clause with anticipatory *it* extraposed, objective clause and predicative clause respectively. Therefore, this section looks at the optional *that* as a subordinator in those clauses where *that* can be omitted, and it is found that optional *that* as a subordinator is far less common in objective clause, predicate clause and subject clause (with anticipatory it extraposed) in students' interpreted English in relation to the original English. This finding suggests that intra-language explicitation of *that* as a subordinator does not exist in students' interpreted English compared with the original English.

To sum up, a statistically significant difference ($p < .05$) exists between students' interpreted English texts and the original English texts with respect to the occurrence of *that*-clauses and the optional *that* as a subordinator. In other words, not only the subordinate clauses introduced by *that* as a subordinator are less likely to occur in students' interpreted English in comparison with the original English, but also the optional *that* as a subordinator is far less common in students' interpreted English in relation to the original English. This finding, in turn, indicates that students do not adopt intra-language explicitation of optional *that* in their interpreted English in relation to the original English.

# Chapter Seven Discussion of the Findings

Chapter Five and Chapter Six investigate inter-language textual explicitations, cohesive devices in particular, performed by Chinese EFL students compared with professional interpreters and intra-language explicitation of students' interpreted English texts in relation to the original English. Chinese EFL students are far less likely to explicitate cohesive markers in comparison with professional interpreters in terms of inter-language explicitation, and their interpreted English manifests less frequency of cohesive devices and *that* as a subordinator in relation to the original English. This chapter not only intends to probe into the reasons for performing explicitation in C-E CI with respect to inter-language explicitation and intra-language explicitation, but also attempts to explore potential motivations behind such explicitation features that distinguish students' interpreted texts from both professional interpreters and the original English in detail.

## 7.1 Reasons for Inter-language Explicitation in C-E CI

The previous studies on explicitation intend to uncover the reasons why the explicitation occurs in translation and interpreting. Researchers more often than not attribute the reasons for performing explicitation to the following most common factors.

(i) Linguistic differences between SL and TL (Klaudy 1998; Pöchhacker 2004; Zhang 2009; Hu & Tao 2009): Language-specific differences often necessitate the obligatory explicitation in syntactic and semantic structures of TL to meet grammatical rules.

(ii) Stylistic preferences in text-building strategies (Vinay & Darbelnet 1995; Blum-Kulka 2004; Klaudy 2010) between SL and TL: such discrepancies usually contribute to optional explicitations in the sense that "grammatical sentences can still be constructed without their application in the target language, although the text as a whole will be clumsy and unnatural" (Klaudy 2008: 106).

(iii) Differences in culture-specific knowledge (Klaudy 1998; Pöchhacker 2004; Baumgarten et al 2008): such discrepancy leads to explicitation in order to explain a cultural concept specific to the SL.

In fact, the three differences mentioned above contribute to the systematic categories of explicitation formulated by Klaudy mentioned in 2.1.3, namely obligatory, optional and pragmatic explicitation respectively. Apart from these differences, other factors that trigger explicitation cover the nature of translation as mediation (Chesterman 2004), preference of individual translators (Baker 2004; Klaudy & Karoly 2005), relative lack of shared information between translators and their audience (Mutesayire 2004), and level of translator's expertise (Englund-Dimitrova 2005). These explanations mostly center on translations of different language pairs, while this section attempts to explore the motivations that account for every subcategory of explicitation in C-E CI with respect to inter-language explicitation.

### 7.1.1 Linguistic differences between Chinese and English

#### 7.1.1.1 Parataxis and Hypotaxis

As is known to all, Chinese and English are radically different languages in terms of lexical device and syntactic structure, and they belong to comparatively different language families. English fall into the Indo-European language family while Chinese belong to Sino-Tibetan language family. In addition, English and Chinese differ in terms of syntactic relation, i.e. hypotaxis and parataxis. Hypotaxis derives from Greek word "hypotassein" (underneath arrangement) whereas parataxis originates from Greek word "paratassein" (side-by-side arrangement). As Halliday (1994: 218) states, hypotaxis refers to "the relation between dependent element and its dominant, the element on which it is dependent". On the contrary, parataxis indicates "the relation between two like elements of equal status one initiating and the other continuing".

It is apparent that, based on the definition above, English is a language which lays more emphasis on hypotaxis while Chinese stresses on parataxis, that is, English is comparatively more hypotactic whereas Chinese is more paratactic. Nida (1983), in his *Translating Meaning*, also points out that the most significant difference in linguistics between English and Chinese is the contrast of parataxis and hyptaxis. In terms of syntactic construction, English is form-oriented and places more emphasis upon formal structures which feature subject-predicate structure as the core, whereas Chinese is meaning-oriented and semantically based which features message-segments logically strung together. In order to achieve the syntactic adaptation in the process of interpreting from Chinese to English, it is necessary to conform to syntactic requirements in the target language. Therefore, the fact that English focuses on hypotaxis, which is form-oriented and Chinese as paratactic, which is meaning-oriented, accounts for the explicitation of referential cohesive devices in C-E CI. The following examples illustrate the syntactic difference between Chinese and

English more clearly.

**Example 7.1**

ST: 中国主管部门采取了一系列的必要的措施，开展了认真、负责的调查，并且已经适时公布了初步的调查的结果。

TT: The competent authorities in China have taken all necessary measures and carried out serious and responsible investigation into the incident. [[They]] have also released the initial investigation results. (Professional)

**Example 7.2**

ST: 公元 1405 至 1433 年，郑和率领庞大的船队，从江苏太仓出发，七下西洋，往返于中国和亚非 30 多个国家之间。

TT: En, since fourteen o five to fourteen thirty three, Zheng He have started their, er, have started his adventure ... from er, Taichang er, in ... of Jiangsu Province en, he...go and returned en from between China and some... er, Asia countries and African countries.And [[he]] had visit more than er, thirty countries. (Student)

In Examples 7.1 and 7.2, the personal pronouns *they* and *he* are regarded instances of explicitation as they are added in English in order to meet the requirement of syntactic structure in English. In both examples, the subjects are absent in the last parts of the sentence in Chinese because Chinese syntactic structure, rather than being confined to subject-predicate construction, seems to be comparatively loose. Only 9% of the Chinese sentences, according to statistical analysis, conform to the subject-predicate structure (Chen 1998: 19). It is apparent that the subjects in the last part of sentences can be inferable from the context even though it is omitted in both examples in Chinese.

The instances of demonstrative pronouns are as follows.

**Example 7.3**

ST: 这是前人留给我们的遗产，是一笔宝贵的资源，它属于龙城、属于中国、属于世界。

TT: This is our forefather left to us, and ... [[these]] are great resources of Long City, of China, and as well as the world. (Student)

**Example 7.4**

ST: 所以和当时中国的国力我认为是不能比的。

TT: So, in terms of national strength, [[those]] countries are no, were no comparison with China, at the time of Zheng He. (Professional)

Likewise, in Examples 7.3 and 7.4 done by a student and a professional respectively, the demonstratives *these* and *those* along with *countries* are explicitated in order to comply with the syntactic rules in English. Both demonstratives function as subjects in the last part of sentences in English, which are absent in the source text, and can be inferable from the context in Chinese.

This section explains the explicitation of referential cohesive devices in C-E CI from the perspective of inter-language explicitation. The following section intends to seek for the explanation for the explicitation of conjunctions in C-E CI.

#### 7.1.1.2 Differences in Forming Logical Relationship

Logical relationship between sentences is relatively significant within a text. Different languages have mainly two ways to embody the logical connection between clauses in a sentence. As Halliday (1994: 218) puts it, "all logical structures in language are either paratactic or hypotatic". As mentioned earlier, Chinese is mainly paratactic, which indicates that the logical relationship between groups of sentences is not confined to using connectives. Instead the logical connection is established thorough the whole context. While English is comparatively hypotactic by using its syntactic forms to convey its semantic meanings, which makes it possible to forge logical relationship by explicit connectives or conjunctions.

English places more emphasis on explicit correlatives, and the logical relationship between clauses or components is mainly achieved through conjunctions such as *because*, *if*, *though*, relative adverbs, prepositions or prepositional phrases. On the contrary, Chinese attaches great importance to covert coherence and contextual meaning, which means the connection between components of a sentence relies on sequential order and intrinsic logic relationship of what is described in the components of a sentence. As Wang Li (1984: 474) points out, in Chinese, the relationship between clauses more often than not resort to semantic cohesion, which does not necessarily rely on conjunctions. For instance, two related clauses can be strung together in a sentence in Chinese without any connective word.

In short, Chinese is comparatively paratactic and logic relations between clauses often depend on internal logical relationship between them, whereas English is mainly hypotactic and logical relationship between clauses usually realized by adding conjunctions. As Halliday and Hasan (2001) point out, conjunction is one of the significant cohesive devices that establish logical relationship among clauses. The logical relationship can be clear to audience and readers alike with the employment of various kinds of conjunctions in English. Therefore, in the process of interpreting from Chinese into English, it is indispensable for interpreters to comply with the English expressive habits, which requires them to explicitate the conjunctions that are absent in Chinese so that the interpreted text can suit the requirement of English expression.

Any text, paragraph, or sentence is composed according to certain logical relationship between its components. In general, logical connections usually include the major logical relation of time and space, cause and effect, etc. The present study investigates the explicitation of causal, adversative and conditional conjunctions in C-E CI. The specific examples retrieved from students' and professional corpora are as follows.

**Example 7.5**

ST: 我可以给你举许许多多的例子,可能需要两个小时。

TT: [[If]] I'm allowed to numerate all the examples without any... restraint, then I'm afraid I will use two full hours. (Professional)

As for Example 7.5, after examing the hidden logic of sentence in Chinese, the professional interpreter adds the conditional conjunction *if* in English in order to explicitate the conditional relationship between first part and second part of the sentence, which is implicit in Chinese.

In summary, the linguistic differences between Chinese and English including Chinese as paratactic and English as hypotactic, and logical relationship between clauses in Chinese and English all contribute to the employment of explicitation in C-E CI. Therefore, in the process of interpreting, in order to make logically acceptable interpretation to the target audience, interpreters are supposed to take linguistic knowledge and logical structure of language pair into account to realize the aim of successful communication. In fact, it would be much better for the interpreters to follow logical reasoning ahead of interpreting so that the interpreted texts are logically valid to the target audience.

## 7.1.2 Nature of Interpreting

### 7.1.2.1 Interpreting Process

The word "interpretation" denotes "interpretive translation", "explaining the implications of the speaker's speech verbally", and "oral translation" in different situations respectively. In fact, interpreting is evolved from translation and it has a much more communicative effect than translation. Otto Kade is the first scholar to put forward the initial definition of interpreting as early as 1960s. Relying on Kade's criteria, the definition is as follows (Pöchhacker 2004: 11):

Interpreting is a form of Translation in which a first and final rendition in another language is produced on the basis of a one-time presentation of an utterance in a source language.

The interpretive theory is sometimes known as "interpretative approach". This theory comes into being with the publication of the doctoral book of Danica Seleskovitch in 1968.Seleskovitch can be regarded the pioneer of the interpretive theory due to his rich experience in conference interpreting. In 1984, Seleskovitch and Lederer co-authored the *Interpreter pour Traduire*, which signified the formal formation of the interpretive theory. The Academy of Translation and Interpretation in Paris adopts this theory, considering that interpreting as paraphrasing, which requires a translator or an interpreter to make explanations of the original text by means of linguistic units based on their own understanding.

The interpretive theory holds that the nature of interpreting lays more emphasis on interpreting the non-verbal sense of discourse instead of its linguistic meaning alone. The theory also believes that interpreting is not a mere trans-coding operation from one language to another, but rather a dynamic communicating process of reformulating the ideas in a coherent way. The interpreting process is not merely direct transcoding from the source language to the target language, but rather converting the implicit information in SL to sense, then through reformulating the sense to the explicit information in TL. Figure 7.1 vividly demonstrates the process of interpreting.

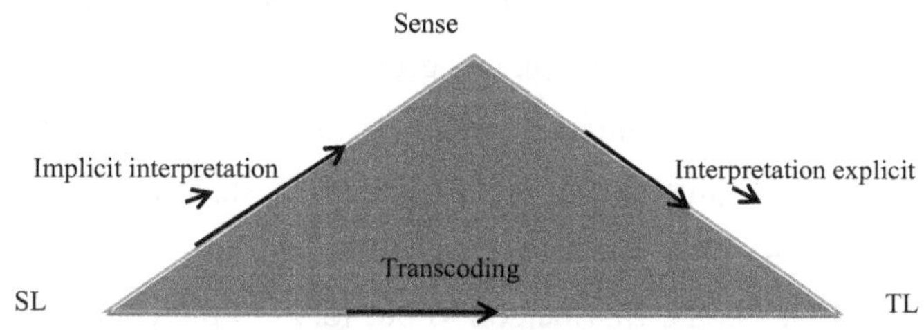


**Figure 7.1 New triangle mode of interpreting**

As seen in Figure 7.1, the interpretation of sense forms the core of the interpreting process. As Lederer (2001: 6) puts it, interpreting "exactly reflects how the linguistic forms of a speech or an article produce sense, and sense converts into interpreter's idea, and then such idea again converts into specific expression in another given language". It is worth mentioning that "sense" here does not refer to "meaning" in semantic scope, but "pragmatic meaning" which is determined by the meaning of component parts of a sentence and the way and situations in which they are combined (Saeed 1997: 10-13). Sense is conveyed by contextual comprehension of the text along with the dynamic combination of linguistic knowledge and non-linguistic knowledge, through the synthetic analysis of the speech.

According to the triangle mode of interpreting above, the information on sense in the interpreting process includes both implicit and explicit information ("explicate" and "implicate" in French) (Lederer 2001: 43). Implicit information indicates implications of language, related to non-linguistic knowledge, while explicit information reveals the specific language used in the text, pertaining to linguistic knowledge. The process of interpreting, largely, works as follows: the organic combination of implicit and explicit information form sense, then reformulating the organic information through sense to make it clear and explicit in the target language. Explicit information in TL facilitates the communication between the speaker and audience.

Interpreting is an act of communication in a particular situational context. In the process of interpreting, interpreters may frequently encounter such situations in which it is hard to find corresponding equivalence in the target language. In that case, the interpreters have to force themselves to find a proper explanation for the audience. The ideas are also relevant to each other by a proper logical relationship catering to the target audience.

Overall, the purpose of interpreting is to serve for communication between two parties. Interpreting is not merely an act of linear decoding of language structures and units from one language to another, but a process of recapturing the contextual meaning with the combination of linguistic and non-linguistic knowledge. Interpreting by essence is interpretive and explanatory based on the Interpretive Theory. Explicitation technique is frequently utilized to "make explanation about the obscure and implicit information in a coherent and proper way" so that the target audience understands the information clearly and accurately. The specific examples of making implicit information explicit can refer back to Example 7.5. On this ground, due to the inherent nature of interpreting as interpretive and explanatory, explicitation strategy is regularly employed in the process of interpreting for both professional interpreters and Chinese EFL students alike.

#### 7.1.2.2 Interpreting Norms

As is known to all, Toury is the first person to put forward the concept of norms applied to translation studies in the late 1970s. According to Toury, norms lay emphasis on "descriptive analysis of translation phenomena" (Toury 1980: 57), more specifically defined as follows (Toury 1999: 14):

> Norms have long been regarded as the translation of general values or ideas shared by a group — as to what is conventionally right and wrong, adequate and inadequate — into performance instructions appropriate for and applicable to particular situations, specifying what is prescribed and forbidden as well as what is tolerated and permitted in a certain behavioural dimension.

In that case, translational norms act as internalized behavioral constraints, which embody the values shared by a community. All decisions that made in the translation process are thus primarily governed by such norms, and not dominantly or exclusively by the two language systems involved.

Some researchers (Shlesinger 1989; Harris 1990; Schjoldager 1995; Gile 1999) propose to extend the concept of norms to interpreting studies. Norms play a vital role in the description of actual translations and interpretations, the formulation of general principles, and practical applications since they are closely relevant to assumptions and expectations about correctness and appropriateness in the target language. In other words, norms not only regulate what translations or interpretations should look like in order to be regarded correct and appropriate, but also concern the specific methods and strategies by which an acceptable translated or interpreted text can be achieved. It seems this kind of norms similar to "operational norms" by Toury (1995: 58).

The major goal of interpreting is that a message makes the same impact on the target audience as was intended by the speaker in the source language (Angelelli 2000). Moreover, the major shaping factors that contribute to interpreters' interpreting performance cover internal cognitive processing and external social and cultural factors in combination. According to Wang (2012), "the major shaping forces of interpreting performance include: the interpreter's interpreting competence, the cognitive conditions on-site and norms of interpreting". The relationship between these major factors and interpreting performance represents the figure as follows.

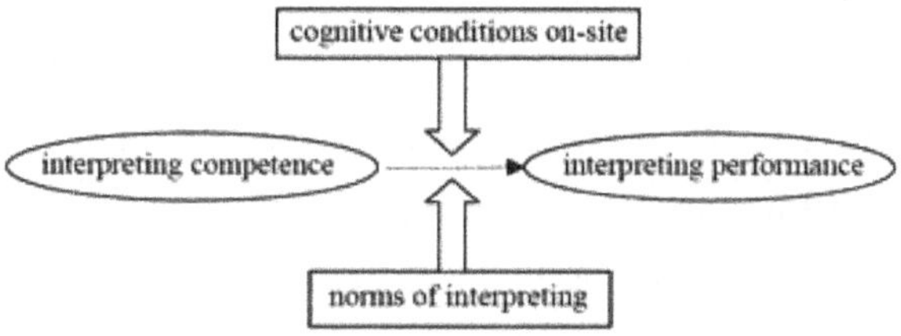


**Figure 7.2 Major shaping forces of interpreting performance** (cited from Wang 2012)

As clearly seen in Figure 7.2, norms of interpreting are regarded one of the crucial factors in deciding interpreting performance. Norm, as a descriptive term, acts as continuum of "socio-cultural constraints" between the two extremes of "idiosyncrasies" and "absolute rules" (Munday 2009: 210). Garzone (2002: 110) also explains norms as "internalized behavioral constraints which govern interpreters' choices in relation to the different contexts where they are called upon to operate". More specifically, Norms of interpreting can be defined as (Wang 2012):

> Norms of interpreting refer to shared values and ideas among interpreters of the profession and users of interpreting service on what the generally-accepted interpreting methods and strategies are and what the right and proper interpreting behaviors are.

Interpreting, as a socially constructed behavior, is assuredly governed by norms. The interpreting norms primarily aim at guiding interpreters, professionals and students alike, in their choice of strategies and methods in interpreting behaviors and make the interpreted texts more appropriate and acceptable in a sociocultural context.

In short, translation and interpreting are regarded norm-governed behaviors and activities in a social, cultural, and historical situation, while norms of interpreting emerge as a potentially successful mechanism to direct interpreters' choice of strategies and methods employed in interpreting. That is to say, norms of interpreting, as internalized behavioral constraint, can account for interpreters' choices on strategies made in interpreting to great extent. Explicitation is one of frequently employed strategies, as interpreters' choice, in translation and interpreting. Explicitation is also a function of norms, and it serves as norm-governed strategy in terms of textual solution.

Several studies on norms of interpreting, C-E CI in particular, support that explicitation of cohesive devices and logic relations is a regularly employed interpreting strategy, which embodies "the actual norms of target-language communication in interpreting" (Wang 2012; 2015). More specifically, through conducting inter-textual comparative analysis of the source texts and the target texts in C-E CI, interpreters get used to form regular pattern in their choice of interpreting strategies, which exemplify norms of interpreting. These strategies include explicitation of cohesive devices, explicit expression of utterance meaning, and explicitation of logic connectives (ibid).

In the process of C-E interpreting, interpreters tend to add either textual cohesive devices or logical connectives to their target texts so that target audiences accurately understand the logic relations in the target texts that are implicit in the source texts. Since explicitation is one of the frequently used strategies in C-E interpreting that triggered by actual norms of target language, thus interpreting norms can be regarded a crucial contributing factor for employment of explicitation in interpreting. That is to say, interpreters, professionals and students alike, are motivated to adopt explicitation strategies in order to conform to the interpreting norms and to optimize the communicative effect of their interpretation so that the target audiences follow the speaker closely in an easy way.

#### 7.1.2.3 Interpreters' Expressive Habits

The word "interpreter" in English comes from Latin *interpres*, which in the sense of "expounder" who can explain what is obscure and difficult to understand, but the semantic root of the word is not clear (Pöchhacker 2004: 9). Some scholars only look at the latter part of the word, and say it derives from *partes* or *pretium* ("price"), thus complies with the meaning of a "middleman", "intermediary" or "commercial go-between" (Franz Pöchhacker 2004: 10), others suggest a Sanskrit root for the word. Despite all this, the Latin root *interpres*, which denotes someone "explaining the meaning", "making sense of" what others have difficulty in understanding, is an appropriate semantic foundation for "interpreter" in our current understanding (ibid).

As the subjects of interpreting practice, interpreters, beyond doubt, are regarded as one the significant decisive factors in C-E CI. On the one hand, the attention paid to the target audience will exert great impact on occurring of explicitation. On the other hand, the strategies and methods interpreters adopted in the process of interpreting will wield enormous influence on the degree of explicitation in interpreting.

In addition, interpretation possesses relatively obvious "impromptu" feature. The speaker talks while thinking without preparation in advance, as the interpreters have to convey the meaning of the speaker's speech in proper target language within short period. In order to make the interpreting activities go uninterrupted, the time for the interpreter's pause should not be too long. During the short period of time, the interpreter fails to think about complex language structure, instead they tend to adopt "explicitation" and use clarifications to convey the meaning of the source text. In general, Chinese tends to use repetitive structures, while English is inclined to employ a referential structure to avoid repetition. Therefore, interpreters more often than not use more simple and convenient connectives to establish the logical relations between sentences in C-E CI.

Explicitation, by its nature, aims at increasing the readability of the target text and offering explanations at syntactic, semantic and pragmatic level of the original text. Blum-Kulka highlights that "successful translation requires complex processing of the text and discourse, and interpreters' effort to offer explanation may make the target text lengthier than the source text" (Blum-kulka 1986: 61).

Ke Fei (2005: 306-310) also puts forward that if the more cultural and social differences exist between two languages, the more possibilities there will be for explanatory explicitation. He points out that, through adequate examples in C-E translations, interpreters tend to employ explanations and interpretive methods in the target text that increases the degree of explicitation of the source text, which makes the audience easily follow the source information.

As is known to us that, as a communicative act, interpretation involves speakers from two sides and an interpreter who functions as abridge for two parties that speak in different languages. In press conference interpreting, the audience is on the spot and their body languages, facial expressions and responses will undoubtedly exert powerful effect on the interpreting strategies employed by the interpreters, covering the explicitation technique as well. In order to help the audience understand the main points of the information that speaker transferred, interpreters opt to use logical connectives or discourse markers to link relations to the language structures followed subsequently. The explicitated interpreting technique enables interpreters to reduce the audience' effort in the process of understanding, thus deliver semantic information in the source speech more clearly to target audience. Just as Slobin (1979: 49) puts forward, in general, it is more likely that audience's response to language structures with connectives is more swift and immediate than that without connectives.

In short, the findings above suggest that, playing a mediatory role, interpreters develop a habit of adopting explanatory and interpretive methods in the interpreting process, as well as employing more connectives or conjunctions to establish explicit logical relations between components of a sentence. As a result, the interpreted texts become more audience-friendly and clear-grounded.

### 7.1.3 Cognitive Explanation

Within the framework of cognitive processing, Gerver (1971: ⅷ) regards the interpreting task as "a fairly complex form of human information processing involving the reception, storage, transformation, and transmission of verbal information". As a result, processing capacity to manage information in interpreting appears to be an extremely complex task. From the perspective of cognitive model, interpreting is actually a kind of communication that requires all participants to work actively at constructing meaning based on evidence offered by speakers.

The role of interpreters within a particular communicative context is characterized as combining the activities of a listener and a speaker. As the two professional pioneers in interpreting studies put it, "To interpret one must first understand" (Seleskovitch 1978: 11), and "each part of each idea should be expressed in the way it would normally be expressed by a good public speaker" (Herbert 1952: 23).

Given the special regard for the mode of CI, Gile ([1995] 2009) construct a series of models that are designed to posit explanations for the cognitive challenges in the process of interpreting so that he can provide available choices for interpreters, and the strategies that maybe employed in order to increase the likelihood of successful interpreting performance. Gile's model for CI includes two phases: "the comprehension phase (or listening and note-taking phase), and the speech production (or reformulation) phase" (Gile 2009: 175). Based on Gile's model, interpreting requires almost all mental energy from interpreters, which takes cognitive processing capacity from a limited available supply.

According to Gile, the Effort Model for CI lays an emphasis on the need to allocate cognitive resources to different mental operations: Listening and Analysis Effort (L), Memory Effort (M) and Production Effort (P). Interpreting can be depicted as "a process which involves a set of operations on successive speech segments" (ibid: 168). Each of the segments is firstly heard and analysized, then the Memory Effort involves with the time between the moment the speech is heard and the moment it is processed mentally, which is relevant to short-term memory, and passed along to the long-term memory. The Production Effort is devoted to generate qualitatively acceptable target texts thorough recalling the successive parts of the original speech from long-term memory.

As is known to all, in interpreting, the first factor to bear in mind when analyzing any aspect is the time constraint. Unlike translators, interpreters have to work at required delivery speed within their information processing capacity. There is apparently a certain limit as to the information retained in interpreter's memory. The function of short-term memory is to process the information after hearing the speech in the first phase of CI: comprehension. The duration of short-term memory is relatively short, only about ± 1 minute, and the capacity of this memory is approximately 7 ± 2 units. Unit here refers to a piece of related information, part of which helps remember another part in the production phase. While the duration of long-term memory is certainly over one minute even for the lifetime, and its capacity for information storage is comparatively large, even limitless.

Consecutive interpreting entails short-term memory in the comprehension phase and long-term memory in the production phase. Both memory efforts are devoted to the storage and processing of the explicit information and the implicit information in the source speech, and this information are interacting as an organic whole in the comprehension of the verbal speech in interpreting practice.

Due to the limited storage capacity for short-term memory, it is unpractical for the interpreter to remember all the linguistic forms of the source speech in interpreting practice. Therefore, what interpreter can remember in CI is the sense of the source speech, and it is feasible for the interpreter to produce the holistic sense of the source speech through recalling the information from the long-term memory.

In the process of interpreting, the interpreter may not interpret based on the whole form of the original language like a translator in translation because what the interpreter can grasp is general idea of the source speech due to memory constraint. Therefore, interpreters often employ interpretive methods rather than literal interpretation to help the target audience understand the logical relations and main information of the original speech.

In short, due to the cognitive operations related to Memory Effort, what the interpreter can remember in CI is the holistic sense of the source speech, not the original linguistic forms, thus it is inevitable for the interpreters to interpret the sense of the source speech. In the process of interpreting, the interpreters can only translate the meaning of the speakers' discourse, because the only content that can remain in the memory after the disappearing of the discourse is meaning. The degree of explanatory interpretation for interpreters is therefore higher than that for the translators, thus the degree of interpretation in interpreting is naturally higher than that of translation.

The way that the human's memory works makes interpreters have to deliver the holistic sense of the source speech but not the original linguistic forms due to the limited memory time. This also makes the use of explicitation possible. Most importantly, explicitation may expect to occur as it refers to "involuntary departure from the information given in the source text, evoked by the specific conditions of cognitive language processing during language mediation" (Baumgarten et al 2008: 181).

## 7.2 Reasons for Intra-language Explicitation in C-E CI

In Chapter Six, it is found that the statistically striking difference lies between students' interpreted English and the original English with respect to the occurrence of referential cohesive devices, subordinating conjunctions and optional *that* as a subordinator. That is to say, there is far less frequency of the referential cohesive devices, subordinating conjunctions and optional *that* as a subordinator in students' interpreted English relative to the original English, which suggests students do not tend to make intra-language explicitation in their interpreted English. This section attempts to seek possible explanations for such findings in the present study.

### 7.2.1 The Influence of the Source Language

As mentioned earlier in 4.2, the subcorpora of students' interpreted English and the original English respectively have roughly the same corpus size and the similar subjects under discussion, which makes the two subcorpora comparable with regard to the occurrence of different cohesive devises and *that* as subordinator in multiple subordinate clauses. The corpus of students' interpreted English consists of multiple interpretations from several same Chinese source speeches, which include speeches given by officials and leaders at the conferences such as the exhibition conference, seminar opening and closing ceremonies in China. While the corpus of the original English is composed of original speech transcriptions of a number of press conferences held by the USA state department.

Interpreted texts, like translations, bear traces of the interpretation process as translators are inclined to write markers down for everything they have construed (Pym 2005). Unlike the original English, students' interpreted English texts are transcriptions of interpreted texts from Chinese, which exert great impact on the formation of interpreted English. As is known to all, English is abundant in frequent usage of personal pronouns and demonstrative pronouns, which are found most notably in the class of pronouns "by reason of their frequency and their grammatical characteristics, as the most important and central class of pronouns" (Quirk et al 1985: 335-336). On the contrary, the personal pronouns that function as grammatical subjects can be absent because of its connective discourse function in Chinese.

In addition, as to personal and demonstrative pronouns, students are less likely to add or explicitate them in their interpreted texts. The detailed information can be referred back to section 5.2. Over half of personal pronouns and demonstratives occurring in interpreted English correspond to their respective pronouns in the source language — Chinese. It seems that students are most likely to adopt literal translation strategy in their C-E interpretation. Students' reliance on the source text is also considered to be determined by their general view of translation in that they generally consider translation to be a replacement of signs between two different languages (Cintrão 2011: 89). That is to say, at most times, the personal pronouns appearing in the interpreted English are the correspondence of respective pronouns in Chinese, resulting in the visibility of the source text structures in the translation (Shreve 2002: 166). The following examples illustrate this point clearly.

**Example 7.6**

ST: 我们希望借鉴和学习国外的先进技术和经验，为国内外广大生产厂家、经销商提供一个交流技术、展示产品的窗口和桥梁。

TT: [[We]] hope to adopt (adapt)... foreign countries' advanced technology and experience to... provide...window and bridge for our manufacturers and ...wholesalers. (Student)

**Example 7.7**

I see a statement from you about this Miss Aung Sun Suu Kyi. It's been a long time now, and do you support democracy or military rule in Burma, because she has been in and out of jails and house arrests and other — when she will be out. (Original)

The examples above are excerpts extracted from students' interpreted English with the corresponding source text and from the original English respectively. It is apparent that the only personal pronoun *we* occurred in a student's interpreted English is the correspondence of its respective pronoun. "我们" in Chinese. In contrast, in the original English, the occurrence of personal pronouns is much higher including first person pronoun *I* once, second person pronoun *you* twice and third person *she* twice, altogether five times in a sentence. Regarding students' interpreted English, it is most likely that the personal and demonstrative pronouns appear either from the interpretation of corresponding pronouns in Chinese or when it is necessary to make the implicit grammatical subject in Chinese explicit in English.

In summary, the source language Chinese wields considerable influence on students' interpreted English with respect to the frequency of pronouns occurring in interpreted English, as expressed in Toury's (2012: 303) law of interference. English and Chinese differ greatly in the way of using pronouns: English exhibits the tendency to repeat personal pronouns, which is improper in Chinese so that where a pronoun is repeated in a text in English, Chinese either drops the pronoun or repeats a noun instead (Liu 1991: 371, quoted from Xiao & Hu 2015: 103). Differences can be observed with respect to the frequency of personal and demonstrative pronouns in interpreted and original texts. Overall, personal and demonstrative pronouns occurred less frequently in students' interpreted English texts compared with the original English texts, which means that the source-language text is credited a dominant role (Lörscher 2009: 13). This finding suggests that interference from Chinese as a source language regarding the usage of pronouns plays a major role in shaping student interpretations with respect to comparatively lower occurrence of personal and demonstrative pronouns.

### 7.2.2 Interpreters' Awareness

Interpreted English texts result from interpreting activities performed by interpreters. Interpreting involves interpreter-mediated interactions, in which the interpreter's decisions influence all participants and potential outcomes (Roy 2000). Interpreter's interpreted texts are composed of more than lexical, phrasal, or syntactic choices. Interpreters' awareness on choices of conjunctions also plays a substantial role in text organization. The choices interpreters make as speakers and hearers "make a significant difference to the progression and cohesion" of the discourse (Wadensjö 1998: 279).

As the subject of interpreting activity, Chinese EFL learners produce students' interpreted English texts. Students' awareness on the use of conjunctions exerts a great impact on the logic of interpreted texts. The use of conjunctions helps target audience make sense of the logical relationship (Hu 1994), which, in turn, informs the organization of linguistic resources in interpreting. To some extent, the inappropriate use of conjunctions could hinder successful communication or even lead to misunderstandings. However, students are not fully aware of the use of conjunctions to produce texts that are not merely correct but meet the expectations of target audience in English.

On the contrary, the original English texts include transcriptions of a number of press conferences held by the US governments. The US leaders deliver speeches in those press conferences, in which they exactly know the logic relies on the proper use of conjunctives within the textual system of cohesion. The leaders who address those speeches in press conferences are native speakers of English. They are fully conscious of the fact that conjunctions will contribute to speech cohesion by overtly expressing the underlying coherence relations holding between the different units of the speech.

In short, the native speakers who address the original English speeches are fully aware of the fact that conjunctions are of great significance to signal the logical relations between ideas (Kintsch & Van Dijk 1978). Chinese EFL student interpreters, by comparison, are less conscious of the importance of conjunctions that are aids for audience to connect sentences in order to get their message across and convey their ideas. The considerable difference between student interpreters and native speakers with regard to the awareness of using conjunctive cohesive devices may contribute to the finding that there are far fewer occurrences of conjunctions in students' interpreted English texts in relation to the original English.

### 7.2.3 Complexity Principle

Rohdenburg (1996: 151) associates the language formality with the complexity principle, which says, "in the case of more or less explicit grammatical options, the more explicit one (s) will tend to be favored in cognitively more complex environments". The principle, in essence, states that more explicit syntactic alternatives prone to occur in cognitively more complex environments. Such complexity factors cover "passive constructions, discontinuous constructions of various kinds, and the length of subjects and objects, and subordinate clauses concerned" (Rohdenburg 1996: 149).

As Pym (2007: 178) puts it, the translated texts cannot assume same degree of shared content as non-translations can. As to degree of planning, the original English speeches delivered in press conferences are more highly planned before they are produced, which are achieved through modifiers, subordinating conjunctions including *that* as a subordinator and the like. On the contrary, the interpreted texts of students have more simple fragmented syntax and less use of subordinating conjunctions, *that* as a subordinator in particular. It can be vividly illustrated in the following examples retrieved from the student's interpreted English and the original English respectively. For instance:

**Example 7.8**

Hm we hope [[that]] we can er hm, we hope er that we can er learn the er good experience, and er er and good sides of the er er abroad, and hm and do something for our er er our our local er market. (Student's interpreted English)

**Example 7.9**

I just spoke to the Secretary's doctor a few minutes ago. I am happy to report [[that]] he's out of surgery, [[that]] everything went fine. (Original English)

As shown clearly in the above examples, the student's interpreted English is associated with the entire range of nonverbal features and paralinguistic features such as repetition, hesitations, false starts and the like, whereas the original English is neatly constructed and its syntactic structure is much more complex with subordinator *that* occurred twice in one sentence. The students' interpreted English is liable to a large quantity of repetitions, pauses and false starts, while there are no repetitions, hesitations and paralinguistic features occurred in the original English.

In addition, as shown in the Example 7.8 retrieved from students' interpreted English, the object clause introduced by *that* as a subordinator precedes with less formal verb *hope* whereas the object clause led by *that* as a subordinator comes with more formal verb *report* in the original English. It is obvious that verbs that are more formal are less common, and less familiar verbs bear a heavier processing burden, therefore the subordinate clauses apparently favor the use of subordinator *that* as "an explicit boundary signal" (Rohdenburg 1996: 160).

In short, the syntactic structure of the original English indicates the greater degree of "complexity" of the original speeches with complex subordinate clauses, whereas the students' interpreted English is far less complex with that-clauses preceded by less formal verbs and a range of repetitions and paralinguistic features. This finding may lead to overall higher frequency of the subordinated clause introduced by *that* in the original English and relatively lower occurrence of *that* as a subordinator in students' interpreted English. The increased employment of *that* as a subordinator with more formal verbs in the original English compared with students' interpreted English probably attribute, partly at least, to the complexity principle.

## 7.3 Explanations for Different Textual Explicitations between Chinese EFL Students and Professional Interpreters

In Chapter Five, a statistically significant difference exists between Chinese EFL students and professional interpreters with regard to inter-language textual explicitation in C-E CI. This section attempts to discuss reasons for such different textual explicitation between students and professional interpreters.

### 7.3.1 Linguistic Competence

The interpreting task requires an excellent knowledge of at least two languages, thus linguistic competence is a prerequisite for performing the interpreting task. Chomsky defined linguistic competence as an idealized understanding of the rules and construction of a given language. This includes grasp of syntactic and semantic rules through which generating infinitely many sentences that conform to these rules. Once a speaker masters this set of rules, he or she can use this grammar to produce new phrases understood by speakers of the same language.

Some linguistic theorists see linguistic competence as a learned behavior rather than an innate function of the human brain. According to the Common European Framework of reference for languages (CEFR 2001: 109), the linguistic competence refers to a learner's "knowledge of and ability to use, the formal resources from which well-formed, meaningful messages may be assembled and formulated". That is to say, linguistic competence is the ability to produce accurate sentences with linguistic knowledge and the ability to infer the meaning of words or sentences with the help of linguistic context. It is the crucial competence to carry out any interpreting task by professional and student interpreters alike.

In interpreting, it is inductive to have some knowledge not only of the language used in the source speech to be interpreted, but also of the target language when it is different, because "interference between those two languages can lead to faulty word usage and syntax as well as unnatural pronunciation which makes comprehension more difficult" (Gile 2009: 87). Therefore, interpreting requires interpreters to possess in-depth knowledge of and potential ability to use both source language and target language. It is essential for professional interpreters and students alike to realize that their language proficiency will allow them to perform the interpreting task adequately, because of the close connection between proficiency in two languages and interpreting.

In short, the linguistic competence involved in interpreting covers the following three components: (i) possibility — the ability to produce grammatical sentences in the target language; (ii) feasibility — the ability to generate sentences decoded by the target audience; (iii) appropriateness — the ability to use correct forms of language in a specific social-cultural context. In addition, interpreters need to comprehend the specific language registers and varieties and respond promptly to this spoken language to transfer the meaning in the target language as fast and faithfully as possible.

Professional interpreters develop comparatively greater linguistic competence involved in interpreting in relation to student interpreters. Professionals tend to have active knowledge and good command of two languages and they conform to most syntax rules and sentence structures in the TL so as to know when it is necessary to explicitate referential cohesive devices and implicit logical relations between clauses in C-E CI. By comparison, student interpreters are far from being competent in two languages and therefore may lack confidence in their interpreting abilities due to time constraint in CI to tap into their target language proficiency. They are less likely to know when it is essential to add the cohesive devices to make explicit the implied logical relations between clauses in interpreting. Thus, the different linguistic competence entailed in interpreting between professional interpreters and Chinese EFL students may contribute to comparatively more explicitations in professional corpus compared with the students' corpus.

### 7.3.2 Interpreting Experience

Expertise in interpreting results from well-refined strategies through practice in each of comprehension, interpretation and reformulation processes, which are specific to the task of interpreting. It seems that, in particular, expert or professional interpreters have developed an ability to manage efficiently their attention between different processes in accordance with specific demand during the task of interpreting. Expert performance refers to "consistently superior performance on a specified set of representative tasks for the domain" (Ericsson & Charness 1997: 6). Thus, expert performance is featured by "stable characteristics" (Englunds-Dimitrova 2005: 16) in interpreters, and characterized by fewer errors, quicker responses and less effort being made.

Experienced interpreters are better at offering more accurate and exhaustive interpretations and they seem to be faster at processing lexical and syntactic information with less effort. The difference between experienced interpreters and students goes beyond accuracy, speed and effort made in interpreting. They also differ in their ability to employ flexible semantic processing strategies, such as the ability to perceive the significance and overall structure of source speech, which in turn may contribute to their success in predicting upcoming information and constructing them into a coherent text.

Liu's (2004) study shows that student interpreters' output is comparatively more fragmented and incoherently linked together than that of expert or professional interpreters. Experience is regarded one of the most powerful predictors of performance in performing a language-related task including interpreting (Bandura 1986; Zeegers 2004; Burton & Dowling 2005; Klomegah 2007). This is because the student internalizes the characteristic of successful or failed experience as one of the main sources of successful performance in the task (Wiedenbeck 2005). Therefore, interpreting is an interpreter-mediated task, and past experience plays an active part in generating more accurate and coherent interpreted texts within required time constraint.

In addition, experienced translators and interpreters are more aware of their readership and target audience (Saldanha 2008: 28). Therefore, they may feel inclined to help their readers and target audience with the use of cohesive devices to establish inter-clausal relationships between sentences. Their concerns with coherence and clarity may prompt them to provide missing links between clauses through conjunctions, lay implicit meanings bare, explain complicated passages and elaborate on the source text (Kruger 2004: 90). Moreover, students with less interpreting experience deliver more fragmented versions compared with their experienced counterparts, and interpreters make use of the speakers' pauses for their interpretations (Barik 1973; 1975). With respect to semantic knowledge, experienced interpreters' semantic interpretation is often relevant to the context of speech and display better organization with more associative conjunctions

(Moser-Mercer et al 2000). These tendencies found in experienced translator and interpreters are relevant to the forms of explicitation employed in translation and interpreting.

The previous research conducted on explicitation studies "has mainly investigated explicitation as textual cohesion" (Sergio & Falbo 2012: 24). Several studies carried out research on explicitation conclude that novice or student translators and interpreters tend to regard each clause or sentence in an isolated manner, and fail to establish logical relations between clauses and to build discourse links (Künzli & Moser-Mercer 1995: 304-306; Englund-Demitrova 2005: 225-227; Gumul 2006; 2007; Tang & Li 2015). Based on these findings, it would be fair to assume that experience in interpreting exerts a substantial impact on the use of explicitation and may contribute to the frequency of explicitation found in students' and professional corpora respectively. That is to say, interpreting experience may lead to the fact that Chinese EFL students make fewer textual explicitations than their professional counterparts do in C-E CI.

### 7.3.3 Cognitive Process

Consecutive interpreting entails a large number of almost concurrent cognitive and affective processes, all of which pose major challenges for the interpreter who has to deal with them simultaneously. The interpreter constantly encounters unexpected situations that require immediate attention while he/she is already working at the limits of his/her available processing capacity (Gile 1995).

Interpreting involves three apparent processes: comprehension, translation, and production (or reformulation). Experienced and novice interpreters, i.e. professional and student interpreters may not differ in "syntactic processing of comprehension, but they do differ in their ability to use more flexible semantic processing" (Liu 2009: 173). Experienced interpreters pay much attention to overall conceptual framework of the source speech. Generally, experienced translators or interpreters have a holistic approach to translation, which means that they are able to focus on the text to be translated as an organic whole (Angelone 2010: 34). Such holistic approach allows experienced translators to produce more effective target texts, such as reordering clauses based on their logical relations or moving semantic units from one paragraph to another (Shreve 2002: 166).

The part of translation process results indirectly from the way interpreters segment the source speech. The studies demonstrated that student interpreters have a tendency to pick out segments in a speech and connect them arbitrarily, which leads to an output lacking coherence (Sunnari 1995), while expert interpreters' output is considered far more coherent, sounded smoother, and more meaningful and natural than student interpreters' (Liu 2001).

In addition, the cognitive processing of experienced translators proceeds in an iterative and non-linear manner (Göpferich & Jääskeläinen 2009: 174), and this kind of parallel processing allow them to have alternatives for a particular text segment even when a translation has already been found (Séguinot 2000: 146). This feature of cognitive processing allows experienced translators to adopt a sense-oriented approach to translation (Lörscher 2009: 15), which allows for a more coherent and natural-sounding target text.

In contrast, inexperienced translators' translation process is primarily restricted to the level of individual words (Cintrão 2011: 89) as the succession of signs, in terms of sentences, clauses and words (Lörscher 2005: 13). Therefore, inexperienced translators demonstrate form-oriented approaches to translation, as they tend to produce translations based on an exchange of language signs (Lörscher 2005: 605), which results in less natural and coherent target texts.

In interpreting, professional interpreters can retrieve relevant domain knowledge and strategies with minimal cognitive effort (Alexander 2003: 3). They can also execute their strategies with greater automaticity (Schneider 1985). Sunnari (1995: 118) also confirms that professionals' strategies are different from those of trainees. Professional interpreters know how and when to use condensing based on macro-processing, while novice or student interpreters focus on the micro-level of the text (SnelTrampus 2002: 44) and fail to produce a coherent message in the target language.

Moreover, in terms of risk involved in translation process, which can be seen as the "probability of undesired outcome" (Pym 2005: 34). Experienced translators, therefore, will aim "to do their best to reduce to a minimum the damage related to the transfer process, and it seems better to end up with some redundancy than with major losses" (Øverås 1998: 576). Inexperienced translators do not perceive the same degree of risk associated with their translations, and from this perspective will thus be less inclined to explicitate in translation.

In short, it is most likely that the differences between professionals and students with respect to semantic processing in comprehension and cognitive processing and risk management involved in translation and interpreting process may contribute to different explicitation tendencies in C-E CI.

# Chapter Eight Conclusion

Drawing on the analytic framework of SFL concerning textual cohesion, and adopting an integrated corpus approach, the present study has investigated the inter- and intra-language textual explicitations found in the C-E interpreting performed by Chinese EFL students. This chapter features a comprehensive summary of major findings on differences between students' textual explicitations and professionals in C-E CI, as well as disparities between students' interpreted English texts and the original English texts with respect to the frequency of textual cohesive devices. The present study also puts forward possible explanations for such findings from linguistic differences, interpreting norms and cognitive aspects. Followed by a discussion of implications and contributions of the study, the chapter concludes by offering potential avenues and alternative suggestions for future studies.

## 8.1 Major Findings

This section summarizes major findings with respect to inter-language textual explicitations found in C-E CI performed by Chinese EFL students in comparison with professional interpreters through a parallel corpus, as well as intra-language explicitation through comparing students' interpreted English with the original English with regard to the frequency of cohesive devices by adopting a comparable corpus. It also attempts to seek explanations that may account for such findings from multiple perspectives including linguistic differences, interpreter awareness, complexity principle and cognitive aspects. The current study responds to research questions put forward in the introductory chapter as follows.

(1) What is specific to Chinese EFL students in C-E CI in terms of categories of inter-language textual explicitations compared with professionals?

The investigations carried out in Chapter Five provide answers for the first question. To answer this question, Chapter Five explores several dimensions of explicitations of cohesive devices on the part of students and professionals in C-E CI, which include personal pronouns, demonstratives and subordinating conjunctions with each classified into multiple subcategories. The statistical results show that there exists a statistically significant difference ($p < .05$) between Chinese EFL students and professional interpreters with respect to inter-language explictitation of textual meaning in C-E CI. The results demonstrate that Chinese EFL students are far less likely to explicitate textual cohesion in comparison with professional interpreters in C-E CI. Professional interpreters, in particular, make considerably more explicitations of conjunctions for clarification of logical relationship between the main clause and subordinate clause than Chinese EFL students do. This finding indicates that Chinese EFL students tend to treat each sentence in an isolated manner and fail to establish relationship between components of a text.

(2) What are the characteristics of intra-language textual explicitation in Chinese EFL students' interpreted English texts in comparison with the original English?

Chapter Six responds to the second question concerning intra-language explicitation of textual meaning, which covers referential cohesive devices, subordinating conjunctions and *that* as a subordinator. The findings reveal that statistically significant differences ($p < .05$) lie between students' interpreted English texts and the original English texts with regard to the frequency of reference, subordinating conjunctions and *that* as a subordinator. The statistical results indicate that those cohesive devices and *that* as a subordinator are far less likely to occur in students' interpreted English compared with the original English, though there are few exceptions to this tendency in some cases. This finding suggests that intra-language explicitation does not exist in students' interpreted English compared with the original English, which is contrary to features of translated language (Baker 1996; Olohan & Baker 2000: 142). Particularly, there is much more frequent occurrence of *that* as a subordinator in the original English than in the interpreted English of Chinese EFL students, especially *that* in the attributive clause, objective clause and the appositive. The findings imply that Chinese EFL students show less tendency to employ subordinating clauses in which *that* as a subordinator.

(3) How do linguistic, cognitive and social factors motivate such explicitation features in C-E CI?

This study explains motivational factors from three perspectives for every type of explicitation: reasons for inter-language explicitation and intra-language explicitation, as well as possible explanations for disparate explicitations between students and professional interpreters respectively.

We argue that the linguistic difference between Chinese as paratactic and English as hypotactic explains the explicitation of referential cohesive devices to meet syntactic requirement of the target language English. The logical connection is established through the context in Chinese, while logic is built through connectives that indicate the logical relationship in English. This makes explicitation of conjunctions possible in C-E interpreting. In addition, inherent feature of interpreting including interpretive theory, interpreting norms and interpreters' expressive habits also account for inter-language explicitation. Finally, cognitive operations related to Memory Effort make interpreters have to deliver the holistic sense of the source speech through interpretive methods, which contribute to the employment of explicitation.

As to intra-language comparison, the interference of Chinese exerts a great impact on students' interpreted English with regard to the lower frequency of pronouns occurring in interpreted English. Moreover, students' inadequate awareness on the use of conjunctions to signal logical relations between clauses possibly account for fewer occurrences of conjunctions in interpreted English, and complexity principle explains more frequent use of *that* as a subordinator in the original English in relation to students' interpreted English.

The possible explanations for the difference between Chinese EFL students and professional interpreters with respect to the use of explicitations cover their linguistic competence, interpreting experience and cognitive processing ability in C-E CI.

## 8.2 Contributions and Implications

As the first attempt made in the field of interpreting studies to incorporate corpus-based approach and students' interpreted texts within the analytical framework of SFL, this research conducts investigations on the inter-language and intra-language explicitation of textual meaning in C-E CI and adds to the growing body of literature on CIS with valuable contributions below.

Theoretically, the multi-layered typology and motivational analysis for explicitation in CI that this study adopts may form a sound theoretical basis for further explicitation studies in other interpreter-mediated activities such as sight interpreting, simultaneous interpreting, etc.

Methodologically speaking, this research employs an integrated corpus approach that includes both parallel corpus and comparable corpus, which allows us to carry out a comprehensive examination of students' interpreted texts in relation not only to their corresponding source texts but also to non-translated texts in the same language. This makes it possible to demonstrate in-depth understanding of Chinese EFL students' language use in C-E CI.

Empirically, this study collects multi-layered data not only on inter-language explicitations between Chinese EFL students and professional interpreters, but also on intra-language comparison between students' interpreted English texts and the original English texts. The multi-dimensional analysis may serve as empirical data for future studies on students' linguistic features of interpreted texts in CI, and the link between the degree of explicitness and interpreter's expertise.

Pedagogically, and most importantly, findings of this study may shed some new light on educational implications for interpreter training in the future in the field of CI, which is also the answer to the research question four below:

Which implications might be possibly put forward for the education of interpreters' training?

The research conducts investigations not only on inter-language explicitations of textual meaning in students' interpreted texts in comparison with professionals in C-E CI, but also on intra-language explicitations of students' interpreted texts in relation to the original texts in English.

This makes it possible to draw a comparison between students' interpreted English texts with professional interpreters and the original English texts respectively. It is the assumption that corpus-based analysis of students' translations will inform us about both translation process and product (Olohan 2004: 39). For instance, as to the explicitation of conjunctions, Chinese EFL students are less likely to perceive the implied logical relations between clauses in a sentence compared with professional interpreters. Therefore, in interpreter training, instructors may try to devise a series of exercises where students can develop the ability to figure out implied inter-clausal relations between clauses. Moreover, compared to the original English texts, there are far fewer occurrences of subordinating clause led by *that* as a subordinator in students' interpreted texts. Based on this finding, to acquire a good command of English in C-E interpreting, students may be encouraged to do more exercises in which they can foster their awareness of using subordinating clauses in their interpreted texts.

In short, the educational implications for the education of interpreters' training might include the following suggestions mentioned below. That is to say, instructors devise a series of interpreting exercises where students can enhance the awareness of correct use of personal pronouns and demonstratives, the ability to assess implied logical relations between clauses, and raise the awareness of proper usage of subordinating clauses in interpreting respectively. In that way, students may come to understand the significance of cohesion in any successful process of interpreting because cohesive ties are helpful in identifying semantic relations in the text and thus can contribute to their valid interpretation.

## 8.3 Limitations and Suggestions for Future Studies

It is worth noting that this study also suffers some limitations in the following aspects. Details are as follows.

Although the study adopts a corpus-based approach, the corpus size is not big enough, comparing to those comprehensive learners' corpora to arrive at an all-sided and general conclusion based on the results yield in this research. Thus the findings presented in this study can only applies to Chinese EFL students majoring in English who attended TEM band eight from the year 2003 to 2007. These results obtained from this study can merely be regarded tentative conclusions with respect to students' explicitation features found in CI.

In addition, it is barely possible to find out exactly the same source speeches interpreted by large number of student interpreters and professional interpreters at the same time while adopting an integrated corpus approach. To minimize the differences, as for parallel subcorpus, the topics under discussion in source speeches both in students' corpus and in professional corpus cover similar subjects related to foreign affairs on formal occasions such as opening and closing ceremonies as well as press conferences. As to comparable subcorpus, it is also the same case in students' interpreted English texts and the original English texts. Yet, there are still some other variables hard to manage, for instance, differences in speed of delivery, voice quality and information density among different speakers, which may exert an impact on the performance of students' interpreting.

Moreover, all the data collected in students' corpus and professional corpus is being processed in the mode of CI. However, it is impossible to have a group of student interpreters and professional interpreters interpreting the same source speech in exactly same interpreting environment on real-life occasions. The original speech in students' corpus is pre-recorded although the speech is in the mode of CI, and students have to interpret sentence by sentence in a TEM band-eight test environment. By comparison, the professional interpreters interpret the original speeches delivered by Chinese government leaders in press conferences. Therefore, the students' performance might be influenced by the lack of perceiving target audience's responses and observing speakers' body language and gestures.

Due to the limited scope of the study, it may still feasible to explore some other possible ways to carry out research on students' explicitation features in translation and interpreting studies in the future. Firstly, this study mainly focuses on explicitation of textual meaning, thus the future research may conduct ideational and interpersonal explicitations and the significant differences between three kinds of explicitation features in CI. Secondly, the future study may invite comparison between translation and different modes of interpreting with respect to explicitation features, motivations and their effect such as in translation, in simultaneous interpreting and sight interpreting etc. Thirdly, future research may attempt to make further exploration with regard to the influence of language directions on explicitation patterns so as to see the potential differences in the frequency, motivations and effect of explicitation between different language directions.

In addition, it might be meaningful and interesting to carry out further research on distinctive features of explicitation on different interpreting occasions such as business negotiations, community interpreting and court interpreting. Moreover, it might be of great value to interpreter training to see whether there is a link between the degree of explicitness and the quality of interpreting.

# References


[1] ADAB B. Discourse analysis as part of translator training: does it work? How do we set about it? A response to Anna Trosborg [J]. Current Issues in Language and Society, 2000, 7(3): 245-28.

[2] ALEXANDER P A. Can we get there from here? [J]. Educational Researcher, 2003 (32): 3-4.

[3] ANGELELLI C. Interpretation as a communicative event: a look through Hymes' Lenses [J]. Meta, 2000,14(4): 580-592.

[4] ANGELONE E. Uncertainty, uncertainty management, and metacognitive problem solving in the translation task [C]// INSHREVE G M, ANGELONE E. Translation and cognition. Amsterdam: John Benjamins, 2010: 17-40.

[5] ASTON G, BERNARDINI S, STEWART D. Corpora and language learners [M]. Amsterdam & Philadelphia: John Benjamins, 2004.

[6] BACHMAN L F. Fundamental considerations in language testing [M]. Oxford: Oxford University Press, 1990.

[7] BAKER M. In other words: a course book on translation [M]. London & New York: Routledge, 1992.

[8] BAKER M. Corpus linguistics and translation studies: implications and applications [C]// M BAKER, G FRANCIS, E TOGNINI-BONELLI. Text and technology: in honour of John Sinclair. Amsterdam & Philadelphia: John Benjamins, 1993: 233-250.

[9] BAKER M. Corpora in translation studies: an overview and some suggestions for future research [J]. Target, 1995, 7(2): 223-243.

[10] BAKER M. Corpus-based translation studies: the challenges that lie ahead [C]// H Somers. Terminology, LSP and translation. Amsterdam: John Benjamins, 1996: 175-186.

[11] BAKER M. Towards a methodology for investigating the style of a literary translator [J]. Target, 2000, 12(2): 241-261.

[12] BAKER M. Contextualization in translator- and interpreter-mediated events [J]. Journal of Pragmatics, 2006, 38(3): 321-337.

[13] BALEGHIZADEH S, SHARIFI A. Explicitation of implicit logical links in Persian-English translation [J]. Translation & Interpreting, 2010, 2(2): 57- 65.

[14] BANDURA A. Social learning theory [M]. New York: General Learning Press, 1977.

[15] BANDURA A. Social foundations of thought and action [M]. Englewood Cliffs, NJ: Prentice-Hall, 1986.

[16] BARIK H C. Simultaneous interpretation: temporal and quantitative data [J/OL]. Language and Speech, 1973, 16: 237-270. http://las.sagepub.com/content/16/3/237.

[17] BARIK H C. Simultaneous interpretation: qualitative and linguistic data [J]. Language and Speech, 1975, 18 (3): 272–297.

[18] BARKHUDAROV L S. Yazykiprevod [language and translation] [M]. Moscow: Mezhdonarodyneotnosheniya, 1975.

[19] BARTOLOMÉ M L. Explicitation in translation memory-mediated environments. Methodological conclusions from a pilot study[J]. Translation & Interpreting, 2011 (3): 45-57.

[20] BASSNETT S, LEFEVERE A. Introduction: Proust's grandmother and the thousand and one nights: The "cultural turn" in translation studies [C]// Bassnett S, Lefevere, A. Translation, history and culture. London & New York: Pinter, 1990: 1-13.

[21] BAUMGARTE N, MEYER B. Explicitness in translation and interpreting: a critical review and some empirical evidence (of an elusive concept) [J]. Across Languages and Cultures, 2008, 9 (2): 177-203.

[22] BECHER V. Abandoning the notion of "translation-inherent" explicitation: against a dogma of translation studies [J]. Across Languages and Cultures, 2010 (1): 1-28.

[23] BECHER V. Explicitation and implicitation in business translation: a corpus-based study of English-German and German-English translations of business texts [D]. Hamburg: University of Hamburg, 2011.

[24] BEIKIAN A, YARAHMADZEHI N, NATANZI M. Explicitation of conjunctive relations in Ghabraei's Persian translation of "the kite runner" [J]. English Language and Literature Studies, 2013 (2): 81-89.

[25] BAUMGARTEN N, MEYER B, OZCENTIN D. Explicitness in translation and interpreting: a critical review and some empirical evidence (of an elusive concept) [J]. Across Languages and Cultures, 2008 (2): 177-203.

[26] BECHER V. When and why do translators add connectives? A corpus-based study [J]. Target, 2011, 23(1): 26-47.

[27] BERNARDINI S, ZANETTIN F. When is a universal not a universal? Some limits of current corpus-based methodologies for the investigation of translation universals [C]// MAURANEN A, KUJAMÄKI P. Translation universals: do they exist? Amsterdam & Philadelphia: John Benjamins, 2004: 51-62.

[28] BIBER D, JOHANSSON S, LEECH G, et al. The Longman grammar of spoken and written English [M]. London: Longman, 1999.

[29] Black T R. Doing quantitative research in the social sciences: An integrated approach to research design, measurement and statistics [M]. London: SAGE Publications. 1999.

[30] Blum-Kulka, Interlingual and Intercultural Communication: Discourse and Cognition in Translation and Second Language Acquisition Studies. Juliane House and Shoshana Blum-Kulka (Eds.). Tübingen: Gunter Narr, 1986. Pp. 292.

[31] BLUM-KULKA S. Shifts of cohesion and coherence in translation [C]//VENUTI L. The translation studies reader. London and New York: Routledge, 2001: 298-313.

[32] BOLTON K, NELSON G, HUNG J. A corpus-based study of connectors in student writing. Research from the international corpus of English in Hong Kong (ICE-HK) [J]. International Journal of Corpus Linguistics, 2002 (2): 165-182.

[33] BOWKER L, BENNISON P. Student translation archive: design, development and application [C]// ZANETTIN E, BERNARDINI S, STEWART D. Corpora in translator education. Manchester: St Jerome, 2003: 103-117.

[34] BURNETT S. A corpus-based study of translational english [D]. Manchester: unpublished MS book, UMIST, 1999.

[35] BURTON L J, DOWLING D G. In search of the key factors that influence student success at university [C]. In Proceedings of the 2005 HERDSA Annual Conference, Sydney: Australia, 2005: 68-78.

[36] CAMPBELL K S. Coherence, continuity and cohesion: theoretical foundations for document design [M]. Hove, UK: Lawrence Erlbaum Associates, 1995.

[37] CAMPBELL S. Translation into the second language. London: Longman, 1998.

[38] CANALE M, SWAIN M. Theoretical bases of communicative approaches to second language teaching and testing [J]. Applied Linguistics, 1980(1): 1-47.

[39] CASTAGNOLI S. Regularities and variations in learner translations: a corpus-based study of conjunctive explicitation [D]. Pisa: University of Pisa, 2010.

[40] CINTRÃO H P. Development of translation competence in novices: a corpus design and key-logging analysis [C]// O'BRIEN S. Continuum studies in translation: cognitive explorations of translation. London: Continuum, 2011: 86-107.

[41] CHEN D. English and Chinese translation — a comparative study[M]. Beijing: China Translation & Publishing Corporation, 1998.

[42] 陈昊泽. 专业译员与学生译员在同声传译中应用逻辑关系显化的比较研究[D]. 北京：北京外国语大学，2014.

[43] CHERNOV V G. Context-free and Context-linked Implication and Problems of Translation[C]// SHVEITSER A D. Tekstiperevod [Text and Translation]. Moscow: Nauka, 1988: 51-63.

[44] CHESTERMAN A. Review of descriptive translation studies and beyond, by Toury G [J]. Target, 1996, 8(1): 197-201.

[45] CHESTERMAN A. The empirical status of prescriptivism[J]. Folia Translatologica, 1999(6): 9-19.

[46] CHESTERMAN A. Beyond the particular [C]// Mauranen A, KUJAMÄKI P. Translation universals: do they exist?. Amsterdam & Philadelphia: John Benjamins, 2004: 33-49.

[47] DONG D, LAN Y. Textual competence and the use of cohesion devices in translating into a second language [J]. The Interpreter and Translator Trainer, 2010, 4(1): 47-88.

[48] CREWE W. The illogic of logical connectives [J]. ELT Journal, 1990 (4): 316-325.

[49] ENGLUND-DIMITROVA B. Semantic Change in Translation — a cognitive perspective [C]// GAMBIER Y, Translation and knowledge. Yves and Jorma Tommola, Turku: Centre for Translation and Interpreting, University of Turku, 1993: 285-296.

[50] ENGLUND-DIMITROVA B. Expertise and explicitation in the translation process [M]. Amsterdam & Philadelphia: John Benjamins, 2005.

[51] ERICSSON K A, CHARNESS N. Cognitive and developmental factors in expert performance [C]// FELTOVICH P J, FORD K M., HOFFMAN R R. Expertise in context, human and machine. Menlo Park, Cambridge MA and London: AAAI Press & The MIT Press, 1997: 3-41.

[52] FABER D, HJORT-PEDERSEN M. Explicitation and implicitation in legal translation — a process study of trainee translators [J]. Meta, 2010, 55(2): 237.

[53] FAIRCLOUGH N. Language and power[M]. London: Longman, 1989.

[54] GAK V G. Typology of Textual Language Transformation in Translation [C]// SHVEITSER A D. Text and Translation. Moscow: Nauka,1988: 63-76.

[55] GAËTANELLE G, PAPP S, DÍEZ-BEDMAR M B. Linking up contrastive and learner corpus research [M]. Amsterdam: Rodopi, 2008.

[56] GERVER D. Aspects of simultaneous interpretation and human information processing [D]. Oxford: Oxford University, 1971.

[57] GILE D. Basic concepts and models for interpreter and translator training [M]. Amsterdam & Philadelphia: John Benjamins, 2009.

[58] GILE D. Norms in research on conference interpreting: a response to Theo Hermans and Gideon Toury [C]// SCHAFFNER C. Translation and norms. Clevedon: Mutlilingual Matters, 1999: 99-105.

[59] GILE D. Teaching conference interpreting: a contribution [C]// TENNENT M. Training for the new millennium: pedagogies for translation and interpreting. Amsterdam and Philadelphia: John Benjamins, 2005: 127-151.

[60] GÖPFERICH S, JÄÄSKELÄINEN R. Process research into the development of translation competence: where are we, and where do we need to go? [J] Across Languages and Cultures, 2009, 10(2): 169-191.

[61] GUTT E A. Translation and relevance: cognition and context[M]. 2nd ed. Manchester: St. Jerome Publishing, 2000.

[62] GRANGER S, A bird's-eye view of learner corpus research [C]// GRANGER S, HONG J, PETCH-TYSON S. Computer learner corpora, second language acquisition and foreign language teaching. Amsterdam & Philadelphia: John Benjamins, 2002: 3-33.

[63] GRANGER S. Computer learner corpus research: current status and future prospects [C]// Connor U, Upton T A. Applied corpus linguistics: a multidimensional perspective. Amsterdam: Rodopi, 2004, 123-145.

[64] Granger S. Learner corpora in foreign language education [C]// DEUSEN SCHOLL N V, HORNBERGER N. Encyclopedia of language and education. Second and foreign language education. Springer, 2008(4): 337-351.

[65] GRANGER S. The contribution of learner corpora to second language acquisition and foreign language teaching [C]// AIJMER K. Corpora and language Teaching. Amsterdam, the Netherlands: John Benjamins Publishing Company, 2009: 13-32.

[66] GRANGER S, TYSON S. Connector usage in the English essay writing of Native and non-native EFL Speakers of English [J]. World Englishes, 1996(1): 17-27.

[67] GUMUL E. Explicitation in simultaneous interpreting: a strategy or a by-product of language mediation? [J]. Across Languages and Cultures, 2006, 7(2): 171-190.

[68] GUMUL E. Explicitation in conference interpreting [C]// Thelen M, TOMASZCZYK B. Translation and meaning. Maastricht: Department of Translation and Interpreting, Maastricht School of International Communication, Zuyd University, 2006.

[69] HADLEY I L. Understanding cohesion — some practical teaching implications [J]. Literacy, 1987, 21 (2): 106-114.

[70] HALLIDAY M A K. Notes in transitivity and theme in English[J]. Journal of Linguistics, 1967, 3(2): 199-244.

[71] HALLIDAY M A K. Exploration in the functions of language [M]. London：Arnold，1973.

[72] HALLIDAY M A K, HASAN R. Cohesion in English [M]. London and New York: Longman, 1976.

[73] HALLIDAY M A K. Language as Social Se-miotics: the social interpretation of language and meaning [M]. London: Edward Arnold, 1978.

[74] HALLIDAY M A K. An introduction to functional grammar [M]. 2nd ed. London: Edward Arnold, 1994.

[75] HALLIDAY M A K, HASAN R. Cohesion in English[M]. Beijing: Foreign Language Teaching and Research Press, 2001.

[76] HALLIDAY M A K, MATTHIESSEN M I M. An introduction to functional grammar[M] 3rd ed. London: Arnold Publishers, 2004.

[77] HALLIDAY M A K, CHRISTIAN M I M. Halliday's introduction to functional grammar[M]. 4th ed. Abington & New York: Routledge, 2014.

[78] HARRIS, B. Norms in Interpretation[J]. Target, 1990, 2(1):115-119.

[79] HATIM B, MASON I. Discourse and the translator[M]. London & New York: Longman, 1990.

[80] HATIM B. Communication across cultures: translation theory and contrastive text linguistics. [M] Shanghai: Shanghai Foreign Language Education Press, 2001.

[81] 贺显斌. 英汉翻译过程中的明晰化现象 [J]. 解放军外国语学院学报, 2004(4): 63- 66.

[82] HERBERT J. The interpreter's handbook: how to become a conference interpreter[M]. Geneva: Georg, 1952.

[83] HERMANS T. Translational norms and correct translations [C]// LEUVEN-ZWART K M V, NAAIJKENS T. Translation studies: the state of the art. Amsterdam: Rodopi, 1991: 155-69.

[84] HERMANS T. Translation in systems: descriptive and system-oriented approaches explained [M].Manchester: St. Jerome Publishing, 1999.

[85] HOLMES J S. The name and nature of translation studies [D]. Amsterdam: Translation Studies Section, Department of General Studies, University of Amsterdam, 1972.

[86] HOUSE J. Explicitness in discourse across languages [J]. To appear in a Festscrift for Professor Heidrun Gerzymisch-Arbogast. Bochum: AKS, 2004: 185-207.

[87] HOUSE J. Using translation and parallel text corpora to investigate influence global english on textual norms in other languages [C]// KRUGER A, WALLMACH K. Corpus-based translation studies. Manchester: St. Jerome, 2011: 187-208.

[88] HU K. Introducing corpus-based translation studies [M]. Springer-Verlag Berlin Heidelberg, 2016.

[89] 胡开宝. 语料库翻译学概论 [M]. 上海: 上海交通大学出版社,2011.

[90] 胡开宝, 朱一凡. 基于语料库的莎剧《哈姆雷特》汉译文本中显化现象及其动因研究 [J]. 外语研究, 2008( 2 ): 72-80.

[91] 胡开宝, 陶庆. 汉英会议口译中语篇意义显化及其动因研究——一项基于平行语料库的研究 [J]. 解放军外国语学院, 2009( 4 ): 67-73.

[92] 胡开宝, 陶庆. 记者招待会汉英口译句法操作规范研究 [J]. 外语教学与研究, 2012(5): 738-750, 801.

[93] 胡显耀, 曾佳. 对翻译小说语法标记显化的语料库研究 [J]. 外语研究，2009(5):72- 79
[94] 胡壮麟. 语言学教程 [M]. 北京：北京大学出版社, 1988.
[95] 胡壮麟. 语篇的衔接与连贯[M]. 上海: 上海外语教育出版社, 1994.
[96] HUANG G W. Hallidiyan linguistics in China [J]. World Englishes, 2002 (2): 281- 290.
[97] 黄立波. 基于汉英／英汉平行语料库的翻译共性研究 [M]. 上海：复旦大学出版社，2007.
[98] 黄立波. 英汉翻译中人称代词主语的显化——基于语料库的考察[J]. 外语教学与研究，2008，40(6): 454- 459.
[99] HUDDLESTON R D. A student's introduction to English grammar. Cambridge, UK: Cambridge University Press, 2005.
[100] KÁROLY K. Referential cohesion and news content: a case study of shifts of reference in Hungarian-English news translation [J]. Target, 2014, 26(3): 406-431.
[101] 柯飞. 翻译中的隐和显 [J]. 外语教学与研究, 2005, 37 (4): 304-307.
[102] KE P. English-Chinese and Chinese-English Translation [M]. Taipei: Bookman, 1994.
[103] KEEN J. Sentence-combining and redrafting processes in the writing of secondary school students in the UK [J]. Linguistics and Education, 2004, 15(1-2): 81-97.
[104] KENNY D. Parallel corpora and translation studies: old questions, new perspectives? Reporting that in Gepcolt. A case study [C]// BARNBROOK G, DANIELSSON P, MAHLBERG M. Meaningful texts: the extraction of semantic information from monolingual and multilingual corpora. Birmingham: University of Birmingham Press, 2005: 154-165.
[105] KINTSCH W, VAN DIJK T A. Toward a model of text comprehension and production [J]. Psychological Review, 1978(85): 363-394.
[106] KLAUDY K. On explicitation hypothesis [C]// KLAUDY K, KOHN J. Transferreneces-seest... current issues of translation theory. Szombathely: Daniel Berzsenyi College, 1993: 69-77.
[107] KLAUDY K. Back-translation as a tool for detecting explicitation strategies in translation [C]// KLAUDY, K., LAMBERT, J. & SOHAR, A. (Eds.). Translation studies in Hungary [C]. Budapest: Scholastica, 1996: 99-114.
[108] KLAUDY K. Explicitation[C]// BAKER M. Routledge encyclopedia of translation studies. London & New York: Routledge, 2008: 80-85.
[109] KLAUDY K. Explicitation[C]// BAKER M, GABIRELA S. Routledge encyclopedia of translation studies[C] 2nd ed. Shanghai: Foreign Language Education Press. 2010:104-108.
[110] KLOMEGAH R Y. Predictors of academic performance of university students: an application of the goal efficacy model [J]. College Student Journal, 2007, 41 (2): 407-415.

[111] KOCH H A functional perspective of cohesion in English [M]. Norderstedt, Germany: GRIN Verlag, 2001.

[112] KOLEHMAINEN L. The translation of null subjects: a test case for the explicitation hypothesis [J]. Across Languages and Cultures, 2014, 15 (1): 25-50.

[113] KOMISSAROV V N. Expliciataion as Problem of Translation [M]. Moscow: TDVK, 1969.

[114] KRUGER A. Corpus-based translation research: its development and implications for general, literary and Bible translation[J]. Acta Theologica, 2004, 22(1): 70-106.

[115] KRUGER H, VAN ROOY B. Register and the features of translated language[J]. Across Languages and Cultures, 2012, 13(1): 33-65.

[116] KRÜGER R. From S-explicitation to T-explicitation? Tracing the development of explicitation concept [J]. Across Languages and Cultures, 2014, 15 (2): 153-175.

[117] KUKHARENKO V A. Expliciataion of the Content of Text during the Process of Translation [C]// SHVEITSER A D. Text and Translation. Moscow: Nauka, 1988: 40-51.

[118] KUNZLI A, MOSER-MERCER B. Human strategies for translation and interpretation [C]// DRESCHLER-FISHCHER L, PRIBBENOW S. KI-95 activities: workshops, posters, demos. Bonn: Gesellschaft Fur Informatike, 1995: 304-306.

[119] LAI F. RI YI ZHONG LI YOUGUANLIANJIECI DE JIAYIXIANXIANG[Phenomenon of Additions of Conjunctions in Japanese-Chinese Translation] [D]. MA thesis, Fujen Catholic University, 1995.

[120] LAVIOSA S. Core patterns of lexical use in a comparable corpus of english narrative prose [J]. Meta, 1998, 43(4): 557-570.

[121] LAVIOSA S. Corpus-based translation studies: theory, findings, applications [M]. New York: Rodopi, 2002.

[122] LAVIOSA S. Universals [C]// BAKER M, SALDANHA G, The routledge encyclopaedia of translation studies. 2nd ed. London, UK: Routledge, 2008.

[123] LAVIOSA S. Learning creative writing by translating witty ads [J]. The Interpreter and Translator Trainer, 2007, 1(2): 197-222.

[124] LEDERER M. 释意学派口笔译理论 [M]. 刘和平, 译. 北京：中国对外翻译出版公司, 2001.

[125] LEE J. Explicitation and implicitation in simultaneous interpreting [J]. Interpretation and Translation, 2014, 16(1): 105-127.

[126] 李德超, 唐芳. 基于类比语料库的英语旅游文本文体特征考察 [J]. 中国外语, 2015 (4): 88-96.

[127] LIU M. Dang Dai Fan Yi Li Lun. Present-day translation studies [M]. Taipei: Bookman,

1993.

[128] LIU M. Expertise in simultaneous interpreting: a working memory analysis [D]. Austin: The University of Texas, 2001.

[129] LIU M. How do experts interpret? Implications from research in interpreting studies and cognitive science [A]. 2009: 159-177.

[130] LIU M, SCHALLERT D L, CARROLL P J, et al. Working memory and expertise in simultaneous interpreting [J]. Interpreting, 2004, 6(1): 19-42.

[131] 刘宓庆. 汉英对比研究与翻译 [M]. 南昌: 江西教育出版社, 1991.

[132] 刘泽权, 陈冬蕾. 英语小说汉译显化实证研究——以《查泰莱夫人的情人》三个中译本为例 [J]. 外语与外语教学, 2010 (4): 8-24.

[133] LONSDALE A. Teaching translation from Spanish to English [M]. Ottawa: University of Ottawa Press, 1996.

[134] LÖRSCHER W. Form-and sense-oriented approaches to translation revisited [J]. Translation Quarterly, 2009(51):1-28.

[135] MASON I. On mutual accessibility of contextual assumptions in dialogue interpreting [J]. Journal of Pragmatics, 2006: 359-373.

[136] MAURANEN A. Strange strings in translated language: a study on corpora [C]// OLOHAN M. Intercultural fault lines, research models in translation studies I: textual and cognitive aspects. Manchester: St. Jerome Publishing, 2000: 119-141.

[137] MAURANEN A. Corpora, universals and interference [C]// MAURANEN A, Kujamäki P. Translation universals do they exist? Philadelphia: J. Benjamins Pub. Co, 2004: 65- 82.

[138] MAURANEN A. Translation universals [C]// BROWN K. Encyclopedia of language and linguistics. 2nd ed. Boston, MA: Elsevier, 2005: 93-100.

[139] MCDERMID C. Cohesion in English to ASL simultaneous interpreting [J]. Translation & Interpreting, 2014, 6 (1): 76-101.

[140] MCENERY T, WILSON A. Corpus linguistics [M]. Edinburgh: Edinburgh University Press, 2001.

[141] MEYER C F. Apposition in contemporary English [M]. Cambridge: Cambridge University Press, 1992.

[142] MOSER-MERCER B, et al. Searching to define expertise in interpreting [C]// ENGLUND-DIMITROVA, HYLTENSTAM K. Language processing and simultaneous interpreting: interdisciplinary perspectives. Amsterdam, Netherlands: the John Benjamins Publishing Company, 2000: 107-131.

[143] MURTISARI E T. The uses of relevance theory for the study of explicitation [D]. Melbourne: Monash University, 2011.

[144] MURTISARI E T. A relevance-based framework for explicitation and implicitation: an alternative typology [J]. Trans-kom, 2013, 6(2): 315-344.

[145] MUTESAYIRE M. Apposition markers and explicitation: a corpus based study [J]. Language Matters, 2004, 35(1): 54-69.

[146] NEUMANN S, Hansen-Schirra S. Corpus methodology and design [C]// HANSEN-SCHIRRA S, NEUMANN S, STEINER, E. Cross-linguistic corpora for the study of translations: insights from the language pair English-German. Berlin: Walter de Gruyter GmbH, 2012: 21-34.

[147] NIDA E A. Toward a science of translating: with special reference to principles and procedures involved in *Bible* translating [M]. Leiden: E. J. Brill, 1964.

[148] NIDA E A. Translating meaning [M]. San Francisco: English Language Institute, 1982.

[149] NILSSON P O. An assessment of the translation-specificity of over-represented multiword patterns in Swedish fiction texts translated from English [J]. Linguistica Antverpiensia, 2002(1): 407-417.

[150] OLOHAN M. Spelling out the optionals in translation: a corpus study [J]. UCREL Technical Paper, 2001 (13): 423-432.

[151] OLOHAN M. Comparable corpora in translation research: overview of recent analyses using the translational English corpus [Z]. LREC Language Resources in Translation Work and Research Workshop, 2002: 5-9.

[152] OLOHAN M. How frequent are the contractions? [J]. Target, 2003,15(1): 59-89.

[153] OLOHAN M. Introducing corpora in translation studies [M]. London & New York: Routledge. 2004.

[154] OLOHAN M, BAKER M. Reporting that in translated English: evidence for subconscious processes of explicitation? [J]. Across Languages and Cultures, 2000, 1(2): 141-158.

[155] ØVERÅS L. In search of the third code: an investigation of norms in literary translation [J]. Meta, 1998, 43(4): 571-588.

[156] PARADIS C. Degree modifiers of adjectives in spoken British English [M]. Lund: Lund University Press, 1997.

[157] PEREGO E. Evidence of explicitation in subtitling: towards a categorization [J]. Across Languages and Cultures, 2003, 4 (1): 63-88.

[158] PETER W K. Translator and interpreter training and foreign language pedagogy [M]. Amsterdam & Philadelphia: John Benjamins, 2008

[159] POPPER K. The logic of scientific discovery [M]. London: Routledge Classics, 1959/2002.

[160] PÖCHHACKER F, SHLESINGER M. The interpreting studies reader [M]. London &

New York: Routledge, 2001

[161] PÖCHHACKER F. Introducing interpreting studies [M]. London: Routledge, 2004.

[162] PUURTINEN T. Assessing acceptability in translated children's books [J]. Target, 1989 (2): 201-213.

[163] PUURTINEN T. Syntax, readability and ideology in children's literature [J]. Meta, 1998, 43(4): 524-533.

[164] PUURTINEN T. Explicitating and implicitating source text ideology [J]. Across Languages and Cultures, 2003a, 4 (1): 53-62.

[165] PUURTINEN T. Genre-specific features of translationese? Linguistic differences between translated and non-translated Finnish children's literature [J]. Literary and Linguistic Computing, 2003b, 18(4): 389-406.

[166] PUURTINEN T. Nonfinite constructions in finnish children's literature: features of translationese contracting translation universals? [C]// GRANGER S, LEROT J, PETCH-TYSON S. Corpus-based approaches to contrastive linguistics and translation studies. Amsterdam & New York: Rodopi, 2003c: 141-154.

[167] PUURTINEN T. Explicitation of clausal relations: a corpus-based analysis of clause connectives in translated and non-translated Finnish children's literature [C]// MAURANEN A, KUJAMAKI P. Translation universals: do they exist?. Amsterdam & Philadelphia: John Benjamins, 2004: 165-176.

[168] PRUNŎ E. priests, princes and pariahs: constructing the professional field of translation [C]// WOLF M, FUKARI A. Constructing a sociology of translation. Amsterdam: John Benjamins, 2007: 39- 56.

[169] PYM A. Explaining explicitation [C]// KÁROLY K. New trends in translation studies, in honour of Kinga Klaudy, 2005.

[170] PYM A. On the social and the cultural in translation studies [C]// PYM A, SHLESINGER M. Sociocultural aspects of translating and interpreting. Amsterdam & Philadelphia: John Benjamins, 2006: 1-27.

[171] PYM A. On Shlesinger's proposed equalizing universal for interpreting [C]// PÖCHHACKER A, JAKOBSEN L, Mees I M. Interpreting studies and beyond: a tribute to Miriam Shlesinger. Copenhagen: Samfundslitteratur Press, 2007: 175-190.

[172] QUIRK R, SIDNEY G, GEOFFREY L, et al. A comprehensive grammar of the English language [M]. London: Longman, 1985.

[173] REID J. A computer text analysis of four cohesion devices in English discourse by native and nonnative writers [J]. Journal of Second Language Writing, 1992, 1(2): 79-107.

[174] ROHDENBURG G. Cognitive complexity and increased grammatical explicitness in En-

glish [J]. Cognitive Linguistics, 1996, 7 (2): 149 -182.

[175] ROY C. Interpreting as a discourse process[M]. New York & Oxford: Oxford University Press, 2000.

[176] SÉGUINOT C. Management issues in the translation process [C]// TIRKKONEN-CONDIT S, JÄÄSKELÄINEN R. Tapping and mapping the processes of translation and interpreting. Amsterdam: John Benjamins, 2000: 143-148.

[177] SAEED J. Pragmatics [M]. London: Blackwell Publishers, 1997.

[178] SALDANHA G. Explicitation revisited: bringing the reader into the picture [J]. Trans-kom, 2008, 1(1): 20-35.

[179] SCHNEIDE R W. Training high performance skills: fallacies and guidelines [J]. Human Factors, 1985, 27(3): 285-300.

[180] SCHJOLDAGER A. An exploratory study of translational norms in simultaneous interpreting: methodological reflections [J]. Hermes, Journal of Linguistics, 1995 (14): 65-87.

[181] SEEBER K G. Cognitive load in simultaneous interpreting [J]. Target-international Journal of Translation Studies, 2013, 25(1): 18-32.

[182] SÉGUINOT C. Pragmatics and the explicitation hypothesis [J]. TTR: Traduction, Terminologie, Rédaction, 1988, 1 (2): 106-114.

[183] SELESKOVITCH D. Take care of the sense and the sounds will take care of themselves or why interpreting is not tantamount to translating languages [J]. The Incorporated Linguist, 1977 (16): 27-33.

[184] SELESKOVITCH D. Interpreting for international conferences [M]. Washington DC: Pen and Booth, 1978.

[185] SELESKOVITCH, D, MARIANNE, L. Interpréter pour traduire [M]. Paris: Didier Erudition, 2001.

[186] SELA-SHEFFY, R, SHLESINGER, M. Identity and status in the translational professions [M]. Amsterdam & Philadelphia: John Benjamins Publishing Company, 2011.

[187] SERGIO F S, FALBO C. Breaking ground in corpus-based interpreting studies [C]. Bern: Peter Lang, 2012.

[188] SCHÄFFNER, C. Norms of translation [A]. In GAMBIER, Y. & VAN DOORSLAER, L. (Eds.). Handbook of translation studies [C]. vol. 1. Amsterdam: John Benjamins, 2010: 235-244.

[189] SHLESINGER M. Extending the theory of translation to interpretation: norms as acase in point [J]. Target, 1989a, 1(2):111-115.

[190] SHLESINGER M. Simultaneous interpretation as a factor in affecting shifts in the position of texts on the oral literature continuum [D]. MA thesis, Tel Aviv University, 1989b.

[191] SHLESINGER, M. Shifts in cohesion in simultaneous interpreting [J]. Translator, 1995, 1(2): 193-212.

[192] SHREVE, G. Knowing translation: cognitive and experiential aspects of translation expertise from the perspective of expertise studies [A]. In RICCARDI, A. (Eds.). Translation studies: perspectives on an emerging discipline [C]. Cambridge: Cambridge University Press, 2002: 150-171.

[193] SHLESINGER, M. Corpus-based interpreting studies as an offshoot of corpus-based translation studies [J]. Meta, 1998, 43(4): 486-493.

[194] SLOBIN, D. I. Psycholinguistics [M]. Glenview, IL: Scott, Foresman Company, 1979.

[195] SNELTRAMPUS, R. Aspects of a theory of norms and some issues in teaching translation [A]. In RICCARDI, A. (Eds.). Translation studies: perspectives on an emerging discipline [C]. Cambridge: Cambridge University Press, 2002: 38-55.

[196] STEWART, D. Poor relations and black sheep in translation studies [J]. Target, 2000, 12(2): 205-228.

[197] SUNNARI M. Processing strategies in simultaneous interpreting: "saying it all" vs. synthesis [C]// TOMMOLA J. Topics in interpreting research. Turku: University of Turku, 1995: 109-119.

[198] SWAN M. Practical english usage [M].Oxford: OUP, 1980.

[199] TANG F, LI D. Explicitation in Chinese-English consecutive interpreting — a comparative study of professional and student interpreters [J]. Foreign Language Teaching and Research, 2013 (3): 442-452.

[200] TANG F, LI D. Explicitation patterns in English-Chinese consecutive interpreting: differences between professional and trainee interpreters [J]. Perspectives, 2015: 235-255.

[201] 唐芳, 李德超. 汉英交替传译中的显化特征——职业译员与学生译员对比研究[J]. 外语教学与研究, 2013 (3): 442- 452.

[202] TANSKANEN S K. Collaborating towards coherence: lexical cohesion in English discourse [M]. Amsterdam & Philadelphia: John Benjamins, 2006.

[203] 陶友兰. 基于语料库的翻译专业口译教材建设 [J]. 外语界, 2010 (4): 2- 8.

[204] TEICH E, FANKHAUSER P. Wordnet for lexical cohesion analysis [C]. In SOIJIKA, P, et al. Proceedings of the 2nd global wordnet conference [C]. Brno, zech Republic: Masaryk University, 2004: 326-31.

[205] TIRKKONEN-CONDIT S. In search of translation universals: non-equivalence or "unique" items in a corpus test [Z]. UMIST/UCL Research Models in Translation Studies Conference, Manchester, 2000: 28-30.

[206] TIRKKONEN-CONDIT S. Translationese — a myth or an empirical fact? a study into the

linguistic identifiability of translated language [J]. Target, 2002, 14 (2): 207-220.

[207] THOMPSON G. Introducing functional grammar [M]. New York: Arnold, 1996.

[208] THOMPSON G. Introducing functional grammar [M]. 3rd ed. London & New York: Routledge, 2014.

[209] TOURY G. In search of translation theory [M]. Tel Aviv: The Porter Institute for Poetics and Semiotics, 1980.

[210] TOURY G. A rationale for descriptive translation studies [C]// HERMANS T. The manipulation of literature: studies in literary translation. London & Sydney: Croom Helm,1985, 16-41.

[211] TOURY G. Descriptive translation studies and beyond [M]. Amsterdam & Philadelphia: John Benjamins Publishing Company, 1995.

[212] TOURY G. A handful of paragraphs on translation and norms [C]// SCHÄFFNER. Translation and norms. London: Short Run Press Ltd, 1999: 9-31.

[213] TOURY G. Descriptive translation studies and beyond [M]. 2nd ed. Amsterdam, Netherlands: John Benjamins, 2012.

[214] TREBITS A. Conjunctive cohesion in English language EU documents — a corpus-based analysis and its implications [J]. English for Specific Purpose, 2009 ( 28 ): 199-210.

[215] TYMOCZKO M. Translation, resistance, activism [M]. Amherst, MA: University of Massachusetts Press, 2010.

[216] VAN DIJK T A. Discourse, ideology and context [J]. Folia Linguistica, 2001, 35 (1): 11-40.

[217] VANLEUVEN-ZWART K M. Translation and original: similarities and dissimilarities [J]. Target, 1989,1 (2): 151-181.

[218] VANDERAUWERA R. Dutch novels translated into English: the transformation of a "minority" literature [M]. Amsterdam: Rodop, 1985.

[219] VASEVA I. Teoriyaipraktikaperevoda [The theory and practice of translation]. Sofia: Naukaiisskustvo, 1980.

[220] VEHMAS-LETO I. Quasi-correctness. A critical study of Finnish translations of Russian journalistic texts [M]. Helsinki: Neuvostoliit-toinstituutti, 1989.

[221] VERIKAITE D. Variation of conjunctive discourse markers across different genres [J]. Man and the Word (Žmogusiržodis), 2005: 68-75.

[222] VINAY J P, DARBELNET J. Comparative stylistics of French and English: amethodology for translation[M]. J C SAGER, M J HAMEL [M] trans. Amsterdam: John Benjamins, 1958/ 1995.

[223] WALLACE C. Investigating explicitation of conjunctions in translated Chinese: a cor-

pus-based study [J]. Language Matters, 2004, 35(1): 95-312.

[224] WANG B. A descriptive study of norms in interpreting: based on the Chinese-English consecutive interpreting corpus of Chinese premier press conferences [J]. Meta, 2012, 57(1): 198-212.

[225] WANG B. Norms of target-language communication in interpreting: a descriptive study based on the corpus of CEIPPC [C]// Translation and cross-cultural communication studies in the Asia Pacific. Brill, 2015: 261-277.

[226] 王克非. 英汉/汉英语句对应的语料库考察 [J]. 外语教学与研究, 2003 : 410- 416.

[227] 王克非. 语料库翻译学探索 [M]. 上海：上海交通大学出版社，2012

[228] 王克非, 秦洪武. 英汉翻译与汉语原创历时语料库的研制 [J]. 外语教学与研究, 2012 (6) : 822- 834.

[229] 王力. 汉语语法理论 [M]. 北京：商务印书馆，1994.

[230] WADENSJÖ C. Interpreting as interaction [M]. London: Longman, 1998.

[231] WADENSJÖ C. The double role of the dialogue interpreter [C]// PÖCHHAKER F, SHLESINGER M. The interpreting studies reader. London: Routledge, 2002: 354-370.

[232] WEISSBROD R. Explicitation in translations of prose-fiction from English to Hebrew as a function of norms [J]. Multilingua, 1992, 11(2): 153-171.

[233] WIEDENBECK S. Factors affecting the success of non-majors in learning to program [Z]. ICER’05, Seattle, Washington, 2005-10-01/02.

[234] WINTERS M. Modal particles explained [J]. Target, 2009, 21(1): 74-97.

[235] WHITTAKER S. “Étude contrastive des syntagmesnominauxdémonstratifs dans des textestraduits du françaisennorvégien et des textes sources norvégiens: stratégie de traductionoutranslationese?” [J]. Forum, 2004, 2(2): 221-240.

[236] 夏云. 英译汉文学语言形合特征的历时研究 [J]. 外语教学与研究，2013,45 (1): 105-116, 161.

[237] XIAO R, HU X. Corpus-based studies of translational Chinese in English-Chinese translation [M]. Berlin & Heidelberg: Springer, 2015.

[238] 肖忠华，戴光荣. 寻求“第三语码”——基于汉语译文语料库的翻译共性研究 [J]. 外语教学与研究，2010,42 (1): 52-58, 81.

[239] YE Z. 英汉翻译理论与实践 [M]. 台北：Bookman, 2000.

[240] ZEEGERS P. Student learning in higher education: a path analysis of academic achievement in science [J]. Higher Education Research and Development, 2004, 23 (1): 35–56.

[241] 张其帆. 中英交替传译之显化现象: 案例分析 [J]. 中国翻译，2009,30 (5): 77- 81.

[242] 张威. 中国口译学习者语料库的副语言标注: 标准与程序[J]. 外语电化教学, 2015 (1): 23-30.

[243] 周红民. 论翻译中的“显化”现象 [J]. 外语研究, 2007 (6): 75- 79.

[244] 赵彦春. 翻译中衔接连贯的映现 [J]. 外语与外语教学, 2002 (7): 23- 27.

[245] 朱纯深,慕媛媛. 以文本解释力为导向的语料库翻译教学——香港城大翻译与双语写作在线教学/自学平台的设计与试用分析 [J]. 中国翻译,2013,34 (2): 56-62.

[246] ZUFFEREY S, CARTONI B. A multifactorial analysis of explicitation in translation [J]. Target, 2014, 26(3): 361-384.

[247] 宗和. “红色翻译”国家队 [J]. 新湘评论, 2012(12): 55-56.